The European Union since 1945

The European Union since 1945

Second edition

Alasdair Blair

Longman
is an imprint of

Harlow, England • London • New York • Boston • San Francisco • Toronto • Sydney • Singapore • Hong Kong
Tokyo • Seoul • Taipei • New Delhi • Cape Town • Madrid • Mexico City • Amsterdam • Munich • Paris • Milan

PEARSON EDUCATION LIMITED

Edinburgh Gate
Harlow CM20 2JE
United Kingdom
Tel: +44 (0)1279 623623
Fax: +44 (0)1279 431059
Website: www.pearsoned.co.uk

First edition published 2005
Second edition published in Great Britain in 2010

© Pearson Education Limited 2005, 2010

The right of Alasdair Blair to be identified as author of this work has been asserted by
him in accordance with the Copyright, Designs and Patents Act 1988.

Pearson Education is not responsible for the content of third party internet sites.

ISBN: 978-1-4082-3452-5

British Library Cataloguing in Publication Data
A CIP catalogue record for this book can be obtained from the British Library

Library of Congress Cataloging in Publication Data
Blair, Alasdair, 1971–
    The European Union since 1945 / Alasdair Blair. – 2nd ed.
        p. cm.
    Includes bibliographical references and index.
    ISBN 978-1-4082-3452-5 (pbk.)
    1. European Union–History.   2. European federation–History.   I. Title.
    JN30.B62 2010
    341.242'2–dc22

                                                                    2010006214

10 9 8 7 6 5 4 3 2 1
06 07 08 09 10

Set in 10/13.5pt Berkeley Book by 35
Printed and bound in Malaysia, CTP-VVP

Introduction to the series

History is a narrative constructed by historians from traces left by the past. Historical enquiry is often driven by contemporary issues and, in consequence, historical narratives are constantly reconsidered, reconstructed and reshaped. The fact that different historians have different perspectives on issues means that there is also often controversy and no universally agreed version of past events. *Seminar Studies in History* was designed to bridge the gap between current research and debate, and the broad, popular general surveys that often date rapidly.

The volumes in the series are written by historians who are not only familiar with the latest research and current debates concerning their topic, but who have themselves contributed to our understanding of the subject. The books are intended to provide the reader with a clear introduction to a major topic in history. They provide both a narrative of events and a critical analysis of contemporary interpretations. They include the kinds of tools generally omitted from specialist monographs: a chronology of events, a glossary of terms and brief biographies of 'who's who'. They also include bibliographical essays in order to guide students to the literature on various aspects of the subject. Students and teachers alike will find that the selection of documents will stimulate discussion and offer insight into the raw materials used by historians in their attempt to understand the past.

Clive Emsley and Gordon Martel
Series Editors

For William

Contents

Publisher's acknowledgements

We are grateful to the following for permission to reproduce copyright material:

Maps

Maps 1–7, adapted from *The Longman Companion to the European Union since 1945* by Alasdair Blair © Alasdair Blair, 1999.

Documents

Document 3 from *The Sinews of Peace. Post-War Speeches by Winston S. Churchill*, Cassell (Randolph S. Churchill (ed.) 1948) pp. 198–202, Reproduced with permission of Curtis Brown Ltd, London on behalf of The Estate of Winston Churchill. Copyright © Winston S. Churchill; Document 5 from '*The first aim of British foreign policy*', Cabinet Memorandum by the Secretary of State for Foreign Affairs, CAB 129/23 (Ernest Bevin 4 January 1948), Public Record Office; Document 6 from http://www.nato.int/docu/basictxt/ b480317a.htm; Document 7 from http://www.nato.int/docu/basictxt/treaty.htm; Document 8 from The Statue of the Council of Europe, 5 May 1949, http:// conventions.coe.int/treaty/en/treaties/html/001.htm, Council of Europe; Document 9 from The Schuman Declaration, http://ec.europa.eu, © European Union, 1995–2010; Document 10 from Déclaration du Gouverneur français René Pleven le 24 Octobre 1950, *Journal Officiel de la République Française*, 10, pp. 7118–19 (1950), Translated by the CVCE. http://www.ena.lu/statement_ rene_pleven_establishment_european_army_24_october_1950-2- 30110 © Translation Centre Virtuel de la Connaissance sur l'Europe (CVCE); Document 11 from Treaty of Paris, http://ec.europa.eu, © European Union, 1995–2010; Document 12 from http://www.ena.lu/treaty_instituting_ european_defence_community_paris_27_1952-2-793 (translated); Document 14 from The Treaty of Rome, http://ec.europa.eu, © European Union,

1995–2010; Document 15(a) extracted from statement by Harold Macmillan on the first British application to the European Economic Community, *Parliamentary Debates*, Fifth Series, Vol. 645, pp. 928–31 (Hansard), House of Commons. Crown Copyright material is reproduced with permission under the terms of the Click-Use License; Document 15(b) from *The Course of My Life* by Edward Heath (© Edward Heath, 1998) is reproduced by permission of PFD (www.pfd.co.uk) on behalf of the Estate of Sir Edward Heath. Document 17 from *1963: A Retrospective of the Political Year in Europe*, WEU Assembly (1964); Document 18 from The Merger Treaty, http://ec. europa.eu, © European Union, 1995–2010; Document 19 from *Bulletin of the European Economic Community*, No. 3, pp. 8–9 (1966), © European Union 1966; Document 20 from *Parliamentary Debates*, Fifth Series, Vol. 746, pp. 310– 14 (Hansard), Crown Copyright material is reproduced with permission under the terms of the Click-Use License; Document 21 from *Bulletin of the European Economic Community*, No. 1, pp. 11–16 (1970), © European Union 1970; Document 22 from *Bulletin of the European Economic Community*, Supplement 11, pp. 26–9 (1970) © European Union 1970; Document 23 from *Bulletin of the European Economic Community*, No. 11, pp. 9–12 (1970) © European Union 1970; Document 24 from *Bulletin of the European Communities*, No. 4, pp. 43–4 (1972) © European Union 1972; Document 25 from *Bulletin of the European Communities*, No. 12, © European Communities, 1974; Document 26 from *Bulletin of the European Communities*, Supplement No. 1, pp. 14–22 (1976) © European Union, 1976; Document 27 © ECSC – EEC – EAEC, Brussels-Luxembourg, 1979, source: *Compendium of Community Monetary Texts*, 1979; Document 28 from *Report of Cases before the Court*, Part 1, case 120/78, pp. 660–5 (Judgement of the Court of 20 February 1979), © European Union, http://eur-lex.europa.eu/; Document 29(a), 30(b) and 33 from *The Downing Street Years*, HarperCollins (Thatcher, M. 1993), Reprinted by permission of HarperCollins Publishers Ltd © 1993 Thatcher, M.; Document 29(b) excerpt by Roy Jenkins from *European Diary 1977–1981* (© Roy Jenkins, 1989) is reproduced by permission of PFD (www.pfd.co.uk) on behalf of the Estate of Roy Jenkins. Document 30(a) from Single European Act, http://ec.europa.eu © European Union, 1995–2010; Document 31 from *International Market Scoreboard*, Edition 19 (July 2009), http://ec.europa.eu, © European Union, 1995– 2010; Document 32 from *The Collected Speeches*, HarperCollins (Thatcher, M. 1997). Reprinted by permission of HarperCollins Publishers Ltd © 1997 Thatcher, M.; Document 34(a) from The Excessive Deficit Procedure, http:// eur-lex.europa.eu/, © European Union, 1998–2010. Only European Union legislation printed in the paper edition of the Official Journal of the European Union is deemed authentic; Document 34(b) from *Protocol (No. 5) on the Excessive Deficit Procedure*, © European Union, http://eur-lex.europa.eu/;

Document 34(c) from Stability and Growth Pact, Annex to Presidency Conclusions, Dublin European Council, 13–14 December 1996, http://www.consilium.europa.eu/, © European Union, 1996; Document 35(a) from *Presidency Conclusions, Copenhagen European Council, 21–22 June 1993*, http://www.consilium.europa.eu/ueDocs/cms_Data/docs/pressData/en/ec/72921.pdf, © European Union, 1993; Document 35(b) from Presidency Conclusions, Luxembourg European Council, December 1997, http://www.consilium.europa.eu/, © European Union, 1997; Document 35(d) after *World Population Prospects*, The 2008 Revision (United Nations 2009) http://www.un.org/esa/population/publications/wpp2008/wpp2008_highlights.pdf; Document 38 from TNS opinion in collaboration with the EP, http://www.europarl.europa.eu/parliament/archive/elections2009/en/turnout_en.html.

In some instances we have been unable to trace the owners of copyright material, and we would appreciate any information that would enable us to do so.

Picture Credits

The publisher would like to thank the following for their kind permission to reproduce their photographs:

Plates 1, 2, 3, 4 and 7 from the Audiovisual Library of the European Commission © European Union, 2010; Plate 5 © Cluff with permission from www.CartoonStock.com; Plate 6 from Stephen Jaffe/Getty Images; Plate 8 Morten Morland / The Times 04.12.2005/ nisyndication.com.

Author's acknowledgements

In preparing this second edition I would like to thank my new colleagues at De Montfort University, particularly Alison Statham, Christopher Goldsmith and Alistair Jones. The series editors and the staff at Longman, particularly Christina Wipf Perry, have been of immense help in delivering the manuscript. Finally, I would like to record my thanks and love to Katherine and William who provide a welcome distraction. As before, it goes without saying that none of these individuals bears the slightest responsibility for the book's remaining deficiencies.

Map 1 The six member states (1957)

Map 2 The nine member states (1973)

Map 3 The ten member states (1981)

Map 4 The 12 member states (1986)

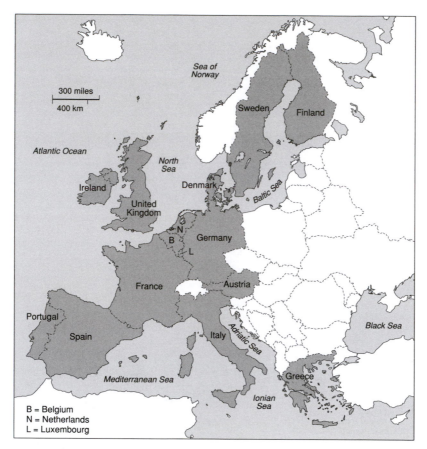

Map 5 The 15 member states (1995)

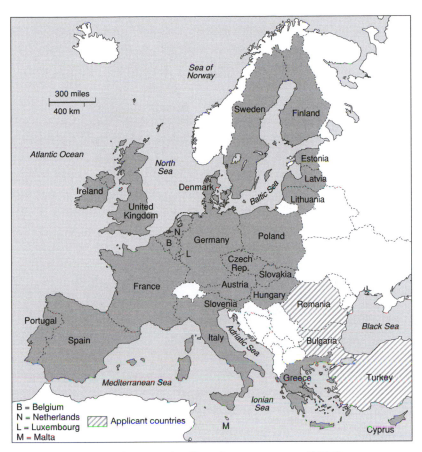

Map 6 The 25 member states and applicant countries (2004)

Map 7 The 27 member states and applicant countries (2009)

Preface to the second edition

When the first edition of this book was published in 2005 the European Union (EU) had just undertaken one of the most momentous enlargements in its history. The expansion in membership from 15 to 25 member states through the accession of eight countries from Central and Eastern Europe and two from the Mediterranean transformed the geographic size, economic importance and political reach of the EU. Enlargement brought about some of the most contentious debates in the history of European integration with regard to what the EU stands for and how far it should or could grow. Heated debates translated into the European integration process stalling as a result of the Dutch and French electorates rejecting the Constitutional Treaty in referenda on 29 May and 1 June 2005. The Treaty was supposed to do more than just 'tidy up' all the loose ends that had emerged with over 50 years of reform and adjustment to the EU; it attempted to set out a clear sense of what the EU could do as well as what powers should remain with the member states. Most significantly, the very use of 'constitution' did not sit well with domestic audiences who often could not relate or did not want to be governed in such a way. From the ashes of this 'Constitutional crisis' member states reached agreement on a Treaty of Lisbon in December 2007 which eventually entered into force on 1 December 2009 after it was ratified by all member states. This proved to be an easier task than the process of ratifying the Constitutional Treaty. This was partly because the Lisbon Treaty merely amends earlier Treaties, whereas the Constitutional Treaty sought to replace all of the previous Treaties. But it was also influenced by the fact that member states shied away from having referendums on the Treaty after the difficulties experienced with the Constitutional Treaty. In the end, when Irish voters endorsed the Lisbon Treaty with a 67 per cent 'Yes' vote in a referendum vote on 2 October 2009, this basically gave the green light to the Treaty entering into force. The Irish referendum was, in fact, their second vote on the Lisbon Treaty, with the electorate having previously voted 'No' some 16 months earlier. Although the change in mood among the Irish electorate had been influenced by some of the developments outlined above, a key factor that appeared to influence the views of voters was the way in which the global economic recession of 2008–09 exposed a fragility in the Irish economy that resulted in a majority of the electorate concluding that they had to vote 'Yes' as the country's fortunes were dependent on European integration.

A feature of the first edition was its attempt to provide an accessible introduction to the study of European integration and the feedback from reviews, colleagues and students was that this goal was met. For this edition I have made a number of changes in response to critics and events. As with all writings on the EU, it is the case that this is a fast-changing landscape and there are always going to be limitations to the extent to which any one book can claim to be fully 'up-to-date'. Those interested in the subject should consult the relevant websites and suggestions for further reading that are indicated at the end of this book.

As I noted in the preface of the first edition, this is a subject matter that is often confused by terminology. The Treaties of Rome created two communities: a European Economic Community (EEC) and a European Atomic Energy Community (Euratom). In 1967 they merged with the European Coal and Steel Community (ECSC) to form a single institutional structure. From the 1970s onwards it was commonplace to refer to all three institutions as the European Community (EC). I have therefore used the term EEC up until the end of the 1960s and from then on the term EC. This is despite the fact that the EEC was not officially renamed the EC until the 1993 Maastricht Treaty on European Union. At this point the EC became a separate entity of the European Union (EU) that was created by the Maastricht Treaty and I therefore use the term EU from 1993 onwards. On occasion, I have adopted the practice of referring to the EEC/EC/EU simply as 'Europe' as this is the term that is often used in debates on the subject.

Abbreviations

ASEAN	Association of Southeast Asian Nations.
Benelux	Benelux Economic Union (Belgium, the Netherlands and Luxembourg)
CAP	Common Agricultural Policy
CFSP	Common Foreign and Security Policy
Comecon	Council for Mutual Economic Assistance
CoR	Committee of the Regions
Coreper	Committee of Permanent Representatives
CSCE	Conference on Security and Cooperation in Europe
DMV	Double Majority Voting
EAGGF	European Agriculture Guidance and Guarantee Fund
EBRD	European Bank for Reconstruction and Development
EC	European Community
ECB	European Central Bank
ECJ	European Court of Justice
ECSC	European Coal and Steel Community
ECU	European Currency Unit
EDC	European Defence Community
EEA	European Economic Area
EEC	European Economic Community
EFTA	European Free Trade Association
EIB	European Investment Bank
EMI	European Monetary Institute
EMS	European Monetary System
EMU	Economic and Monetary Union
EPC	European Political Cooperation
ERDF	European Regional Development Fund
ERM	Exchange Rate Mechanism
ESCB	European System of Central Banks
ESDI	European Security and Defence Identity
ESF	European Social Fund

ESPRIT	European Strategic Programme for Research and Development in Information Technology
EU	European Union
Euratom	European Atomic Energy Community
GATT	General Agreement on Tariffs and Trade
GDP	gross domestic product
GNP	gross national product
IGC	intergovernmental conference
JHA	justice and home affairs
MEP	Member of the European Parliament
NATO	North Atlantic Treaty Organization
OECD	Organisation for Economic Cooperation and Development
OEEC	Organisation for European Economic Cooperation
QMV	qualified majority voting
SEA	Single European Act
SEM	Single European Market
TEU	Treaty on European Union
UEF	European Union of Federalists
USA	United States of America
WEU	Western European Union
WTO	World Trade Organization

Chronology

1945

February Yalta conference deals with questions relating to the post-war settlement.

8 May Victory in Europe Day. Formal surrender of Germany.

July–August Potsdam conference on post-war settlement.

1946

5 March Winston Churchill's 'iron curtain' speech.

19 September Winston Churchill's 'United States of Europe' speech.

December Formation of the European Union of Federalists (UEF).

1947

4 March Treaty of Dunkirk.

12 March Truman Doctrine.

17 March Benelux Treaty.

14 May European Movement is created.

5 June Marshall Plan.

1948

1 January Benelux customs union.

17 March Signature of Brussels Treaty (collective alliance of Britain, France and Benelux).

16 April Organisation for European Economic Cooperation (OEEC) is created.

7–11 May Movement for European unity held European Congress in The Hague.

24 June Commencement of Berlin blockade.

1949

4 April Creation of North Atlantic Treaty Organization (NATO).

5 May Council of Europe founded.

1950

9 May Schuman Declaration.

20 June Start of negotiations to establish the European Coal and Steel Community (ECSC).

19 September European Payments Union.

24 October Pleven Plan for a European Defence Community (EDC).

1951

15 February Commencement of negotiations to establish a European Defence Community.

18 April ECSC Treaty is signed by Belgium, France, Germany, Italy, Luxembourg and the Netherlands (otherwise known as 'the Six').

1952

27 May EDC Treaty signed in Paris by 'the Six'. Treaty of Association signed with UK.

23 July ECSC comes into operation.

10 August ECSC High Authority takes office.

1953

1 January Start of the ECSC levy. It is the first European tax.

10 February Establishment of the ECSC Common Market for coal and iron ore.

15 March Establishment of the Common Market for scrap iron.

1954

30 August French National Assembly reject the EDC Treaty.

23 October Brussels Treaty is amended to create the Western European Union (WEU).

21 December First ruling from the European Court of Justice.

1955

5 May Germany joins NATO.

1–2 June Messina Conference of 'the Six' foreign ministers establishes the Spaak Committee to look at ways in which 'a fresh advance towards the building of Europe'.

8 December　Council of Europe adopts the blue flag with 12 golden stars as its emblem, which subsequently becomes the emblem of the European Community.

1956

6 May　Spaak Report proposing the creation of the European Economic Community (EEC) and European Atomic Energy Community (Euratom).

29 May　Approval of the Spaak Report.

26 June　Start of negotiations to establish the EEC and Euratom.

31 October　Franco-British intervention in the Suez Canal.

1957

25 March　Signing of the Treaties of Rome.

1958

1 January　Treaties of Rome come into effect.

7 January　Walter Hallstein is appointed the first President of the European Commission.

10 February　EEC harmonised tariff for coal and steel.

7 October　European Court of Justice in Luxembourg replaces the ECSC Court of Justice.

1959

1 January　First tariff reductions and quota enlargements in the common market take place.

20 March　European Investment Bank (EIB) grants its first loans.

1960

4 January　Signature of the European Free Trade Area Association (EFTA) convention in Stockholm by Austria, Denmark, Norway, Portugal, Sweden, Switzerland and the UK.

3 May　Stockholm Convention creating EFTA enters into force.

20 September　Establishment of European Social Fund.

14 December　Organisation for Economic Cooperation and Development (OECD) replaces the OEEC.

1961

July–August Denmark, Ireland and the UK apply for EEC membership.

1 September First regulation on the free movement of workers.

2 November Fouchet Plan for a European political community.

1962

14 January Agreement on a common agricultural policy (CAP).

17 April Collapse of the Fouchet Plan negotiations.

1 July Reduction of customs duties between the member states to 50 per cent of their 1957 level.

30 July Regulations establishing the CAP enter into force.

1963

14 January France vetoes UK application to join the Community.

22 January Franco-German Treaty of Friendship.

5 February European Court of Justice rules in the Van Gend en Loos case that the Community is a new legal order.

20 July Yaoundé Convention is signed.

1964

4 May Start of the Kennedy round of General Agreement on Tariffs and Trade (GATT) negotiations.

1 June Yaoundé Convention enters into force.

1 July Establishment of the European Agriculture Guidance and Guarantee Fund (EAGGF).

15 July In Costa/ENEL the European Court of Justice rules that Community law supersedes national law.

1965

8 April Merger Treaty.

1 July Start of empty chair crisis.

1966

28–29 January Luxembourg Compromise.

29 March French government announced that French force assignments to NATO would end on 1 July 1966 and that Allied military forces and headquarters would have to be removed from France by 1 April 1967.

1967

9 February Council of Ministers agree to harmonise indirect taxes in the Community and to adopt the principle of value added tax system.

2 May UK reapplies to join the Community and is followed by Ireland and Denmark and, a little later, Norway.

1 July Merger of the Community Executives into a 14-member Commission.

27 November French President Charles de Gaulle stresses the incompatibility of the UK economy and the EEC.

1968

1 July Customs union completed 18 months ahead of schedule.

1969

28 April Resignation of French President Charles de Gaulle.

29 July Signature of the Second Yaoundé convention.

1–2 December 'The Six' agree to complete, enlarge and strengthen the Community at 'The Hague summit'.

1970

22 April Treaty of Luxembourg is signed introducing a system of own resources.

7–8 October Werner Report for economic and monetary union.

27 October Davignon Report for European Political Cooperation (EPC).

1971

1 January Second Yaoundé Convention and Arusha Agreements come into force.

1 February Common Fisheries Policy takes effect.

22 March Member states agree on a plan to achieve Economic and Monetary Union (EMU) by 1980.

1972

24 March Introduction of the currency 'snake' between Belgium, France, Germany, Italy and the Netherlands.

24 April Basle Agreement enters into force establishing the system for the narrowing of the margins of fluctuation between the currencies of the Community, otherwise known as the 'snake' (margins of 2.25 per cent) in the tunnel (plus of minus 2.25 per cent). The participating countries are Belgium, France, Germany, Italy, Luxembourg and the Netherlands.

24–25 September Norway withdraws its application to join the Community after a referendum vote against entry.

19–21 October Paris summit of the Nine prepares a blueprint for the future development of the Community.

1973

1 January Accession of Denmark, Ireland and the UK to the EEC.

3–7 July First session of the Conference on Security and Cooperation in Europe (CSCE).

1974

January Creation of European Social Fund (ESF) and European Regional Development Fund (ERDF).

4 June UK outlines details of its terms of renegotiation of EEC membership.

9–10 December Paris summit agrees to the principle of direct elections to the European Parliament and establishment of the European Council.

1975

28 February Lomé Convention is signed, thereby replacing and extending the Yaoundé Conventions and the Arusha Agreement.

18 March European Regional Development Fund (ERDF) established.

5 June UK referendum on EC membership – 17.3 million vote 'Yes' to stay in the EEC, 8.4 million vote 'No' to withdraw (67.2 per cent of voters are in favour of membership).

12 June Greece applies for accession to the Community.

1 August Final act of the Conference on Security and Cooperation in Europe (CSCE) is signed by states in Helsinki.

29 December Tindemans Report on political cooperation.

1976

1 April Entering into force of the EEC–ACP Convention which had been signed in Lomé on 28 February 1975 (otherwise known as the Lomé Convention).

1977

28 March Portugal applies for Community membership.

28 July Spain applies for Community membership.

1978

9 March   European Court of Justice Simmenthal ruling maintains and consolidates the principle of the supremacy of Community law over national law.

6–7 July   European Council summit in Bremen approves the Franco-German plan to establish the European Monetary System (EMS).

1979

13 March   European Council meeting in Paris brings the European Monetary System into operation.

7–10 June   First direct elections to the European Parliament.

31 October   Second Lomé Convention (Lomé II).

1980

1 October   EEC–ASEAN Cooperation Agreement.

1981

1 January   Greece becomes the tenth member of the Community.

6–12 November   Genscher–Colombo initiative to further develop European political cooperation.

1982

23 February   As a result of a consultative referendum, Greenland decides to withdraw from the Community (having become a member of the Community through being part of Denmark).

30 May   Spain joins NATO and became its 16th member.

1984

1 January   EEC–EFTA free trade area.

14–17 June   Second direct elections to the European Parliament.

25–26 June   Fontainebleau European Council produces agreement on the UK budget rebate.

13 July   Signing of the Franco-German agreement on the abolition of border checks.

8 December   Third Lomé Convention.

1985

7 January   Jacques Delors takes office as head of a new European Commission.

1 February   Greenland leaves the Community, being the only country ever to withdraw.

9 March	Dooge committee recommends the convening of an intergovernmental conference (IGC) to examine the reform of the Treaty of Rome.
14 June	Schengen agreement on the gradual abolition of frontier controls.
15 June	Lord Cockfield presents his timetable for the completion of the internal market.
28–29 June	Milan European Council meeting approves the European Commission's project to complete the internal market. The meeting also established an intergovernmental conference to look at the wider reform of the Treaty.
2–3 December	Luxembourg European Council reaches agreement on the Single European Act (SEA).

1986

1 January	Portugal and Spain join the Community.
17 and 28 February	Foreign ministers sign the SEA in Luxembourg and The Hague.
1 May	Third Lomé Convention between the EEC and the ACP countries comes into force.

1987

14 April	Turkey formally applies to join the European Communities.
1 July	SEA comes into existence.

1988

27–28 June	EEC member states agree at the Hanover European Council to establish the Delors committee on Economic and Monetary Union. Agreement was signed between the EC and Comecon that enabled the two organisations to recognise each other.
24 October	European Council agrees to establish a Court of First Instance to reduce the work of the European Court of Justice.

1989

12 April	Delors Report proposes a three-stage route to EMU: linking the currencies, integration between states and the creation of a European Central Bank (ECB).
15–18 June	Third direct elections to the European Parliament.
17 July	Austria formally applies to join the European Community.
9 November	Collapse of the Berlin Wall.

1990

5 February	Action programme for the development of relations between the Community and the countries of Central and Eastern Europe (PHARE).
19 June	Schengen Agreement signed by Belgium, France, Germany, the Netherlands and Luxembourg.
1 July	Start of Stage 1 of EMU. German Union Treaty also comes into force.
3 October	German reunification.
8 October	UK joins the ERM of the EMS.
22 November	Transatlantic Declaration between the United States and the EU.
27 November	Italy signs the Schengen Agreement.
14–15 December	Rome European Council launches intergovernmental conferences on EMU and Political Union.

1991

14 April	Establishment of European Bank for Reconstruction and Development (EBRD).
16 May	Start of civil war in Yugoslavia due to ethnic and political tensions.
22 August	Failure of the attempted coup in the Soviet Union.
1 September	Fourth Lomé Convention.
21 October	Agreement on the establishment of the European Economic Area (EEA) between the Community and EFTA.
9–10 December	Maastricht European Council reaches agreement on the Treaty on European Union.
16 December	'Europe Agreements' signed between the Community and Poland, Hungary and Czechoslovakia.
25 December	Mikhail Gorbachev resigns as President of the Soviet Union.

1992

7 February	Treaty on European Union is signed.
2 June	Danish referendum rejected the Treaty on European Union.
December	Completion of the internal market programme.

1993

1 January	Single European Market comes into effect.
February–March	Europe Agreements signed with Bulgaria and Romania.
18 May	Second Danish referendum approves the Treaty on European Union.

21–22 June   Copenhagen European Council produces agreement on the accession of Austria, Finland, Sweden and Norway by 1 January 1995.

1 November   Treaty on European Union (Maastricht Treaty) formally comes into effect.

21–22 June   Copenhagen European Council produces agreement on the accession criteria for applicant nations.

1994

1 January   Agreement establishing the EEA comes into effect.

26–27 March   Ioannina compromise resolved disputes surrounding institutional questions as a result of the implication of enlarging the EU.

9, 12 June   Fourth direct elections to the European Parliament.

1 July   Start of second stage of EMU.

28 November   Norwegian electorate reject membership of the EU.

1995

1 January   Austria, Finland and Sweden become EU members and thereby increased the number of member states from 12 to 15. The population of the EU increases from 345 million to 368 million.

1 February   Europe Association Agreements between the EU and Bulgaria, Romania, the Slovak Republic and the Czech Republic.

26 March   Schengen Agreement comes into effect.

13–14 December   Dublin European Council reaches agreement on a stability pact for the single currency.

16 December   Bulgaria applies to join the EU.

1996

29 March   Start of IGC negotiations to revise the Maastricht Treaty on European Union.

13–14 December   Dublin European Council reaches agreement on a stability pact for the single currency.

1997

16–17 June   Amsterdam European Council reaches agreement on the IGC negotiations to revise the Treaty on European Union, resulting in a Treaty of Amsterdam.

2 October   Treaty of Amsterdam is signed.

1998

25 March   European Commission recommends that 11 member states adopt the single currency from 1 January 1999, having met the necessary convergence criteria. The 11 countries are Austria, Belgium, Finland, France, Germany, Ireland, Italy, Luxembourg, the Netherlands, Portugal and Spain. Denmark, Sweden and the UK had taken an earlier decision not to join the single currency. Greece was deemed not to have met the necessary convergence criteria.

2–3 May   A meeting of finance ministers in Brussels agrees that the 11 countries recommended by the European Commission in March had met the necessary economic criteria to adopt the single currency on 1 January 1999.

1999

1 January   Third stage of EMU. Euro is launched in 11 member states.

16 March   Resignation of the Santer Commission after publication of a critical report on corruption and mismanagement.

24–25 March   Agenda 2000 agreed by European Council.

1 May   Treaty of Amsterdam comes into effect.

10–13 June   Fifth direct elections to the European Parliament.

2000

March   Lisbon European Council produces agreement on an approach to assist economic modernisation.

7–9 December   Nice European Council marks the conclusion of the intergovernmental conference negotiations that started in Brussels in February 2000.

2001

2 January   Greece became the 12th member of the eurozone.

June   Ireland rejects the Treaty of Nice in a referendum.

11 September   Terrorist attacks on the United States resulted in the collapse of the World Trade Center building in New York and spurred the US into a 'war on terror'.

2002

1 January   Changeover to the use of euro banknotes and coins in the eurozone.

February   Convention on the Future of Europe begins in Brussels.

28 February	End of the period of dual circulation of currencies, with the euro the sole currency within the 12 participating member states of the eurozone.
31 May	EU ratifies the Kyoto Protocol on climate change.
June	ECSC comes to an end after 50 years of existence.
9 October	European Commission recommends that ten countries should conclude their accession negotiations by the end of 2002 with a view to being ready for EU membership from the start of 2004: Cyprus, Czech Republic, Estonia, Hungary, Latvia, Lithuania, Malta, Poland, Slovak Republic and Slovenia.
19 October	In a second referendum the Irish electorate vote in favour of the Treaty of Nice.

2003

1 February	Treaty of Nice comes into effect.
20–21 June	Thessalonica European Council meeting in Greece discusses the draft Constitutional Treaty produced by the Convention on the Future of Europe that was chaired by Valery Giscard d'Estaing and which commenced work in February 2002.
14 September	Swedish electorate reject the euro in a referendum vote.
4 October	IGC negotiations on the Future of Europe commence in Rome.

2004

29 March	Bulgaria, Estonia, Latvia, Lithuania, Romania, Slovakia and Slovenia become full NATO members.
1 May	Cyprus, the Czech Republic, Estonia, Hungary, Latvia, Lithuania, Malta, Poland, Slovakia and Slovenia become members of the European Union, which now totals 25 member states.
10–13 June	Sixth direct elections to the European Parliament held in 25 member states.
17–18 June	Brussels European Council reaches agreement on the EU Constitution.
29 June	Brussels Council reaches agreement that José Manuel Durão Barroso will succeed Romano Prodi as President of the Commission. Also agreed that Javier Solana will be appointed as Secretary-General of the Council and High Representative for CFSP and that on the day of entry into force of the EU Constitution he will be appointed EU Minister for Foreign Affairs.
29 October	Heads of State and Government and EU Foreign Ministers sign the Treaty establishing the Constitution for Europe.

2005

12 January	European Constitution is approved by the European Parliament.
16 February	Kyoto Protocol on climate change enters into force.
20 February	Spanish electorate accept the Constitutional Treaty in the first referendum vote in the EU.
13 April	European Parliament agrees to the accession of Bulgaria and Romania to the EU.
29 May	French electorate reject the Constitutional Treaty in a referendum vote.
1 June	Netherlands electorate reject the Constitutional Treaty in a referendum vote. The 'no votes' in France and the Netherlands put the ratification of the Treaty in doubt.
10 July	Luxembourg votes 'Yes' in a referendum vote on the Constitutional Treaty.

2006

11 July	Council agrees to allow Slovenia to join the euro area from 1 January 2007.
5 December	Finnish Parliament ratifies the Constitutional Treaty.

2007

1 January	Slovenia adopts the euro as its currency.
10 July	EU Council of Finance Ministers approve that Cyprus and Malta can adopt the euro from 1 January 2008.
23 July	Representatives from EU member states meet in Brussels for the start of an IGC on a draft reform treaty to make changes to the EU Treaties.
13 December	Signing of the Treaty of Lisbon.
21 December	Enlargement of the Schengen area to include the Czech Republic, Estonia, Hungary, Latvia, Malta, Poland, Slovakia and Slovenia.

2008

1 January	Cyprus and Malta adopt the euro. This brings the number of member states in the eurozone to 15 countries which is equivalent to a population of some 320 million people.
12 June	54 per cent of the Irish electorate vote 'No' to the Lisbon Treaty in a referendum vote.

2009

1 January	Slovakia is the 16th member state to adopt the euro.
4–7 June	European Parliament elections are held across the EU. 736 MEPs are elected, with a voter turnout of 43.2 per cent.

23 July Iceland applies for EU membership.

2 October 67 per cent of the Irish electorate vote 'Yes' in a referendum on the Lisbon Treaty, thereby overturning the previous 'No' vote recorded some 16 months earlier.

2 November Ruling by the Czech constitutional court that the Lisbon Treaty is in line with the country's constitution. This ensures that the Czech Eurosceptic President Vaclav Klaus will no longer oppose the Treaty.

19 November At an informal meeting in Brussels, EU heads of state and government appoint the Belgian Prime Minister Herman Van Rompuy as the first permanent president of the EU, and the British EU Trade Commissioner Catherine Ashton to be the EU's High Representative for Foreign Affairs and Security Policy. Both posts were created by the Lisbon Treaty. The new President will serve for two and a half years, with this position bringing to an end the previous system of rotating presidency every six months.

1 December Treaty of Lisbon enters into force.

Who's who

Adenauer, Konrad (1876–1967): First Chancellor of the Federal Republic of Germany 1949–63. Negotiated German entry into the EEC and NATO; developed a close relationship with France that resulted in the 1963 Treaty of Friendship between the two nations.

Ashton, Catherine (b. 1956): Since 1 December 2009 has served as EU High Representative for Foreign Affairs and Security Policy and vice-president of the European Commission.

Barroso, José Manuel (b. 1956): President of the European Commission since 1 November 2004. Previously Prime Minister and Foreign Minister of Portugal.

Bevin, Ernest (1897–1976): UK Labour Foreign Secretary 1945–51. Played an influential role in the Brussels Treaty and Britain's entry to NATO.

Bidault, Georges (1899–1983): French Foreign Minister under de Gaulle. Although he played an important role in the creation of the OEEC and NATO, he was primarily concerned with Germany's revival.

Blair, Anthony (b. 1953): UK Labour Prime Minister 1997–2007. A committed pro-European, he attempted to raise the UK's profile in Europe, although his premiership was overshadowed by his support for the US-led invasions of Afghanistan in 2001 and Iraq in 2003.

Brandt, Willy (1913–92): Socialist Chancellor of the Federal Republic of Germany from 1969–74; leader of the Social Democratic Party (SDP) from 1964–87; developed an active foreign policy towards Eastern Europe and the Soviet Union (referred to as *Ostpolitik*).

Briand, Aristide (1862–1932): As French Foreign Minister, he was one of the first advocates of a European Federal Union through a proposal to the League of Nations on 5 September 1929. A lack of support from other member states and Briand's death in 1932 brought his proposals to an end.

Chirac, Jacques (b. 1932): Gaullist politician and President of France 1995–2007. Previously Prime Minister 1974–76 and 1986–88.

Churchill, Winston (1874–1965): UK Prime Minister 1940–45 and 1951–55. After the landslide Labour Party victory in the 1945 general election, he led the Conservative Party in opposition, during which time he advocated closer European integration, urging for the construction of a United States of Europe in 1946.

Cockfield, Lord Arthur (1916–2007): UK Conservative Secretary of State for Trade from 1982 to 1983. Member of the European Commission with responsibility for the Internal Market 1985–88.

Davignon, Viscount Etienne (b. 1932): As political director of the Belgian foreign ministry in the 1970s he chaired the committee which devised the report that laid the foundations of European Political Cooperation (EPC). He later served as a European Commissioner from 1977 to 1985.

de Gasperi, Alcide (1881–1954): A founding father of Europe, he was Prime Minister of Italy from 1945 to 1954, during which time he pursued the modernisation of the Italian economy. He steered a pro-western foreign policy, being a committed supporter of greater European integration.

de Gaulle, Charles (1890–1970): Leader of the Free French during the Second World War and President of France 1958–69. Attached great emphasis to European integration, partly to lessen the reliance on the US. He threw the Community into crisis with the French boycott in the Council of Ministers January–June 1965. He also vetoed UK applications to join the Community in 1963 and 1967.

Delors, Jacques (b. 1925): President of the European Commission 1985–95. Played a significant role in developing the EEC, both in terms of widening membership and increasing the scope of the policies it embraced.

Giscard d'Estaing, Valéry (b. 1926): President of France 1974–81. Influential in the institutionalisation of summit meetings of Community heads of state and government and supported the development of the European Monetary System. Chaired the discussions on the Convention on the future of Europe that took place between March 2002 and June 2003.

Gorbachev, Mikhail (b. 1931): General Secretary of the Soviet Union 1985–91. He was instrumental in the change in Soviet policy that was reflected in the policies of *glasnost* and *perestroika*. Established close relations with the United States and Western Europe.

Hallstein, Walter (1901–82): First President of the European Commission, holding office 1958–67. His views often clashed with those of the French

President, Charles de Gaulle, who did not share Hallstein's desire for the Commission to be the main motor of European integration.

Heath, Edward (1916–2005): UK Conservative Prime Minister 1970–74. A committed pro-European, he was in charge of the UK's first application for membership.

Jenkins, Roy (1920–2003): President of the European Commission 1977–81, having previously served as UK Home Secretary and Chancellor of the Exchequer for the Labour Party. As Commission President he was a keen advocate of the European Monetary System (EMS) and helped to steer the Community out of a period of Eurosclerosis.

Kohl, Helmut (b. 1930): Chancellor of the Federal Republic of Germany 1982–98. A key figure in the development of the Community, he enjoyed a strong relationship with President François Mitterrand of France, though his relations with the UK Prime Minister, Margaret Thatcher, were not as positive.

Macmillan, Harold (1894–1986): UK Conservative Prime Minister 1957–63, having succeeded Anthony Eden after the Suez crisis. He advocated membership of the European Community, a policy that failed when de Gaulle vetoed the application in 1963.

Major, John (b. 1943): UK Conservative Prime Minister 1990–97. His period of office was marked by severe splits over the issue of European integration.

Marshall, George C. (1880–1959): US Secretary of State 1947–49. Author of the June 1947 Marshall Plan for the economic rehabilitation of Europe.

Mitrany, David (1888–1975): Romanian-born scholar who was the founding father of functionalism. He regarded nationalism as a major threat to world and European peace and argued that states should cooperate in such policy sectors as agriculture, science and transport.

Mitterrand, François (1916–1996): President of France 1981–85. Played a significant role in the deepening of European integration, including the development of a European single currency. Established a close relationship with the German Chancellor, Helmut Kohl.

Monnet, Jean (1888–1979): Key figure in the European integration process after 1945. As head of the French Planning Commission he highlighted the need for European nations to recover through a joint strategy. An advocate of a gradual approach to European integration, he was a significant influence behind the Schuman Plan and was appointed the first President of the High Authority of the European Coal and Steel Community.

Ortoli, François-Zavier (1925–2007): French President of the Commission 1973–77, continuing to serve as a member of the Commission until 1984. As President he struggled to manage the economic problems that stifled the Community's growth through the 1970s.

Pompidou, Georges (1911–74): President of France from 1969 until his death in 1974. An influential figure behind the December 1969 Hague summit which fostered a climate of optimism in the Community.

Prodi, Romano (b. 1939): Italian President of the European Commission 1999–2004. Served as Prime Minister of Italy 1996–98 and 2006–08. His period as Commission President was not as dynamic in reforming the EU policy-making process as many would have liked.

Reagan, Ronald (1911–2004): As President of the United States 1981–89 he played a key role in the events that resulted in the end of the Cold War and the collapse of the Soviet Union. Reagan believed that military strength and confidence in US leadership was a prerequisite for peace. He oversaw a dramatic increase in US defence spending and a return to Cold War conflict with the Soviet Union after the era of détente that dominated much of the 1970s.

Santer, Jacques (b. 1937): President of the European Commission 1995–99, having previously served as Prime Minister of Luxembourg from 1984–95. His period as Commission President was tarnished by a March 1999 fraud report by a Committee of Independent Experts which criticised the operation of the Commission.

Schmidt, Helmut (b. 1918): Chancellor of the Federal Republic of Germany 1974–83. Played an important role in the development of the EEC, being one of the principal advocates of the European Monetary System that was endorsed by the European Council in 1978.

Schuman, Robert (1886–1963): Prime Minister of France 1947–48; Foreign Minister 1948–55. On 9 May 1950 he advanced the Schuman Plan that resulted in the establishment of the European Coal and Steel Community. President of the European Movement 1955–61; head of the European Parliamentary Assembly 1958–60.

Solana, Javier (b. 1942): Served as Secretary-General of the Council of the European Union, Secretary-General of the Western European Union and the EU's High Representative for the Common Foreign and Security Policy 1999–2009. A former Spanish Minister for Foreign Affairs (1992–95), he also served as Secretary General of NATO 1995–99.

Spaak, Paul-Henri (1889–1972): An important figure in the furtherance of European integration who held the office of Prime Minister and Foreign

Minister of Belgium on various occasions after 1945. He was influential in the creation of the Congress of Europe in 1948 and the European Movement. At the 1955 Messina Conference he was charged with the responsibility of chairing a committee that would examine proposals for a European Community (Spaak Report).

Spinelli, Altiero (1907–86): A key figure in federalist organisations throughout the 1940s and 1950s who advocated a federal United States of Europe. He established the European Federalist Movement in Milan in 1943 and the European Union of Federalists in 1946. He was a member of the European Commission 1970–76 and later served as a member of the European Parliament 1979–86.

Thatcher, Margaret (b. 1925): UK Conservative Prime Minister 1979–90. A tough negotiating stance on the budget and her forthright personality accentuated the nation's position as an 'awkward partner'.

Thorn, Gaston (1928–2007): President of the European Commission 1981–85, a period characterised by an absence of significant developments in the furtherance of European integration.

Tindemans, Leo (b. 1922): Prime Minister of Belgium 1974–78 and Foreign Minister 1981–89. Member of the European Parliament 1979–81 and 1989–99. Author of the 1975 Tindemans Report on European Union.

Truman, Harry (1894–1972): President of the United States 1945–53. Played an important role in the reconstruction of Europe, of which his key initiatives included the Truman Doctrine, the Marshall Plan and the creation of NATO.

Van Rompuy, Herman (b. 1947): On 19 November 2009 he was elected the first President of the European Council, a position that he will occupy for two and half years. Prior to his appointment he had served as Prime Minister of Belgium since December 2008.

Wilson, Harold (1916–95): UK Labour Prime Minister 1964–70 and 1974–76. Oversaw the UK's second application for EEC membership in 1967 and in 1974 renegotiated the terms of entry that Edward Heath had obtained. In 1975 he held a referendum on Community membership.

Glossary

Accession: The process by which countries join the EU. The treaties that cover the conclusion of the negotiations between applicant countries and the EU are known as 'Treaties of Accession'.

Acquis communautaire: The assortment of legislation, treaties and rulings of the European Court of Justice that constitute the legal identity of the EU. Referred to as simply the 'acquis'.

Agenda 2000: The plans that were set out by the European Commission in 1997 in response to the enlargement of the EU Central and Eastern Europe. This included proposals for the reform of the CAP and cohesion policy.

Area of Freedom, Security and Justice (AFSJ): The Treaty of Amsterdam brought the Schengen agreements into the European Community. This provided for the abolition of frontier controls, the free movement of people and cooperation between judicial and police authorities to combat cross-border crime.

Assent procedure: The procedure whereby the European Parliament's assent, by means of an absolute majority of its members, is necessary before certain important decisions can be adopted.

Association agreement: An agreement between the EU and non-member countries that fosters a close economic and political relationship.

Atlanticism: When the interests of a nation state are maximised by a close relationship with the US.

Barriers to trade: The elimination of tariffs and quotas among member states.

Beyen Plan: On 4 April 1955 the Netherlands Foreign Minister, Johan Beyen, proposed the creation of a customs union among 'the Six' members of the European Coal and Steel Community (ECSC).

Bipolar: When two states are in competition for dominance over the other. The Cold War competition between the US and the Soviet Union was regarded as being a bipolar struggle.

Brezhnev Doctrine: When politicians in the former Czechoslovakia put in place reforms that undermined the Communist system in 1968, the Soviet Union responded by invading the country to suppress the changes. Soviet willingness to maintain pro-Moscow governments in Central and Eastern Europe was formally outlined in 1969 by the announcement of the Brezhnev Doctrine which advanced the concept of limited sovereignty for the pro-Moscow states.

Brussels Treaty: Signed on 17 March 1948 by Belgium, France, Luxembourg, the Netherlands and the UK to provide a system of collective self-defence.

Co-decision procedure: Introduced in the 1993 Treaty on European Union. Increases the powers of the European Parliament by allowing it to prevent a proposal being adopted if its views are not taken into consideration by the Council.

Cohesion fund: Introduced in the Treaty on European Union to provide financial assistance to poorer member states.

Cold War: The rivalry between the US and the Soviet Union after the end of the Second World War, which continued until the collapse of Communism in 1989 and the break-up of the Soviet Union in 1991.

Committee of the Regions (CoR): Comprises representatives of local and regional authorities who are appointed by national governments and not directly by any regional authority.

Common Agricultural Policy (CAP): Established in 1962 to support agricultural production. Today it accounts for approximately 45 per cent of the EU budget.

Common Foreign and Security Policy (CFSP): Although the 1993 Treaty on European Union established a commitment to develop the foreign and security capacity of the EU, subsequent years demonstrated the difficulty of the EU member states being able to operate as a cohesive group. This became known as the 'capability-expectations gap'.

Commonwealth: A voluntary organisation established in 1931 that comprises former members of the British Empire. By 2009 it had 53 members, the majority of whom have joined since 1945 as a result of the granting of independence.

Communism: A political ideology that emphasises the common ownership of property and the absence of class divisions. Applied in the Soviet Union until its collapse in 1991.

Conference on Security and Cooperation in Europe (CSCE): Established in 1975 with 35 members as part of the period of détente to provide a forum for dialogue between the Warsaw Pact and NATO. It was renamed the Organisation for Security and Cooperation in Europe (OSCE) in 1990.

Constitutional Treaty: Emerging out of the work of the Convention on the Future of Europe, member states reached agreement on a Constitutional Treaty in June 2004 that attempted to provide a clearer structure to the EU by consolidating all previous Treaties into a single document. Reaction to the Treaty was mixed, with many being concerned about the creation of a 'European Constitution' and this eventually resulted in the Treaty being rejected in referendum votes in France and the Netherlands in June 2005.

Consultation procedure: Requires an opinion from the European Parliament before the Council can take a decision.

Convention on the Future of Europe: Established in 2002, chaired by former French President Valéry Giscard d'Estaing. A draft Constitutional Treaty was published in June 2003 which set out possible routes for future European integration in light of the 2004 enlargement of the EU.

Convergence criteria: The economic conditions that member states have to meet before they can participate in the single currency. The criteria are: (1) an average rate of inflation of not more than 1.5 per cent higher than that of the three best performers; (2) a budget deficit of not more than 3 per cent of GDP and a public debt ratio not exceeding 60 per cent of GDP; (3) participation in the narrow bands of the ERM for two years without severe tension or devaluation; (4) average nominal long-term interest rate not more than 2 per cent higher than that of the three best-performing states.

Cooperation procedure: Introduced in the SEA to provide the European Parliament with a greater input to the legislative process so as to reduce the democratic deficit. The Parliament has to be consulted twice before a legislative proposal from the European Commission takes effect.

Council of Europe: Strasbourg-based organisation established in May 1949 to assist with the maintenance of the rules of law and democracy, being separate from the EU.

Council of Ministers: Comprising ministers from member states, it is the main decision-making body of the EU, having legislating and decision-making powers.

Court of Auditors: Monitors the management of the finances of the Community.

Customs Union: When two or more countries establish a free-trade policy among themselves by lifting duties and creating a common external tariff.

Davignon Report: Published in November 1970, it recommended that closer foreign-policy cooperation among member states should be achieved trough the mechanism of European Political Cooperation.

Decisions: A form of EU legislation that has direct applicability in member states without the need for additional national enactment. Decisions could be applied to member states, companies and individuals.

Decolonization: A process that has mainly taken place since the end of the Second World War, whereby colonial powers have granted independence to their former colonies.

Deepening: The advances made in European integration from the initial customs union to the creation of the eurozone.

Democratic deficit: The belief that the EU lacks sufficient democratic and parliamentary supervision. Often used in connection with the desire to increase the powers of the European Parliament.

Détente: The improvement in relations between the US and the Soviet Union that took place in the 1970s and was associated with a number of measures to limit and contain the spread of nuclear and conventional weapons.

Directives: Targeted at member states, requiring them to adopt appropriate legislation, though they are able to decide on the method and form of implementation.

Dunkirk Treaty: A 50-year Treaty of Alliance and Mutual Assistance signed by France and the UK on 5 March 1947 to counter against the possibility of renewed German aggression. Subsequently replaced by the Brussels Treaty.

Economic and Monetary Union (EMU): Although a formal commitment to EMU was established in the Maastricht Treaty on European Union, member states had discussed the idea of monetary union since the 1970 Werner Report.

Empty chair crisis: A period when the Community was brought to a standstill by France's refusal to participate in meetings of the Council of Ministers between July and December 1965.

Enhanced cooperation: Permits those member states that wish to develop deeper forms of integration than others.

Enlargement: The preamble of the Treaties of Rome contains reference to the determination 'to lay the foundations of an ever closer union among the peoples of Europe'.

Europe Agreements: Agreements that have been concluded between the EU and Central and Eastern European countries since 1991.

European Atomic Energy Community (Euratom): Commenced operating on 1 January 1958 to develop nuclear energy, conduct research, create a common market for nuclear fuels and supervise the nuclear industry.

European Central Bank (ECB): Based in Frankfurt, it is responsible for the monetary policy of the eurozone. Its main objective is the maintenance of price stability.

European Coal and Steel Community (ECSC): First example of supranational cooperation among European nations when it commenced operations in 1952.

European Commission: The executive body of the EU and guardian of the Treaties. It has the task of initiating EU legislation and implementing policies that have been agreed on. It also plays an important role in negotiating on behalf of the EU on trade matters and with respect to relations with Third World countries. It can refer matters to the ECJ when agreed policies have not been implemented by member states.

European Communities: A phrase that symbolises the ECSC, EEC and Euratom. Since the Merger Treaty of 1967, each of the three Communities has shared the same institutional structure. The 1993 Maastricht Treaty on European Union officially renamed the EEC the European Community (EC), at which time the EC became a central component of the European Union (EU).

European Council: Provides political direction to the EU. Comprises heads of state or government of the member states and the president of the European Commission.

European Court of Human Rights: Based in Strasbourg within the Council of Europe and hears cases relating to states that have ratified the European Convention on Human Rights.

European Court of Justice: Final arbiter of all legal issues, including the resolution of disputes between EU member states as well as between firms and individuals within the EU.

European Defence Community (EDC): An unsuccessful attempt to create a common European army that failed because of the refusal of the French National Assembly to support it in 1954.

European Economic Area (EEA): Permits the free movement of goods, capital, services and workers between the EU and the countries of the European Free Trade Association (EFTA).

European Economic Community (EEC): Created by the 1957 Treaties of Rome. Revised by negotiations such as the Single European Act (SEA) and

Treaty on European Union (TEU). When the latter entered into force on 1 January 1993, the EEC was renamed the European Community and formed part of the European Union (EU).

European Free Trade Association (EFTA): Created in 1960 to provide a less supranational trading group than the EEC. Its relevance has declined as many EFTA members have joined the EU and at the time of writing its membership is limited to Iceland, Liechtenstein, Norway and Switzerland.

European Monetary System (EMS): A forerunner of the single currency. Established in 1979 as a 'zone of monetary stability'. It comprised the ERM, which was a parity grid for restricting the fluctuation of currencies, the ECU and the European Monetary Cooperation Fund (EMCF).

European Parliament: Comprises Members of the European Parliament (MEPs) who are directly elected for a five-year term of office from each member state, with the number of national MEPs being in proportion to population. The most important area of the European Parliament's influence is its power to amend and adopt legislation via the co-decision procedure, while its approval is also necessary for appointments to the European Commission.

European Political Cooperation (EPC): Cooperation by EC foreign ministers in the field of foreign policy began in 1970 and was replaced with the Common Foreign and Security Policy (CFSP).

European System of Central Banks (ESCB): Responsible for managing the single currency, comprising the European Central Bank and the national banks of all EU member states irrespective of whether they have adopted the euro or not.

European Union (EU): An economic and political union of member states (presently 27). The EU was formally established by the Treaty on European Union and covers a wide range of policies from internal market to the single currency. The origins of the EU can be traced back to the European Coal and Steel Community (ECSC).

Europeanisation: The impact that the EU has had on member states, whereby the pressure of common policies and structures forces a degree of uniformity.

Eurosceptic: Used to describe those that are opposed to European integration as a result of a concern about the loss of national sovereignty. Eurosceptics often favour economic independence rather than deeper European integration.

Eurosclerosis: A term that is generally used in reference to the 1970s when there was little growth in the pace of European integration.

Eurozone: Consists of the member states which have adopted the euro as the single currency.

Exchange Rate Mechanism (ERM): A central component of the European Monetary System (EMS) that was established in 1979. The ERM acted as a stabilizing mechanism for reducing currency fluctuations among the participating countries whose currencies were given an exchange rate set against the European Currency Unit (ECU).

Federalism: In the EU context it is a theory of integration that places emphasis on the building of supranational institutions which in turn limit the influence of nation states.

Flexibility: A concept that is used to highlight a situation whereby all member states are not committed to a specific EU policy, such as the single currency.

Fouchet Plan: A draft Treaty for political union published on 2 November 1961 by a committee chaired by Christopher Fouchet of France. Proposed the creation of a council of Heads of Government or Foreign Ministers where decisions would only be taken by unanimity and the establishment of an international secretariat composed of officials taken from national Foreign Ministries. The plan was opposed by all member states apart from France.

Free trade area: An area where barriers to trade such as customs duties and restrictive trading measures have been removed between two or more countries.

Functionalism: A theory of integration that advocates cooperation between nation states through the creation of organisations that encourage integration in economic, social and technical policies.

Genscher–Colombo Plan: In 1981 the German and Italian foreign ministers, Hans-Dietrich Genscher and Emilio Colombo, set out a plan to extend European Political Cooperation to cover security and defence issues.

Glasnost: Mikhail Gorbachev championed 'openness' as a means of advancing reform in the Soviet Union from the mid-1980s onwards.

Gross domestic product: The total value of the goods and services produced in a country over a period of one year. It excludes foreign-exchange earnings.

Hallstein Doctrine: Named after Walter Hallstein, this policy stipulated that the Federal Republic of Germany (FRG) was the sole representative of Germany because, in contrast to the government in the German Democratic Republic (GDR), the FRG's government had been democratically elected.

Harmonisation: The process of bringing states closer together by the setting of common European standards from which they cannot deviate.

High Authority: The administrating body of the ECSC and forerunner of the European Commission.

High Representative for Foreign Affairs and Security Policy: Introduced in the Treaty of Lisbon, this new post combines the previous jobs of High Representative and the European Commissioner for External Affairs. The High Representative is responsible for conducting the EU common foreign and security policy, including presiding over the Foreign Affairs Council and having responsibility for the EU External Action Service and EU delegations in third countries and international organisations.

Interest groups: Often used in the same context as pressure groups, they are essentially a group of individuals who aim to exert influence on political decisions.

Intergovernmental conference (IGC): A negotiating forum comprising representatives of all member states with the aim of making changes to the EU's activities.

Intergovernmentalism: An approach to European integration which emphasises the centrality of member states and which seeks to limit the influence of supranational institutions.

Internal market: The EU internal market where member states have deepened cooperation beyond the initial customs union to create 'an area without frontiers in which the free movement of goods, persons, services and capital is ensured'.

Iron curtain: Used during the Cold War to refer to the East–West division of Europe.

Justice and Home Affairs (JHA): Introduced in the TEU to increase co-operation among member states on matters of asylum policy, the crossing of the external borders of member states, immigration policy, combating drugs, combating international fraud, judicial cooperation in civil and criminal matters, customs cooperation and police cooperation.

League of Nations: Established in April 1919 as a result of the atrocities of the First World War, its efforts to promote collective security failed because of the aggression of Germany and Japan during the interwar period.

Liberal intergovernmentalism: A theoretical account that places emphasis on the manner in which the EU has been transformed by a series of inter-governmental bargains. This theory states that integration will take place only when there exists enough domestic political support for further integration and when there is a convergence in the preferences of governments.

Luxembourg Compromise: An informal agreement that was created in January 1966 as a means of overcoming France's boycott of the Community (the so-called empty chair crisis).

Marshall Plan: In June 1947 US Secretary of State, General George C. Marshall, set out a plan to improve the economic recovery of European states by means of US financial assistance. During 1948–51 the plan distributed just over $12,500m in aid.

Merger Treaty: Established a single Council of Ministers and a single Commission for Euratom, the ECSC and the EEC, which came into force on 1 July 1967.

Multi-level governance: The range of different actors that have an input to EU politics at the European, national and sub-national (regional/local) level.

Multi-speed Europe: When there are variations in the pace of European integration between member states.

Mutual recognition: The principle that a product sold in one EU member state should be able to be sold in any EU member state.

Neo-functionalism: A theory of European integration that considers the path of integration to be an incremental one that involves the spillover of integration from one sector to another.

Net contributor: EU member states that obtain less funding out of the EU than they contribute to its budget.

Net recipients: EU member states that obtain more funding out of the EU than they contribute to its budget.

Non-tariff barriers: Barriers that hinder trade between countries which can include rules on product specifications, technical standards, and rules of origin.

North Atlantic Treaty Organization (NATO): Founded in 1949, it includes all the EU states (apart from Austria, Finland, Ireland and Sweden), Canada, Iceland, Norway, Turkey and the United States. At the heart of NATO is an Article 5 Treaty commitment that an attack on one member is an attack on all members.

Opt-out: A situation when it has been decided that a member state does not want to join others in a specific EU policy area.

Organisation for European Economic Cooperation (OEEC): Established in 1948 to administer assistance provided by the Marshall Plan to Western European countries. Succeeded by the Organisation for Economic Cooperation and Development (OECD).

Ostpolitik: The policy towards Eastern Europe that was adopted by the coalition government of Social Democrats and Liberal Free Democrats that came to power in the Federal Republic of Germany (FRG) in 1969. The policy was described as 'change through rapprochement' and replaced the Hallstein Doctrine.

Own resources: The Community was provided with an ability to raise its own finances in April 1970 rather than being dependent on the financial support of the member states. They have four elements: (1) customs duties based on the imports from non-EU member states; (2) agricultural duties and the sugar and isoglucose levies; (3) the VAT resource based on a portion of the revenue of each member state's VAT; (4) and a percentage of the GNP of a member state.

Perestroika: Just as Mikhail Gorbachev advanced *glasnost* to promote openness, he also championed restructuring through *perestroika*. The process of reform set off a tidal wave of unrest that resulted in the downfall of the Soviet system.

Permanent representation: Each EU member state has a permanent representation to the EU that is based in Brussels and which acts as the national basis for conducting EU negotiations and forms a linkage between national capitals and the EU.

Pillar framework: The Treaty on European Union introduced a three-pillar structure that reflected a Greek temple, with the EU sitting astride each pillar. Pillar one consisted of the European Community which included the EEC, the ECSC and Euratom. Pillar two consisted of the Common Foreign and Security Policy (CFSP) and pillar three Justice and Home Affairs (JHA). Cooperation in pillars two and three was based on intergovernmental methods that did not include the supranational cooperation of the first pillar.

Pleven Plan: The Plan for a European Defence Community that was put forward by the French Prime Minister René Pleven on 24 October 1950.

President of the European Council: Introduced in the Treaty of Lisbon, the President is elected for a period of two and a half years, thereby replacing the previous system whereby the Presidency rotated between among EU member states on a six-monthly basis.

Price support mechanism: The system of agricultural support for farmers that often results in higher food prices.

Qualified majority voting (QMV): A process of decision-taking where it is possible for decisions to be passed if there is sufficient backing for the initiative, with votes being divided among member states in proportion to their relative size.

Red lines: In EU negotiations this term emphasises the policy areas that governments are unwilling to compromise on.

Referendum: Governments often ask their electorate to register their vote on policies and decisions. In the EU context referendums have sometimes been used when a member state has applied for membership as well as to approve significant changes, such as joining the single currency.

Regulations: A form of EU legislation (others are decisions and directives) that are directly applicable and fully binding on those that the regulation is applicable to. This includes the administrations of member states.

Resolutions: A method that the Council uses to highlight a political commitment and does not require any need for binding legislation. They do not require the Commission to propose them.

Schengen Agreement: Signed in the Luxembourg town of Schengen in 1985 to remove border controls between EU member states. The initial signature countries were Belgium, France, Germany, Luxembourg, the Netherlands, Portugal and Spain. The Agreement was incorporated into it by the Treaty of Amsterdam.

Schuman Plan: Signed on 9 May 1950 and resulted in the establishment of the European Coal and Steel Community (ECSC).

Second Cold War: After the era of détente that dominated much of the 1970s there emerged a period of superpower tension during 1979–85 which became known as the Second Cold War.

Sectoral integration: A view of integration that takes an incremental approach sector by sector.

Sinatra Doctrine: After the collapse of the Berlin Wall the Soviet Union adopted a policy of non-intervention in Central and Eastern Europe. Known as the Sinatra Doctrine by alluding to the song 'My Way' from the famous American singer Frank Sinatra.

Single European Act (SEA): Played a key role in advancing the internal market programme, widening the scope of the competence of the EC and advancing the cause of Economic and Monetary Union (EMU).

'Snake in the tunnel': A March 1972 agreement that limited the fluctuation of currencies of European nations by means of restricting movement against the US dollar at a rate of 1.25 per cent on either side.

Social Charter: Adopted in December 1989 at the Strasbourg European Council, it was a non-legally binding agreement that emphasised the need to develop a social dimension to the internal market programme.

Solemn Declaration: At the June 1983 Stuttgart European Council member states agreed to a 'Solemn Declaration' which emphasised the international identity of the Community and noted the desire to develop foreign-policy cooperation beyond European Political Cooperation (EPC).

Sovereignty: Nation states have the right to take responsibility for the decisions within their own borders. Eurosceptics argue that European integration has undermined national sovereignty.

Spheres of influence: The ability of a country to exercise influence over other countries. It is a term that has been used to highlight the influence that the Soviet Union and United States exercised over countries during the Cold War.

Spillover: The neo-functionalist view that sectoral integration in one area would have an impact on other areas.

Stability and Growth Pact: At the December 1996 Dublin European Council agreement was reached on a set of conditions that necessitated members to adhere to strict budget and fiscal policies to ensure that they could participate in the single currency.

State aids: Finance provided by member state governments to companies to support their operations, which can provide them with an unfair advantage vis-à-vis companies in other member states. EU competition law requires such support be subject to scrutiny by the European Commission, with the European Court of Justice being the final arbiter.

Structural funds: Promotes cohesion between EU member states. Structural funds are the European Social Fund, the European Regional and Development Fund and the guidance section of the European Agricultural Guidance and Guarantee Fund.

Subsidiarity: The concept that decisions should be taken at the lowest level of government. It that is not possible then the decision should be passed up to the next, or most appropriate, level of government.

Subnational: Decisions that are taken below the level of central government, such as local and regional government.

Superpower: Countries that have resources that are far greater than others. During the Cold War it was recognised that the only superpowers were the US and Soviet Union.

Supranational: National governments share sovereignty with each other and establish supranational institutions above the nation state to co-ordinate policies.

Third countries: Any state that is not a member of an organisation such as the EU.

Third World: An expression that is used to refer to those less developed countries that are mainly to be found in Africa, Asia and Latin America. Such countries tend to be reliant on producing primary products and generally suffer from poor infrastructure.

Transparency: The degree of openness within the EU institutions. Includes ensuring that there is access to information and documents, and that information is easy to read. Questions about transparency often reflect a view that the EU decision-making is remote and inaccessible.

Transposition: The process whereby EU law is written into national legislation, being required for Directives.

Treaty of Amsterdam: Signed in 1997, it came into effect in 1999. It widened the scope of the co-decision procedure, increased the use of qualified majority voting, improved the effectiveness of foreign policy cooperation, incorporated the Schengen Agreement into the Community and established an employment chapter.

Treaty of Lisbon: After the failure of the Constitutional Treaty, member states agreed to a Treaty of Lisbon on 13 December 2007 which entered into force on 1 December 2009. Key provisions of the Treaty include the creation of the post of President of the European Council, the new position of High Representative, a redistribution of weighting of votes among member states and a removal of national vetoes in a number of policy areas, the creation of a smaller European Commission and the strengthening in the powers of the European Parliament.

Treaty of Nice: Signed in 2001, it came into effect in 2003. It attempted to reform the EU to take account of enlargement. Notable changes included reform to the European Commission and the weighting of votes in the Council for decisions by a qualified majority.

Treaties of Rome: Signed in 1957 and came into effect in 1958. Established the European Economic Community (EEC) and the European Atomic Energy Community (Euratom).

Treaty on European Union (TEU): Signed in 1992, it came into effect in 1993 and is otherwise known as the Maastricht Treaty. Among other measures it increased the powers of the European Parliament, established the pillar framework and set a deadline for monetary union.

Truman Doctrine: The commitment made by US President Truman in March 1947 to maintain freedom throughout the world by limiting the spread of Communism.

Two-speed Europe: Describes a situation when a group of member states choose to advance at a faster pace of integration than other member states.

Unanimity: A form of voting in the Council. Requires that no member state can vote against a proposal, though it is possible to have abstentions.

Warsaw Pact: Established in 1955 as the Soviet Union's response to NATO. Following the ending of the Cold War, the Warsaw Pact was dissolved on 1 April 1991.

Werner Report: Published in October 1970, it set out a three-stage process for the creation of monetary union within a period of ten years.

Western European Union (WEU): Established in 1955 to coordinate foreign and security policy among Western European nations, it was quickly over-shadowed by NATO. It was reactivated in the 1980s and was heavily involved in strengthening the foreign and defence identity of the EC. In 1999 the WEU took the decision to relinquish its military headquarters and its responsibility in crisis management as a result of the decision by EU member states to strengthen the European Security and Defence Policy (ESDP).

Yaoundé Convention: A trade agreement between 'the Six' and the 18 nations of the Associated African States and Madagascar which was signed in 1963 in Yaoundé, Cameroon. Entering into force in 1964, the Convention was renegotiated in 1969 and was superseded by the Lomé Convention.

Part 1

BACKGROUND

1

The Context of European Integration

On the afternoon of 9 May 1950 in the elaborate clock room of the French foreign ministry in Paris, the French Foreign Minister, **Robert Schuman**, proposed the creation of an organisation that would take responsibility for Franco-German coal and steel production [**Document 9, p. 119**]. Barely five years after the end of the Second World War, the Declaration aimed to link the interests of European states by establishing a common organisation to oversee coal and steel production. The choice of coal and steel was deliberate because they represented the most important economic industries at the time and were the basis for military power. More than six decades later, observers may find it difficult to understand the true significance of the proposals that Schuman advanced: not only did they provide a structure to unite countries that had spent much of the previous century at war with each other, but they represented a departure from the tactics employed after the First World War when French attempts to suppress German power had failed.

Schuman's plans were attractive to France and Germany for different reasons. For France, they offered the prospect of leadership in Europe and a method of controlling (but not suppressing) Germany. For Germany, they offered the chance to cleanse the horrors of the Third Reich and to be treated as an equal partner with other European countries. Apart from the support of France and Germany, Schuman's proposals were warmly received in the capitals of Belgium, Italy, Luxembourg and the Netherlands and resulted in 'the Six' countries agreeing on 18 April 1951 to establish a **European Coal and Steel Community** (ECSC) which eventually came into operation on 25 July 1952. Five years later, in March 1957, the same six countries signed the Treaties of Rome that created the **European Economic Community** (EEC) and **European Atomic Energy Community** (Euratom) [**Document 14, p. 123**].

In the years that have passed, numerous reforms and changes have enhanced the influence of the institutions that govern the European Union (EU) of today. There has also taken place an increase in membership, from

Schuman, Robert (1886–1963): Prime Minister of France 1947–48; Foreign Minister 1948–55. On 9 May 1950 he advanced the Schuman Plan that resulted in the establishment of the European Coal and Steel Community. President of the European Movement 1955–61; head of the European Parliamentary Assembly 1958–60.

European Coal and Steel Community (ECSC): First example of supranational cooperation among European nations when it commenced operations in 1952.

European Economic Community (EEC): Created by the 1957 Treaties of Rome. Revised by negotiations such as the Single European Act and Treaty on European Union. When the latter entered into force on 1 January 1993, the EEC was renamed the European Community and formed part of the European Union (EU).

European Atomic Energy Community (Euratom): Commenced operating on 1 January 1958 to develop nuclear energy, conduct research, create a common market for nuclear fuels and supervise the nuclear industry.

Federalism: In the EU context it is a theory of integration that places emphasis on the building of supranational institutions which in turn limit the influence of nation states.

Spinelli, Altiero (1907–86): A key figure in federalist organisations throughout the 1940s and 1950s who advocated a federal United States of Europe. He established the European Federalist Movement in Milan in 1943 and the European Union of Federalists in 1946. He was a member of the European Commission 1970–76 and later served as a member of the European Parliament 1979–86.

de Gasperi, Alcide (1881–1954): A founding father of Europe, he was Prime Minister of Italy from 1945 to 1954, during which time he pursued the modernisation of the Italian economy. He steered a pro-western foreign policy, being a committed supporter of greater European integration.

the six states of the ECSC to 27 member states as of 2009, while Croatia, Turkey and the Former Yugoslav Republic of Macedonia are candidate countries for membership [**Document 35, p. 142**]. This process of enlargement has resulted in the EU's population swelling by 2008 to some 497 million, a figure that will only increase in the future [**Document 35, p. 142**]. The likelihood of further enlargement brings with it a redefinition of the boundaries of the EU, with many studies raising the question of 'So where, then, is Europe?' (McCormick, 2008: 35). Up until the late 1980s the Cold War division of Europe made this a straightforward task. However, in a post-Cold War world, the experience of enlargement to former Eastern bloc countries has resulted in many other countries seeking membership, with Iceland in 2009 being the latest to express an interest. The end result is that EU membership could possibly increase to 36 member states (or even more).

At the same time, there has occurred a growth in the number of policies that are now tackled at the EU level, from matters relating to consumer affairs and the environment to international trade policy and the single currency. And although some of these developments have been the product of incremental change over the last six decades, a great many more have been undertaken in the period since 1986. There has therefore been a considerable quickening in the pace of European integration in recent times, as evidenced by the creation of the single currency and the fact that the EU's membership has more than doubled in the period since 1990. More and more decisions that were once taken at the national level are now taken at a European level, involving the input of the supranational institutions of the European Commission and European Parliament as well as the member states in the form of the Council of Ministers. Member states are also faced with the impact of rulings by the European Court of Justice which emphasises the fact that European law has supremacy over national law.

In evaluating the history of European integration, academics have sought to chart the events that have occurred as well as to offer theoretical models to provide a fuller explanation of events and processes. Theories are of particular importance because they move us away from merely describing events to instead creating structures that provide the opportunity to make decisions about the relevancy of information. This is particularly important in a European context where students are faced with a tidal wave of material and as such theories enable a student to make judgements between relevant and irrelevant information (Blair and Curtis, 2009: 125).

In the early days of European integration, **federalism** was advocated by many to be a worthwhile model because the World Wars of the first half of the twentieth century emphasised that nation states could not be relied on to provide stability, peace and security for their populations. To overcome this situation, federalists such as **Altiero Spinelli** and **Alcide de Gasperi** argued that nation states should be embedded in a broader political system, that of a federal Europe. However, many European governments were opposed to the idea of transferring power to new federal institutions.

The federal vision was soon replaced by **functionalism**, which was developed in the 1930s by **David Mitrany**. Functionalist theory argued that integration should take place in specific sectors of the economy, such as coal or agriculture, with supranational organisations therefore being established to tackle particular economic or technical problems. But while functionalists believed that governments would be willing to surrender some sovereignty in specific policy areas to new functional bodies where there was no direct threat to the nation state, the view that it would be possible to separate functional cooperation from domestic political interests did not reflect reality. A consequence of this was the adaptation of functionalism into a revised theory of **neo-functionalism** which emphasised the fact that the integration process involved bargaining and compromise, and that cooperation among member states in less contentious areas of policy would result in pressure building up for cooperation in others. Although this so-called 'spillover effect' meant that neo-functionalism held sway in the early years of European integration, its shine began to fade by the mid-1960s as it could not account for the slowdown in integration that arose out of France not taking part in the Community's affairs in 1965. This was a period known as the 'empty chair crisis' and was resolved by a compromise that gave member states a veto over policies that impinged on their national interests. In other words, the future of integration was very much dependent on the ability of member states to agree among themselves, with this view being advanced in an approach that became to be known as **intergovernmentalism**. This focus on the importance of member states was further refined in the **liberal intergovernmentalism** approach that has been particularly applied to the study of key periods in the history of European integration, most notably **intergovernmental conference** (IGC) negotiations which are particularly influenced by the interests of member states.

Although such theories are of great use in helping to structure arguments by enabling us to explain in more detail patterns of activity rather than just describing events, it is nevertheless the case that as the European integration process has developed it has become increasingly difficult for any one particular theory to offer an accurate picture of the EU. The reality of this situation is that many scholars prefer to analyse the EU through the concept of '**multi-level governance**', which conveys a picture of policies being agreed to at the supranational level above the state, at the national level, as well as at the **subnational** level. Additionally, in recent years scholars have also made use of the concept of **Europeanisation**, which refers to the way in which European integration affects domestic political structures by necessitating

Functionalism: A theory of integration that advocates cooperation between nation states through the creation of organisations that encourage integration in economic, social and technical policies.

Mitrany, David (1888–1975): Romanian-born scholar who was the founding father of functionalism. He regarded nationalism as a major threat to world and European peace and argued that states should cooperate in such policy sectors as agriculture, science and transport.

Neo-functionalism: A theory of European integration that considers the path of integration to be an incremental one that involves the spillover of integration from one sector to another.

Intergovernmentalism: An approach to European integration which emphasises the centrality of member states and which seeks to limit the influence of supranational institutions.

Liberal intergovernmentalism: A theoretical account that places emphasis on the manner in which the EU has been transformed by a series of intergovernmental bargains. This theory states that integration will take place only when there exists enough domestic political support for further integration and when there is a convergence in the preferences of governments.

Intergovernmental conference (IGC): A negotiating forum comprising representatives of all member states with the aim of making changes to the EU's activities.

Multi-level governance: The range of different actors that have an input to EU politics at the European, national and sub-national (regional/local) level.

Subnational: Decisions that are taken below the level of central government, such as local and regional government.

Europeanisation: The impact that the EU has had on member states, whereby the pressure of common policies and structures forces a degree of uniformity.

Sovereignty: Nation states have the right to take responsibility for the decisions within their own borders. Eurosceptics argue that European integration has undermined national sovereignty.

Regulations: A form of EU legislation (others are decisions and directives) that are directly applicable and fully binding on those that the regulation is applicable to. This includes the administrations of member states.

organisations to adopt structures and policies that enable them to respond to and be able to influence decisions that are taken at the European level. This is a situation that has been characterised by Tanja Börzel and Thomas Risse as one of 'uploading' the preferences of national actors to the supranational EU and the 'downloading' of the EU's supranational policies to the national level (Börzel and Risse, 2003: 62).

But while such approaches offer value to academic analysis, they often have little impact on the wider public or for that matter policy makers. Thus, rather than picturing European integration as a process of Europeanisation, some individuals may conclude that the cumulative effect of these changes has been an unacceptable transfer of power away from national governments and a reduction in national **sovereignty** that can only be rectified by a member state withdrawing from the EU. Yet, as has been argued elsewhere, the concept of a state being completely sovereign over its affairs is out of date. In the area of economic affairs, virtually all of the world's economies are dependent on international trade and are affected by the vagaries of financial markets, demand, investment opportunities and so on that can take place on the other side of the world. The most obvious recent example of this was the way in which the international financial crisis that took hold in 2008 emerged in the sub-prime housing market of the US and yet necessitated European governments to take individual and collective response. In other fields, such as legal affairs, nation states are also influenced by decisions that are taken outside of their borders. This includes the decisions taken by the United Nations Security Council on international security.

Concerns about loss of sovereignty tend to be linked to claims that the cost of EU membership for some member states outweigh the benefits. In crude terms, they pay in more money than they get out. It is an argument that has been used to considerable effect by the UK Independence Party in European Parliamentary elections. In the most recent elections of 2009 they obtained 13 out of a total of 72 UK MEPs, which was an increase on the 2004 elections when they obtained 11 out of a total of 78 UK MEPs (a reduction in the number of total MEPs was the result of a redistribution of MEPs across the EU to take account of enlargement) [**Document 36, p. 144**]. The simplicity of this argument responds to fears among the electorate that interference from 'Brussels' has led to unnecessary legislation that would not otherwise be implemented if the country was outside the EU. Such an argument fails to consider that there are often good reasons to have common regulation, while it would also be naïve of eurosceptics to think that national governments are not capable of excessive **regulations**. For example, much of the interference that affects everyday life is the source of decisions taken at a national level, a factor that is particularly evident in the area of health and safety legislation.

Some critics of European integration appreciate that certain benefits accrue from membership. This principally constitutes the ability to trade and move freely within Europe, while initiatives that seek to deepen European integration into other policy areas are steadfastly resisted. In contrast to these viewpoints, other individuals consider that the EU does not possess enough power, influence and resources for it to be able to effectively deal with the challenges that it faces. The argument here is that the series of negotiations that have shaped the EU have been determined by the need to achieve compromise and as such the EU's influence and abilities have often been deliberately limited to appease member state concern.

As ever, there is an element of truth in each of these categorisations. On the one hand, EU rules can appear to be overly burdensome, and yet at the same time the EU is often ill equipped to deal with its challenges. Beneath these differing views is the greater reality that the EU's structure and scope of policy competences have been the product of the decisions taken by member state governments. Indeed, when we examine the 'so-called' history-making decisions that came out of IGC negotiations, it is evident that member state governments agreed to all the outcomes of the Single European Act, Treaty on European Union, Treaty of Amsterdam and Treaty of Nice (Peterson, 1995). Similarly, the expansion in the European Commission's responsibility into matters relating to the **internal market**, and the agreement to make greater use of the **qualified majority voting** (QMV) procedure within the Council of Ministers, were also judged to be appropriate developments by member state governments.

It is not only that member state governments have agreed to the key strategic decisions that have affected the history of European integration, it is also that they have often been over-enthusiastic when it comes to implementing EU rules and regulations in their own country. The frustration that business communities and individuals have at what they perceive to be unnecessary EU legislation is often because the member state government has over-implemented EU legislation by exceeding the minimum requirements. This is commonly referred to as 'gold-plating', whereby national governments extend the scope of European legislation by going beyond the specific guidelines that have been set when they commence the process of the **transposition** of European decisions into national legislation. Other examples of over-implementation include 'regulatory creep' as a result of over-zealous implementation and what is known as 'double banking' whereby a member state government fails to rationalise the overlap between existing national legislation and EU-sourced legislation. Yet, as with many other points relating to the EU, the possibility of being critical of such a process is not as clear cut as you might think. This is because there can be good reasons for a government to take a decision to over-implement EU legislation. Thus

Internal market: The EU internal market where member states have deepened cooperation beyond the initial customs union to create 'an area without frontiers in which the free movement of goods, persons, services and capital is ensured'.

Qualified majority voting (QMV): A process of decision-taking where it is possible for decisions to be passed if there is sufficient backing for the initiative, with votes being divided among member states in proportion to their relative size.

Transposition: The process whereby EU law is written into national legislation, being required for Directives.

although the UK adopts a policy of imposing an annual MOT test on all cars that are three or more years old, the minimum EU requirement is that cars should be tested for road-worthiness every other year when they are four or more years old. In basic terms, the UK over-implements this aspect of EU legislation. Critics could point to the financial savings to be achieved by having a less rigorous policy that still met the EU standard. However, a decision to adopt such a policy would potentially result in a lessening in road-safety standards and lead to an increase in accidents. So in cases such as this the costs and benefits of meeting or exceeding the EU requirement need to be clearly thought through.

Whatever the outcome of decisions such as that on MOT testing requirements, which in the case of the UK has remained unchanged since 1968, member states can influence the shaping of the EU and the way in which the policies that emerge at the European level impact on the national level. This evidence of member states acting as the key decision-maker contrasts with the initial views held by Robert Schuman and **Jean Monnet** (later president of the ECSC). They argued that once member states had enjoyed the benefits of integration in one area they would inevitably agree to extend cooperation into other policy areas through a form of domino effect. According to this idea of spillover, the experience of integrating coal and steel industries would in time lead to the joining together of defence industries which would in turn forge the creation of a common foreign and defence policy. Such an approach has come to be known as the 'Monnet method'. But integration has been neither inevitable nor automatic. This was initially demonstrated by the collapse of the **European Defence Community** (EDC) in 1954 [**Document 12, p. 121**]. A decade later, France's refusal to accept European Commission proposals to enhance the powers of the European Parliament and extend the use of QMV resulted in the government in Paris refusing to take part in meetings of the Council of Ministers in the second half of 1965. This period, which is referred to as the 'empty chair crisis', directly led to the Luxembourg compromise of January 1966 which cemented the position of member states and limited the opportunity for further European integration until the mid-1980s [**Document 19, p. 128**]. Thus, moves towards the taking of decisions at a European level and the transfer of power away from member states have been greatly influenced by the decisions of member states.

In taking such a path, member state governments have for the most part concluded that a fundamental benefit of European integration has been the ability to tackle problems that could not be adequately dealt with by any one individual state. Hence, in the post-war period many countries were willing to engage in new forms of cooperation and to create supranational structures to administer common policies purely because they considered that individual

Monnet, Jean (1888–1979): Key figure in the European integration process after 1945. As head of the French Planning Commission he highlighted the need for European nations to recover through a joint strategy. An advocate of a gradual approach to European integration, he was a significant influence behind the Schuman Plan and was appointed the first President of the High Authority of the European Coal and Steel Community.

European Defence Community (EDC): An unsuccessful attempt to create a common European army that failed because of the refusal of the French National Assembly to support it in 1954.

governments were not able to cope with the challenges that Western Europe faced. In examining the factors that motivated states to engage in such a process of integration, Alan Milward has emphasised the point that the creation of the ECSC represented a desire to satisfy French national interests by ensuring the continued economic recovery of France (Milward, 1984). Germany was equally keen to participate in the ECSC (as was Italy) because it provided a means of rehabilitation, while the smaller nations of Belgium, Luxembourg and the Netherlands realised that they could not economically afford to distance themselves from the markets of France and Germany. A number of years later, the British government concluded that the economic benefits of participating in the EEC far outweighed the impact that integration would have on national sovereignty. This focus on the national interest has led Milward to argue that European integration took place only when it was demanded by nation states and that supranational institutions were established for specific purposes and not as a means of eclipsing the nation state (Milward, 1992).

But while there is great strength in this argument, member states have not acted as free agents in the European-integration process. Thus, just as Monnet and Schuman were influenced by the Second World War, it is also the case that the decisions taken at the outset of European integration had a significant impact in determining subsequent decisions. In other words, the work of Monnet and Schuman set the European integration project on a certain path of travel. Consequently, even though the Monnet method may not have been successful, the decisions that were taken in the early years have proven to be very influential. This has been commonly referred to as a path-dependency approach.

A casual observer might be forgiven for thinking that a cumulative effect of over 60 years of European integration and the continued desire of countries to join the EU would be reflected in the Union having a high degree of popularity within the member states. One might also conclude that the experience of doing business with each other would produce a convergence of views among the member states. Yet for both questions the opposite has been the case. Eurosceptic causes have taken hold in all member states, while there additionally appears to be a decline in interest in European affairs among the electorate. Thus, the average level of voting fell for the seventh time running at the June 2009 European Parliamentary elections. Of the 'established' member states, the UK has traditionally had one of the lowest voter turnouts and this trend continued in 2009 with just 35 per cent of the electorate voting. Surprisingly, however, this was still higher than some of the new member states, where the low election results that were recorded in the 2004 elections did not result in significant improvement in the 2009 elections. For instance, only one in five of the electorate voted in Slovakia [**Document 37, p. 145**].

This, of course, raises the question as to the reasons for such an outcome. Are low turnouts in European elections the result of voter apathy? Does the electorate appreciate the many benefits of EU membership? Or is it simply the case that we should not be surprised by the lack of support for and awareness of European integration? In this sense, should we just accept the fact that the transfer of power away from member states is likely to be greeted with concerns about the erosion of sovereignty among a national electorate that continue in their eyes to be governed and influenced by law and policies that are shaped within a member state? Key policies such as taxation and education continue to be set by national governments. Up till now a European army or police force has not been created, although tellingly the pressure among member states of having to respond to conflicts in Iraq and Afghanistan in the first decade of the twenty-first century have increased the desire among some member states (particularly France) to establish a European army. And while this may signal the creeping influence of European integration, the practical realities of having to respond to common threats among all member states can necessitate such decisions being taken. Thus, European citizens are presented with a picture that highlights the continued influence of member states and at the same time the erosion in their ability to individually determine many policies. It is a confusing picture that raises a number of important questions. Why have member states been willing to share the responsibility for taking decisions with other member states? Why have particular member states adopted a more **eurosceptic** approach than others? What are the implications of some member states participating in certain policy areas while others choose not?

The preceding summary provides a superficial examination of some of the key issues and questions that concern the study of European integration. Nevertheless, students may begin to appreciate the complex nature of the study of the European Union. The chapters that follow provide an overview of the history of European integration without entering into the blow-by-blow account that would be impossible in such a concise book. Readers are therefore encouraged to consult the other studies that are listed at the end of the book for more detailed explanations of the policies and personalities that are highlighted in this text.

Eurosceptic: Used to describe those that are opposed to European integration as a result of a concern about the loss of national sovereignty. Eurosceptics often favour economic independence rather than deeper European integration.

Part 2

ANALYSIS

2

The Road to Rome: 1945–57

Three linked but distinct issues dominated European politics in the immediate post-war period. The first of these concerned the need to tackle the economic and physical destruction caused by war. A second and related issue was how Germany – which had been at the forefront of the two world wars – could be rehabilitated into a peaceful post-war Europe. The third and final issue concerned the threat posed to Europe by the Soviet Union, as emphasised by the bipolar division of Europe into Eastern and Western **spheres of influence**.

THE EMERGENCE OF EUROPEAN UNITY

Despite the fact that the ideal of European unity was overwhelmingly influenced by the impact of the Second World War, the plan of a united Europe that overcame national jealousies was not a new idea. In the inter-war years of 1918–39 a number of plans were produced that sought to create new forms of cooperation among European nations. This included the Pan-European Union that was founded in 1923 by the Austrian Count Richard Coudenhove-Kalergi, who had argued the previous year for the creation of a European federation in his book *Paneuropa*. In the aftermath of the devastating impact of the First World War, the Pan-European Union acquired a loyal following that included individuals who shaped European integration in the post-1945 era – such as **Konrad Adenauer** and **Georges Pompidou** – as well as leading politicians of the time. The latter included **Aristide Briand**, who, as French Foreign Minister, proposed a scheme to create a confederal bond between European states at the League of Nations in September 1929. Some months later, these ideas were outlined in the Briand Memorandum of 1 May 1930. It argued that European governments should establish a union within the

Spheres of influence: The ability of a country to exercise influence over other countries. It is a term that has been used to highlight the influence that the Soviet Union and United States exercised over countries during the Cold War.

Adenauer, Konrad (1876–1967): First Chancellor of the Federal Republic of Germany 1949–63. Negotiated German entry into the EEC and NATO; developed a close relationship with France that resulted in the 1963 Treaty of Friendship between the two nations.

Pompidou, Georges (1911–74): President of France from 1969 until his death in 1974. An influential figure behind the December 1969 Hague summit which fostered a climate of optimism in the Community.

Briand, Aristide (1862–1932): As French Foreign Minister, he was one of the first advocates of a European Federal Union through a proposal to the League of Nations on 5 September 1929. A lack of support from other member states and Briand's death in 1932 brought to an end his proposals.

League of Nations: Established in April 1919 as a result of the atrocities of the First World War, its efforts to promote collective security failed because of the aggression of Germany and Japan during the interwar period.

de Gaulle, Charles (1890–1970): Leader of the Free French during the Second World War and President of France 1958–69. Attached great emphasis to European integration, partly to lessen the reliance on the US. He threw the Community into crisis with the French boycott in the Council of Ministers January–June 1965. He also vetoed UK applications to join the Community in 1963 and 1967.

Customs Union: When two or more countries establish a free-trade policy among themselves by lifting duties and creating a common external tariff.

Cold War: The rivalry between the US and the Soviet Union after the end of the Second World War, which continued until the collapse of Communism in 1989 and the break-up of the Soviet Union in 1991.

structure of the **League of Nations** and would include the creation of a permanent political committee and supporting secretariat [**Document 1, p. 114**]. Despite the historical significance of Briand's proposals, there was a conspicuous lack of support from other leading European nations. The lack of interest from the likes of Britain, Germany and Italy, combined with Briand's death in March 1932, brought to an end the proposals that had been outlined in the Briand Memorandum.

The remainder of the 1930s saw little progress towards European unity and it would take the horrors of the Second World War to revive interest in European integration. In 1941 the anti-fascists who had been imprisoned by the Italian dictator Benito Mussolini published the Ventotene Manifesto, which called for a European Federation to provide new structures because of the perceived failure of nation states to maintain peace and stability in the first half of the twentieth century. The Free French, led by General **Charles de Gaulle**, also expressed an interest in some form of European cooperation, with de Gaulle inviting Europeans on 11 November 1942 'to join together in a practical and lasting fashion'. Nearly two years later, the leaders of Belgium, Luxembourg and the Netherlands announced in September 1944 that they wished to establish a Benelux **customs union** (eventually established in January 1948). Such initiatives, according to Hoffman, were greatly influenced by the wartime resistance movement which had 'an acute awareness of the dangers of nationalist celebrations and national fragmentation in Western Europe' (Hoffman, 1966: 870). Thus, having fought against the nationalist forces that were the cause of the conflict, the resistance movement concluded that peace could only be secured through the creation of some form of European framework (Lipgens, 1982: 44–58). This directly led to the formation in December 1946 of the European Union of Federalists (Européenne des Fedéralistes), which argued for the creation of a united states of Europe and the creation of a constitution for this purpose (Harrison, 1974: 47).

Over and above all other factors, European integration in the post-war period was shaped by two key developments. The first concerned the need to tackle the dire economic situation that affected European nations as a result of the war having inflicted massive infrastructure damage that obliterated houses, factories and roads. This difficult economic situation impacted on the ability of European nations to defend themselves, as emphasised in February 1947 when Britain was incapable of providing support to Greece at a time when the government in Athens was threatened by the attempts of Communist guerrillas to take power. The second key factor was the emerging **Cold War** bipolar division of Europe, which became evident at the summit meetings that took place in 1945 between the United States, the Soviet Union and Britain in an attempt to reach agreement on the post-Second World War settlement. At the Yalta summit of 4–11 February 1945 it was agreed that Germany would be divided into four occupation zones that would be governed by the United States, Soviet Union, Britain and France. This was the first outward sign of the division of Europe into 'spheres of influence', a policy which had itself initially been reflected in the October 1944 agreement in which UK Prime Minister **Winston Churchill** and Soviet leader Joseph Stalin agreed to a 50:50 division of Yugoslavia and a 90:10 division of Greece in Britain's favour. But while the Western Allies may at the time have viewed the division of Europe to be a temporary affair, it rapidly became apparent that the Soviet Union regarded the division to be a permanent fixture and ensured that governments favourable to its interests were installed in those countries that fell within its sphere of influence. The reality of this state of affairs prompted Churchill to observe in his March 1946 '**iron curtain**' speech at Fulton, Missouri that 'an iron curtain has descended across the [European] continent' [**Document 2, p. 114**]. Some months later, in September 1946, Churchill spoke of the need to 'build a kind of United States of Europe' around a Franco-German axis to provide a structure to promote peace and stability [**Document 3, p. 115**]. In arguing for a strong Franco-German axis, Churchill continued with the line of reasoning that he had advanced before the war that Britain was 'with Europe but not of it. We are interested and associated, but not absorbed' (Zurcher, 1958: 6). Although a Franco-German Treaty of Friendship was not signed until 1963, the relationship between France and Germany not only provided the initial impetus to closer European unity in the post-1945 era, but also acted as the key driving force behind the process of European integration [**Document 17, p. 127**].

One response to these developments was for the British Foreign Secretary, **Ernest Bevin**, and the French Foreign Minister, **Georges Bidault**, to discuss in 1946 and 1947 the merits of forming a 'third force'. In Bevin's eyes this would involve establishing close relations with the **Commonwealth** to establish a body that was capable of matching the influence of the Soviet Union and the United States. Such a proposal was doomed to failure on three counts. First, the economic and social destruction of the war meant that European economies were unable in the short term to match America and the Soviet Union. Second, the war had brought to the fore demands for **decolonization** that by 1946 were well under way. Finally, the growing pressures of the Cold War meant that European nations quickly realized the fallacy of establishing a third force that could challenge the USA (upon which they relied for security). In this sense, 'rather than seeking to match American strength Western Europe soon looked to Washington for protection from the Soviet Union' (Young, 1991: 30).

The combination of Europe's difficult economic situation and the threat posed by the Soviet Union produced a swift American response. In March

Churchill, Winston (1874–1965): UK Prime Minister 1940–45 and 1951–55. After the landslide Labour Party victory in the 1945 general election, he led the Conservative Party in opposition, during which time he advocated closer European integration, urging for the construction of a United States of Europe in 1946.

Iron curtain: Used during the Cold War to refer to the East–West division of Europe.

Bevin, Ernest (1897–1976): UK Labour Foreign Secretary 1945–51. Played an influential role in the Brussels Treaty and Britain's entry to NATO.

Bidault, Georges (1899–1983): French Foreign Minister under de Gaulle. Although he played an important role in the creation of the OEEC and NATO, he was primarily concerned with Germany's revival.

Commonwealth: A voluntary organisation established in 1931 that comprises former members of the British Empire. By 2009 it had 53 members, the majority of whom have joined since 1945 as a result of the granting of independence.

Decolonization: A process that has mainly taken place since the end of the Second World War, whereby colonial powers have granted independence to their former colonies.

Truman, Harry (1894–1972): President of the United States from 1945–53. Played an important role in the reconstruction of Europe, of which his key initiatives included the Truman Doctrine, the Marshall Plan and the creation of NATO.

Truman Doctrine: The commitment made by US President Truman in March 1947 to maintain freedom throughout the world by limiting the spread of Communism.

Marshall, George C. (1880–1959): US Secretary of State 1947–49. Author of the June 1947 Marshall Plan for the economic rehabilitation of Europe.

Marshall Plan: In June 1947 US Secretary of State, General George C. Marshall, set out a plan to improve the economic recovery of European states by means of US financial assistance. During 1948–51 the plan distributed just over $12,500m in aid.

Bipolar: When two states are in competition for dominance over the other. The Cold War competition between the US and the Soviet Union was regarded as being a bipolar struggle.

1947 US President **Harry Truman** pledged America's support for 'free peoples who are resisting subjugation by armed minorities or by outside pressures'. The **Truman Doctrine**, as it came to be known, marked the start of a more active US foreign policy, where Western Europe was the most immediate beneficiary. Yet an exhausted Europe was not only incapable of defending itself from the Soviet threat, it was also unable to support itself in terms of its food requirements. The stark reality of the dire economic situation that faced Europe was not lost on the United States, which quickly concluded the need to construct a plan that would enable European economic recovery. In a speech at Harvard University in June 1947, US Secretary of State General **George Marshall** outlined a plan to offer economic assistance to aid the recovery of all European states, declaring that 'Europe's requirements for the next three or four years of foreign food and other essential products – principally from America – are so much greater than her present ability to pay that she must have substantial additional help or face economic, social and political deterioration of a very grave character' [**Document 4, p. 116**]. The plan, which proved to be a tremendous success, aimed to promote intra-European trade and create a marketplace that was similar to the US. In aiming to speed up the process of European economic recovery, the United States hoped that an upturn in Europe's fortunes would lessen the dependence on American aid (Lundestad, 1998: 18). To avoid criticism that the **Marshall Plan** was part of a broader US anti-communist policy (an argument that was levelled at the Truman Doctrine), the plan was open to a large number of countries [**Document 4, p. 116**]. But only West European governments accepted the aid, which was in itself a highly predictable outcome. As De Porte comments, 'Though the American offer was nominally open to the Soviet Union as to other European countries, there could have been little expectation that it would join in the required cooperative response or, if it did, that the programme would have received congressional and public support in the United States' (De Porte, 1986: 135).

It is therefore evident that barely two years after the end of the Second World War there was a **bipolar** division of Europe based on Soviet and US spheres of influence. This situation would continue for a further four decades until the dramatic break-up of the Soviet-dominated Eastern bloc in 1989–90. The intervening Cold War proved to be the defining feature of international politics and the institutions that emerged during this period – which in the case of Western Europe included the **North Atlantic Treaty Organization** (NATO) and the EEC and in the case of Eastern Europe included the Warsaw Treaty Organization (or **Warsaw Pact**) and the founding of the Comecon – served to demonstrate both the division of Europe along East–West lines and the role each **superpower** played in underpinning these institutions. It was accordingly the case that the combination of this division and the tension between the two superpowers proved to be both the defining feature of international politics and an instrumental factor in fostering the origins of European integration.

Superpower influence within the European arena was reflected in the rapid assertion of Soviet influence in Eastern Europe: by 1948 Czechoslovakia, East Germany and Poland were under Moscow's influence and in time the Soviet grip on Eastern Europe would become known as the **Brezhnev Doctrine**. In March 1948 the Soviet Union commenced a policy of restricting Western access to Berlin, which materialised into a total blockade of land access to the city by June of that year. This was in essence an economic war, with the method of warfare being starvation and represented an attempt by the Soviet Union to exercise pressure not just on Berlin but on the West in general. Indeed, a future Soviet leader, Nikita Khrushchev, would comment that 'Berlin is the testicle of the West' and 'when I want the West to scream, I squeeze on Berlin'. This 'Berlin blockade' would result in 1.6 million tons of clothing, food, fuel and other necessities being airlifted to the city and provided the first real flash point of the Cold War that demonstrated the potential for superpower conflict. And although the Soviets lifted their blockade on 12 May 1949, the Berlin crisis highlighted the need for the countries of Western Europe to be protected by some form of collective defence system. In this sense, the blockade acted as a key factor in institutionalising the Cold War, a point that in itself would be most noticeable by the erection of the Berlin Wall in 1961. Consequently, the background of the blockade influenced the decision of Britain, France, Belgium, Luxembourg and the Netherlands to sign the **Brussels Treaty** in March 1948, committing the participating members to a system of collective self-defence [**Document 6, p. 117**]. Just over one year later, in April 1949, the principle of collective self-defence would evolve into the signing of the North Atlantic Treaty in Washington by Belgium, Canada, Denmark, France, Iceland, Italy, Luxembourg, the Netherlands, Norway, Portugal, the United Kingdom and the United States. NATO was significant not just because of the commitment to collective self-defence, whereby if one member was attacked then all the other members would be obliged to respond, but because US involvement provided an important balance of power within Europe [**Document 7, p. 118**].

In addition to military and security developments, the division of Europe was highlighted by economic factors. The **Organisation for European Economic Cooperation** (OEEC) was established in April 1948 with the purpose of supervising the Marshall Aid programme, which provided just over $12.5 billion in aid to Europe between 1948 and 1951 (Milward, 1984: 94). Based on a method of cooperation known as intergovernmentalism, the OEEC managed to lower trade barriers among European nations and provided the first small step towards European economic cooperation. But despite

---

North Atlantic Treaty Organization (NATO): Founded in 1949, it includes all the EU states (apart from Austria, Finland, Ireland and Sweden), Canada, Iceland, Norway, Turkey and the United States. At the heart of NATO is an Article 5 Treaty commitment that an attack on one member is an attack on all members.

Warsaw Pact: Established in 1955 as the Soviet Union's response to NATO. Following the ending of the Cold War, the Warsaw Pact was dissolved on 1 April 1991.

Superpower: Countries that have resources that are far greater than others. During the Cold War it was recognised that the only superpowers were the US and Soviet Union.

Brezhnev Doctrine: When politicians in the former Czechoslovakia put in place reforms that undermined the Communist system in 1968, the Soviet Union responded by invading the country to suppress the changes. Soviet willingness to maintain pro-Moscow governments in Central and Eastern Europe was formally outlined in 1969 by the announcement of the Brezhnev Doctrine which advanced the concept of limited sovereignty for the pro-Moscow states.

Brussels Treaty: Signed on 17 March 1948 by Belgium, France, Luxembourg, the Netherlands and the UK to provide a system of collective self-defence.

Organisation for European Economic Cooperation (OEEC): Established in 1948 to administer assistance provided by the Marshall Plan to Western European countries. Succeeded by the Organisation for Economic Cooperation and Development (OECD).

Supranational: National governments share sovereignty with each other and establish supranational institutions above the nation state to co-ordinate policies.

the success of the OEEC, many countries argued that it lacked the necessary **supranational** structures to bring long-term changes to the economic and political situation in Western Europe. This was a view shared by Schuman and Monnet. Monnet commented: 'I could not help seeing the intrinsic weakness of a system that went no further than mere cooperation between governments . . . The countries of Western Europe must turn their national efforts into a truly European effort. This will be possible only through a federation of the West' (Monnet, 1978: 272–3). To remedy this situation, 'a start would have to be made by doing something more practical and more ambitious. National sovereignty would have to be tackled more boldly and on a narrower front' (Monnet: 1978: 274). For Monnet, the successful integration of Europe could be achieved only by the creation of institutions.

Not all European nations were willing to accept the loss of sovereignty that supranational cooperation required. Britain, Portugal and many of the Scandinavian countries favoured intergovernmental cooperation that did not lessen the authority of their elected governments. The British position could partly be defended on economic grounds. It continued to be a relatively vibrant trading nation with many interests beyond the European theatre: its coal and steel production after 1945 far exceeded that of other European countries. A perception that Britain was a significant power led Churchill in the early 1950s to advance the concept of 'three great circles among the free nations and democracies' – that embraced the Commonwealth, the English-speaking world and Europe – and crucially, Britain played a key role in each of them. Churchill therefore argued that Britain's leadership of the Commonwealth, special relationship with the United States, and connection to Europe meant that Britain was 'the only country which has a great part in every one of them'.

Yet while it was perfectly true that Britain did have a role in each of these circles, it was not a permanent one. It is hard to disagree with David Reynolds' view that 'In the decade from 1955 Britain's relationship with America became one of dependence, the Commonwealth and Sterling Area crumbled, and Western Europe was transformed by the creation of the EEC without British participation. Underlying all three developments was the country's rapid and catastrophic decline' (Reynolds, 2000: 190). Other European nations, by contrast, came to a far quicker understanding that their interests were best served through the creation of new institutional structures. The Benelux states, France and Italy had come to the conclusion that supranational cooperation offered a number of advantages that more than offset any loss of national sovereignty. Italy, for instance, considered that the new structures would offer it a degree of legitimacy in the international community, which it needed because of its alliance with Germany during the Second World War.

THE HAGUE CONGRESS

Much of the impetus behind supranational beliefs was in fact a product of wartime resistance movements that directly led to the formation of the European Union of Federalists (UEF) in December 1946 (Lipgens, 1982). In the early post-1945 period the dominant approach to European integration was federalism. The federalist approach envisaged the creation of a federal constitution for Europe whereby a federal parliament, government and court would be entrusted with certain powers over such policy areas as security and trade, with the remaining policies to be dealt with by the different levels of government within the member states. The crux of the plan was that the member states would be linked by certain common policies that would be governed by an institutional structure at a level above national governments. The desire of the federalists to create an appropriate constitution resulted in the decision to hold a conference of interested parties, eventually held in The Hague in May 1948.

The Hague Congress attracted 750 delegates from a range of nongovernmental organisations. Its Honorary President was Winston Churchill, who in 1946 had called for a 'United States of Europe' [**Document 3, p. 115**]. But while Churchill considered that France and Germany should form the key partnership in the reconstruction of Europe (a view shared by Monnet), his views did not extend to Britain taking a leading role in such a union. This mirrored the then Labour government's standpoint that favoured a policy of independence; relations with Europe were placed within the context of Britain's extensive network of trading linkages to the Commonwealth and America. Moreover, whereas France favoured the establishment of new structures to control Germany, this was less of a concern to policy-makers in London who tended to view European cooperation within the wider context of resisting Soviet influence [**Document 5, p. 116**]. But even in the realm of military affairs Britain had come to the conclusion that its security interests were best served by its relationship with America rather than with a war-beaten Western Europe. As a consequence Britain championed the 1949 North Atlantic Treaty Organization (which crucially involved a US commitment) [**Document 7, p. 118**] and at the same time showed no interest in the discussions that took place at the Hague. Yet when these discussions led to the formation of the **Council of Europe** in May 1949 [**Document 8, p. 118**], Britain, despite its reservations, was one of the ten founder members.

The Council of Europe, which by 2009 had 47 members and played an important role in promoting human rights through the **European Court of Human Rights**, met on an annual basis and provided the first opportunity for the rehabilitation of West Germany when it became a member in 1950. But while the Council of Europe aimed 'to achieve a greater unity between

Council of Europe: Strasbourg-based organisation established in May 1949 to assist with the maintenance of the rules of law and democracy, being separate from the EU.

European Court of Human Rights: Based in Strasbourg within the Council of Europe and hears cases relating to states that have ratified the European Convention on Human Rights.

its Members', the fact that it sought to do this 'by discussion of questions of common concern and by agreements and common action in economic, social, cultural, scientific, legal and administrative matters and in the maintenance and further realisation of human rights and fundamental freedoms' meant that there was an extremely broad and vague remit for discussion [**Document 8, p. 118**]. As one commentator has noted: 'This was so vague as to be virtually meaningless: in practice there was nothing in the Council structure which facilitated action as distinct from talk' (Henig, 2002: 23). Moreover, in contrast to the wishes of the federalists who had provided the initiative behind The Hague meeting, the structure of the Council of Europe was based on intergovernmental rather than federal designs. As such it did not involve the transfer of power and influence away from nation states that was so desired by the federalist movement, whose members quickly realised its powerlessness. At the time, British ministers and officials could have come to the conclusion that its preference for intergovernmental structures had triumphed over federalist desires for the reconstruction of Europe. Such an assessment was boosted by two further factors. First, the establishment of strong post-war welfare policies in most European states lessened the demand for the European solutions that the federalists advocated. Second, the United States had reservations over solutions to European integration that sprang from resistance and/or communist initiatives and pressure.

THE COAL AND STEEL COMMUNITY

By the end of the 1940s it was increasingly clear that a strong Germany was central to the economic rehabilitation of Europe and vital in the emerging Cold War conflict with the Soviet Union. The implication here was clear: if Germany was going to take on a greater role and become an 'equal' partner with other European states, the restrictions imposed on it at the end of the war would have to be removed. For Konrad Adenauer, the first Chancellor of the Federal Republic of Germany, this was the crux of the matter: he 'believed that Germany's interests were essentially identical with those of the Western powers and that they would be willing to grant Germany a genuine partnership by gradually dismantling the discriminatory status of the occupation regime' (Paterson, 1994: 142).

Britain and America were particularly supportive of the reintegration of Germany and of the need to lift the restrictions. France was less keen and had refused to merge its occupation zone in Germany with that of Britain and America (the latter two had merged to create the Bizone in December 1946). For obvious reasons, France had been keen to maintain its control over the coal resources of the Ruhr as a means of restricting the resurgence of German power and as a way of assisting with the modernisation of the French economy. Yet British and American pressure to lift restrictions on Germany, combined with British reluctance to take the lead in Europe, meant that by 1949 France was in search of a new policy that sought to permit German economic recovery and reconcile French security concerns about a resurgent Germany (Monnet, 1978: 292).

How was this to be accomplished? In the absence of British leadership, France took the lead in addressing the combined issues of Europe's need to contain Germany and Germany's need for equality (Lundestad, 1998: 23). For these twin objectives of political integration and the normalisation of closer relations between France and Germany to occur Monnet proposed the creation of a supranational coal and steel community. Coal and steel were chosen because they were the most important economic industries at the time and had been influential in the friction that resulted in two world wars. Monnet lost no time in managing to persuade the French Foreign Minister, Robert Schuman, to adopt his proposals and these were made clear in the opening gambits of the **Schuman Plan** of 9 May 1950: 'The French Government proposes that Franco-German coal and steel production should be placed under a common High Authority in an organisation open to the other countries of Europe' [**Document 9, p. 119**]. As Monnet himself commented: 'The Schuman proposals are revolutionary or they are nothing . . . The indispensable first principle of these proposals is the abnegation of sovereignty in a limited but decisive field . . . Any plan which does not involve this indispensable first principle can make no useful contribution to the solution of the grave problems that face us . . . What must be sought is a fusion of the interests of the European peoples . . .' (Monnet, 1978: 316). The significance of the declaration lay in the desire of France to forfeit an amount of national sovereignty through the creation of new supranational structures in an effort to create peace (Gillingham, 1991: 231) and as such it is generally regarded as 'a first decisive act in the construction of Europe' (Willis, 1968: 80).

Schuman Plan: Signed on 9 May 1950 and resulted in the establishment of the European Coal and Steel Community.

This 'functionalist' approach to integration was notably different from the federalist approach that had been behind The Hague Congress. The functionalist approach was based on the principle of a gradual transfer of sovereignty from nation states in specific policy areas that Monnet thought would be acceptable to the member states. Influenced by the work of David Mitrany, functionalism was less ambitious and far-reaching than the federalist viewpoint (Mitrany, 1946). The great hope was that peace could be achieved through the furtherance of integration in specific sectors of the economy, such as agriculture or coal, with these sectors governed by supranational institutions. Although methods of decision-making would be determined by member states outside the specific sector of the economy, functionalists nonetheless considered that the success of integration in one sector would create '**spillover**' pressures that would result in a demand for more integration in other areas (Haas, 1968: 283). Monnet's assumption was that in an effort to capitalise on the benefits of integration, member states would agree to other policy areas being incorporated into the European fold. But although Monnet's approach was successful initially, the underlying assumption that European integration would proceed on a logical and rational path in the manner of a 'domino effect' was not borne out by the events of later years.

Spillover: The neo-functionalist view that sectoral integration in one area would have an impact on other areas.

Belgium, Italy, Luxembourg and the Netherlands responded positively to the Schuman Declaration, not least because it provided a useful mechanism to accelerate the process of industrial modernisation (Milward, 1992). Germany was particularly enthusiastic as it combined the means to develop the German coal and steel industry with allaying French security concerns in the light of the support offered by the American government. Britain, by contrast, while aware of the benefits offered by the Schuman Plan in forging closer Franco-German cooperation, felt no compulsion to get involved in a process that centred on the decisions of a new higher authority being binding on the participating member states (Diebold, 1959: 49). Matters were not helped by the fact that Schuman had deliberately not consulted Britain about the proposal as a result of his fear that London would thwart the initiative. Yet it is extremely unlikely that Britain would have responded in any other manner even if it had been specifically consulted. This was because the Schuman Declaration was not merely concerned with the coordination of coal and steel production. It stressed that 'the pooling of coal and steel production will immediately ensure the establishment of common bases for economic development as a first step in the federation of Europe, and will change the destinies of those regions which have long been devoted to the manufacture of arms, to which they themselves were the constant victims' [**Document 9, p. 119**].

Britain, which had been content with the intergovernmental structures of the OEEC, did not feel the need to re-establish itself in a new form of organisation. The diversity and 'relative' strength of Britain's trade – after 1945 it produced approximately two-thirds of the steel of what would become 'the Six' – meant that it did not consider its influence on world events would be enhanced by joining forces with other countries. Such a viewpoint contrasted the position of many of the governments of 'the Six' who, faced with a combination of domestic economic difficulties, the threat of Soviet **communism** and a decline in Europe's influence in the world economy, regarded participation in a new organisation to be the only means to overcome these challenges. It is a point that Alan Milward has made in arguing that European integration took place as a result of the demands of the nation states

Communism: A political ideology that emphasises the common ownership of property and the absence of class divisions. Applied in the Soviet Union until its collapse in 1991.

(Milward, 1992). Both Italy and Germany, for instance, considered European integration to be a central means by which they could re-establish themselves, while for other nations, such as France, it reduced their fear of a revived Germany.

Britain's policy of favouring loose association rather than integration with Europe was shaped by a refusal to accept Schuman's condition that all member states had to agree to the principle of supranational cooperation *prior* to engaging in the talks that were to work out the details of the Schuman Plan (Diebold, 1959: 1; Milward, 1984: 405). The government consequently 'turned the Schuman Plan down flat on the grounds that its supranationalism would prejudice her national sovereignty' (Nutting, 1961: 31). But while Britain's policy of non-participation 'is widely regarded as the most crucial of the opportunities which the Labour government allegedly missed between 1945 and 1951', the nature of the Schuman Plan 'left the British government with no real alternative' (Warner, 1984: 72). Upon reflection it is nonetheless evident that the decision taken by Britain not to participate in the ECSC discussions resulted in France being the key driving force in the early years of European integration, while in the longer term the most important power axis centred on the Franco-German relationship.

Britain was absent when 'the Six' states of Belgium, France, Germany, Italy, Luxembourg and the Netherlands met at the beginning of June 1950 to commence discussions on the Schuman Plan. Jean Monnet, who chaired the talks, stressed the importance of progressing beyond the national negotiating position: 'We are here,' he said, 'to undertake a common task – not to negotiate for our own national advantage, but to seek it in the advantage of all. Only if we eliminate from our debates any particular feelings shall we reach a solution. In so far as we, gathered here, can change our methods, the attitude of all Europeans will likewise change' (Monnet, 1978: 323).

The outcome of these negotiations was the formation of a European Coal and Steel Community Treaty that was designed to last for 50 years and whose founding treaty was signed in Paris by the representatives from Belgium, France, Germany, Italy, Luxembourg and the Netherlands on 18 April 1951; the process of ratification was completed by the end of June 1952 [**Document 11, p. 121**]. The underlying objective of the Treaty was to foster 'economic expansion, growth of employment and a rising standard of living' in the member states by means of creating a common market in coal and steel that would be managed by joint institutions on the basis of agreed policies. Such policies would embrace consumption, development, expansion, prices, production, trade and the economic and social conditions of employees working within the industry. One impact of these policies was the immediate abolition of all coal and steel import and export duties and the removal of all national subsidies for these commodities.

Despite the fact that the Treaty focused only on a specific sector of the economy, the preamble demonstrated the desire of the founding fathers to move beyond coal and steel to create a wider Community by means of functional integration and political spillover. 'The idea was to create a federal prototype. Once "a practical community of interests" had been created, mentalities would change, other steps would become possible, a new dynamic would begin to operate and finally, step by step, lead to a federal destination' (Duchêne, 1996: 55). Thus, at the heart of the ECSC lay a sector-by-sector approach to European integration. In this context, the founding member states 'resolved to substitute for age-old rivalries the merging of their essential interests; to create, by establishing an economic community, the basis for a broader and deeper community among peoples long divided by bloody conflicts; and to lay the foundations for institutions which will give direction to a destiny henceforward shared' [**Document 11, p. 121**]. This, combined with the supranational institutional structure of the ECSC, ensured that it was distinguishable from other efforts to promote European cooperation, such as the Council of Europe.

High Authority: The administrating body of the ECSC and forerunner of the European Commission.

Monnet, who had chaired the talks, was elected the first President of the ECSC (1952–56). The four institutions that governed it included a **High Authority** (subsequently the European Commission), which Monnet argued should be independent of the member states. Moreover, as an executive institution Monnet stressed that it should take responsibility for the coal and steel industries of 'the Six' (members) and establish common policies on such issues as working conditions and prices. The Treaty also established a Council of Ministers, composed of one representative from each member state and which had to be consulted by the High Authority. A Court of Justice was also created to resolve disputes among the member states and between them and the ECSC, and although a Common Assembly was created to inject a degree of democracy, the pattern of weak democratic control was established and this 'democratic deficit' would in later years become a particularly contentious issue.

In short, the significance of the ECSC lay in the capacity for European integration to progress beyond initiatives such as the Council of Europe, whose vague aims did little to unite European nations. The ECSC thus offered a new form of organisation where nation states agreed to surrender an element of their sovereignty to a supranational institution. Yet at the same time it had a limited membership and many OEEC members, such as Britain, were not part of the ECSC. Its structures also did not reflect the full federation for which many had campaigned. But despite this compromised outcome, it provided the first attempt to integrate the states of Europe in a structure that differed from the intergovernmental principles of the OEEC and NATO.

THE FAILURE OF THE EUROPEAN DEFENCE COMMUNITY

Just as the economic concerns of a post-war Germany provided the impetus behind the ECSC, the security concerns of a future remilitarised Germany were central to the development of the **European Defence Community** (EDC). In the climate of the Cold War, the US was particularly keen to revive German military power and for the country to become a member of NATO as a means of countering the threat of the Soviet 'Red Army' in the European theatre. At the same time, the wider global tension between the US and the Soviet Union had been accentuated by the successful Soviet atomic test in the autumn of 1949 and the outbreak of the Korean War in 1950. A militarily revived Germany would nonetheless be a matter of concern for France, which initially opposed the American plans for German rearmament. Indeed, as a significant proportion of the French army had been involved in Indo-China since 1946, German rearmament would quickly result in it having the largest army in Western Europe. Once again Monnet found a solution to this problem when he advocated that the principle of supranational cooperation could be extended into the remit of defence. Monnet's idea was therefore to mimic the example of the Schuman Plan to promote the creation of a European defence system (Fursdon, 1980: 78–84). In turn, the premier of France, René Pleven, suggested in October 1950 that France, Germany and other interested countries should establish a supranational European Army of 100,000 soldiers. Thus, just as supranationalism had been used to control German industry, so too would it be used to control German rearmament. As Alistair Cole has written, 'The EDC provided the second example of a supranational solution that would enhance German sovereignty' (Cole, 2001: 8).

Such a proposal built on the **Dunkirk Treaty** of March 1947 and the Brussels Treaty of March 1948 [**Document 6, p. 117**]. (The latter had committed Britain, France and the Benelux nations to a common defence system at a time when the stability of Europe was threatened by the Soviet Union, most notably in the form of the Berlin blockade of 1948 and before NATO was founded.) Britain, which had been absent from the ECSC discussions, reacted negatively to the **Pleven Plan** with its proposal for a multinational force that would be responsible to a European Assembly and a European minister of defence (Warner, 1984: 75). But for other countries, the Plan's attractions lay in the fact that it locked Germany into a defence system [**Document 10, p. 119**]. It was with this in mind that Belgium, France, Germany, Italy and Luxembourg commenced a process of negotiations in February 1951 that would eventually result in the signing of the European Defence Community Treaty in May 1952 [**Document 12, p. 121**]. The

European Defence Community (EDC): An unsuccessful attempt to create a common European army that failed because of the refusal of the French National Assembly to support it in 1954.

Dunkirk Treaty: A 50-year Treaty of Alliance and Mutual Assistance signed by France and the UK on 5 March 1947 to counter against the possibility of renewed German aggression. Subsequently replaced by the Brussels Treaty.

Pleven Plan: The Plan for a European Defence Community that was put forward by the French Prime Minister René Pleven on 24 October 1950.

Netherlands, which was the remaining member of 'the Six' ECSC nations, joined the EDC discussions in October 1951.

The outlook for European integration in 1952 initially appeared to be positive. But within a short time it became ever more gloomy and underscored the limitations of Monnet's approach to European integration. France was particularly keen to exercise its stamp on the shape of post-war Europe and did not view its relationship with Germany as that of an equal. Thus, while the EDC Treaty stressed that Germany should not have an independent military command, the other members were able to keep their own defence structures, albeit with the armed forces placed under a new supranational structure. This meant that all parties to the Treaty would have to forgo some degree of their capacity for independent action. This was something to which many politicians in France, particularly the Gaullists, were opposed as it implied the relinquishing of national command of the French army. Such nationalist arguments were influential behind the failure of the French National Assembly on 30 August 1954 to ratify the EDC Treaty. Indeed, it was only in the 1990s that member states were prepared to extend the EC's competence into defence matters and it can therefore be seen that the failure of the ambitious EDC plan – which would have led also to the creation of a European Political Community – was a notable setback for Monnet's approach to European integration and progress towards the building of supranational institutions. In this sense, it provided an early lesson that achieving a 'balance between European integration and preserving national autonomy would prove a delicate equilibrium to achieve' (Blair and Curtis, 2009: 272).

Western European Union (WEU): Established in 1955 to coordinate foreign and security policy among Western European nations, it was quickly overshadowed by NATO. It was reactivated in the 1980s and was heavily involved in strengthening the foreign and defence identity of the EC. In 1999 the WEU took the decision to relinquish its military headquarters and its responsibility in crisis management as a result of the decision by EU member states to strengthen the European Security and Defence Policy (ESDP).

Nevertheless, the underlying issue of German remilitarisation remained an important topic on the European political landscape. To deal with this problem, the British Foreign Secretary (from 1955 Prime Minister), Anthony Eden, put forward a Foreign Office scheme which proposed that the 1948 Brussels Treaty (which had committed Britain, France and the Benelux states to a common defence system) should be expanded to include West Germany and Italy. For Britain, the key advantage of the proposal to create a new defence organisation – to be known as the **Western European Union** (WEU) – was that its intergovernmental structure meant that it did not contain the supranational features of the EDC, with the new policy being accepted by Belgium, France, Germany, Italy, Luxembourg, the Netherlands and Britain as a result of the modification of the Brussels Treaty by the Paris Agreements of 23 October 1954. In addition to this championing of the WEU, Eden argued that the crucial issue of German rearmament should take place within NATO, which Germany eventually joined in May 1955. And it would be this security dependence on the USA via NATO, rather than the WEU, which would act as the formal check on German armament.

The absence of supranational structures in the WEU represented a bitter blow to the federalist movement. The WEU differed little from the loose intergovernmental structure of the Brussels Treaty, with the only addition being a Consultative Assembly that would be attended by the same national delegates to the Common Assembly of the Council of Europe. From such a beginning the WEU never matured into a major security structure in the way that NATO did, but then again it was not meant to. It was clear from the outset that the WEU was not formed to duplicate the work of other organisations, while the military responsibility of the Council was handed over to NATO from the very beginning. In short, the collapse of the EDC and its replacement by the WEU demonstrated the decline of the attractiveness of the Community idea advanced by Monnet and Schuman.

This state of affairs, combined with the desire of France to strengthen the position of the member states within the ECSC, influenced Monnet's decision to announce his resignation as President of the ECSC in November 1954. Impatient for further advances in European integration, he had become disenchanted with the resistance of some member states. In a statement to the ECSC Common Assembly in Strasbourg, Monnet stressed that 'It is for Parliaments and Governments to decide on the transfer of new powers to the European institutions. The impulse must therefore come from without. [In resigning as President], I shall be able to join in the efforts of all those who are working to continue and enlarge what has begun' (Monnet, 1978: 400). To do this, Monnet established a pressure group of like-minded Europeans known as the 'Action Committee for the United States of Europe', formed on 13 October 1955 with Monnet serving as President until his resignation on 9 May 1975.

Monnet's departure from the ECSC proved to be a significant shock to the national governments and raised the key question of what would now happen. The response was to come from the Benelux governments. In a memorandum that was drafted on their behalf by the Belgian Foreign Minister, **Paul-Henri Spaak**, they advocated the taking of further steps towards integration by establishing a common market and creating an atomic energy community. This in turn formed part of the discussions that took place at a meeting in Messina in June 1955.

Spaak, Paul-Henri (1889–1972): An important figure in the furtherance of European integration who held the office of Prime Minister and Foreign Minister of Belgium on various occasions after 1945. He was influential in the creation of the Congress of Europe in 1948 and the European Movement. At the 1955 Messina Conference he was charged with the responsibility of chairing a committee that would examine proposals for a European Community (Spaak Report).

THE TREATIES OF ROME

In June 1955 the foreign ministers of 'the Six' met in Messina (Italy) to discuss proposals for further European integration, of which the fields of transport and atomic energy were considered to be two possible options. As

France was the only country to possess a nuclear-energy programme, it had been the main champion of Euratom, a policy which it hoped to dominate within the Community. Moreover, as the costs associated with the policy were considered to be too great for just one country, France hoped to benefit from the greater levels of funding available from the Community. In essence, French support for European integration was shaped by its desire to secure its national interests. The end product was a **resolution** that noted that 'The Governments of the Federal Republic of Germany, Belgium, France, Italy, Luxembourg and the Netherlands believe the time has come to make a fresh advance towards the building of Europe. They are of the opinion that this must be achieved, first of all, in the economic field' [**Document 13, p. 122**].

To take the Messina Resolution forward, a committee was formed that included relevant experts and government representatives, chaired by Spaak. Other leading figures in the discussions included Monnet and the Dutch Foreign Minister, Johan Beyen. His contributions proved to be particularly crucial, as the **Beyen Plan** argued for the creation of a customs union and common market that reduced trade barriers between 'the Six'. This approach differed from the widely held viewpoint that progress should proceed by means of **sectoral integration** alone and Beyen's plans were therefore more ambitious.

Not all states shared Beyen's view of European integration. Britain was particularly hostile to the creation of a common market, which according to the then Chancellor of the Exchequer, Rab Butler, 'was not going to work'. The government believed plans to create a customs union represented a form of protectionism that did not mirror Britain's preference for open and multilateral trading relationships. Such economic concerns masked a far more important reason for Britain's refusal to participate in the EEC: a rejection of the supranational powers of the Community's institutions. Britain's preferences were framed within the context of 'cooperation without commitment' and government ministers hoped to be able to steer the outcome in a non-supranational direction. Yet it was a highly unrealistic objective as the Spaak Committee's thoughts clearly involved the principle of some loss of national sovereignty. The longer Britain continued to take part in the discussions, the harder it would be for the British government to distance itself from being committed to the result. Britain therefore withdrew from the discussions in November 1955 when the government concluded that its proposal to establish a **free trade area** was not acceptable to 'the Six'. Spaak would later comment that 'little by little the British attitude changed from one of mildly disdainful scepticism to growing fear' (Spaak, 1971: 232). Where did this leave Britain?

As an alternative, the British government pushed for intergovernmental cooperation within the OEEC. It was an approach that nevertheless proved

---

Resolutions: A method that the Council uses to highlight a political commitment and does not require any need for binding legislation. They do not require the Commission to propose them.

Beyen Plan: On 4 April 1955 the Netherlands Foreign Minister, Johan Beyen, proposed the creation of a customs union among 'the Six' members of the European Coal and Steel Community (ECSC).

Sectoral integration: A view of integration that takes an incremental approach sector by sector.

Free trade area: An area where barriers to trade such as customs duties and restrictive trading measures have been removed between two or more countries.

unacceptable to the other member states (which Britain had wrongly thought would be unwilling to accept the objective of a common market) because they wanted a supranational rather than intergovernmental solution. And although Britain further clarified its position by drawing up a proposal for an alternative free trade association in November 1956, the Spaak Committee had already recommended in its April 1956 report that a common market and atomic energy community should be created. Such a conclusion was the product of the argument put forward by the Spaak Committee that further sectoral integration on the model of the ECSC would not work. As such, the Committee's report took the extremely significant step of abandoning further sectoral integration and instead advocated the creation of an Atomic Energy Community and a separate customs union. The Spaak Committee's report in turn formed the basis of the subsequent intergovernmental negotiations of 'the Six' that commenced in June 1956 and ended in February 1957. The negotiations, which were often of a difficult nature, produced common agreements that resulted in the creation of the EEC and Euratom. The agreements were signed in Rome by the six member states of the ECSC on 25 March 1957 [**Document 14, p. 123**]. Robert Marjolin, who as a close colleague of Monnet played an important role in the creation of the two Treaties of Rome, was able to reflect that 'this date represents one of the greatest moments of Europe's history. Who would have thought during the 1930s, and even during the ten years that followed the war, that European states which had been tearing one another apart for so many centuries and some of which, like France and Italy, still had very closed economies, would form a common market intended eventually to become an economic area that could be linked to one great dynamic market?' (Marjolin, 1989: 306). The **Treaties of Rome** were swiftly ratified by the national parliaments and came into effect on 1 January 1958 and in so doing marked a key moment in the history of Europe.

Treaties of Rome: Signed in 1957 and came into effect in 1958. Established the European Economic Community (EEC) and the European Atomic Energy Community (Euratom).

3

Constructing the Community: 1958–70

European Communities: A phrase that symbolises the ECSC, EEC and Euratom. Since the Merger Treaty of 1967, each of the three Communities has shared the same institutional structure. The 1993 Maastricht Treaty on European Union officially renamed the EEC the European Community (EC), at which time the EC became a central component of the European Union (EU).

N early 13 years after the end of the Second World War, the European Economic Community and European Atomic Energy Community took effect on 1 January 1958. Combined with the ECSC they formed the core of the **European Communities**. But while the Treaty expressed a desire 'to lay the foundations of an ever closer union among the peoples of Europe' [**Document 14, p. 123**], it was less precise on a number of other matters that would in time be the subject of subsequent negotiations. As Nugent notes, 'such references as there were to specific sectoral policies – as, for example, with the provisions for "the adoption of a common policy in the sphere of agriculture", and the statement that the objectives of the Treaty "shall . . . be pursued by Member States within the framework of a common transport policy" – were couched in somewhat general terms' (Nugent, 2003: 42).

European Commission: The executive body of the EU and guardian of the Treaties. It has the task of initiating EU legislation, implementing policies that have been agreed on and also plays an important role in negotiating on behalf of the EU on trade matters and with respect to relations with Third World countries. It can also refer matters to the ECJ when agreed policies have not been implemented by member states.

INSTITUTIONAL DESIGN

In 1958 the leaders of 'the Six' were faced with three bodies that sought to grapple with the problems and concerns of post-war Europe: the ECSC, Euratom and the EC. In terms of administrative structure, it was not surprising that the new organisations drew heavily on the existing ECSC, of which the High Authority's influence from the mid-1950s had been increasingly challenged by the national governments of 'the Six'. The experience of the ECSC consequently influenced the minds of the framers of the Treaties of Rome: their keenness to create a supranational institutional structure that would bind the member states together was tempered by a desire to ensure that the interests of national governments were reflected in the decision-making structure. In practical terms, the Treaties of Rome provided the EEC with four main institutions: a **European Commission**, a **Council of**

Ministers, a **European Court of Justice** and an Assembly (the latter two were shared with the ECSC and Euratom). An Economic and Social Committee was additionally created to act as a consultative body for the Council and Commission. The different institutional apparatus of the three institutions would continue to exist until June 1967 when they were merged to create a single Council of Ministers and a single Commission for the three European Communities [**Document 18, p. 127**].

The main supranational aspect of the EEC and its central administrative body consisted of a Commission (replacing the ECSC High Authority) whose primary task was to ensure that the provisions of the Treaty and the policies that flowed from it were properly administered, and to initiate and recommend policies to the Council of Ministers. This was a responsibility that the Commission performed in the early years under the leadership of its first President, **Walter Hallstein** (who had been Monnet's main collaborator in the negotiation of the ECSC Treaty). The Commissioners (who headed individual departments) were, despite their appointment by member states, technically not representatives of the member states. Symbolically, this was a point that was emphasised by each Commissioner taking an oath of loyalty to the EEC and swearing 'neither to seek nor to take instructions from any government or body'. This was inevitably a rather unlikely state of affairs given that each Commissioner will have been recommended for appointment by a governing political party. As Simon Hix notes, 'Almost all commissioners are career politicians, with links to national parties, and have strong views about what types of legislation they would like the Commission to propose' (Hix, 2008: 125). Nonetheless, federalists hoped that the Commission would act as the driving force behind European integration and that it would not be constrained by the politicking of member states. This was a position that was not shared by de Gaulle who did not accept the federalist vision and who, on his return to power in June 1958, would argue against the enhancement of the Commission's powers. Indeed, it was evident that in the early years the Commission deliberately avoided upsetting the relationship with and between member states. For example, even though the Commission's remit extended into challenging the legitimacy of national policies, in the first ten years of the Community the Commission only brought 27 cases against the member states (Alter, 2001: 11–14).

Although the Commission contained an explicit supranational design, it was not the only institution that had a supranational focus. Observers could be forgiven for assuming that as the national interests of member states were reflected in the Council of Ministers (the second major EEC institution), the Council was devoid of supranationalism. To be sure, the Council's composition of national government ministers – with varied membership depending on the agenda – reflected an intergovernmental design that was further

Council of Ministers: Comprising ministers from member states, it is the main decision-making body of the EU, having legislating and decision-making powers.

European Court of Justice: Final arbiter of all legal issues, including the resolution of disputes between EU member states as well as between firms and individuals within the EU.

Hallstein, Walter (1901–82): First President of the European Commission, holding office 1958–67. His views often clashed with those of the French President, Charles de Gaulle, who did not share Hallstein's desire for the Commission to be the main motor of European integration.

Unanimity: A form of voting in the Council. Requires that no member state can vote against a proposal, though it is possible to have abstentions.

Merger Treaty: Established a single Council of Ministers and a single Commission for Euratom, the ECSC and the EEC, which came into force on 1 July 1967.

Permanent representation: Each EU member state has a permanent representation to the EU that is based in Brussels and which acts as the national basis for conducting EU negotiations and forms a linkage between national capitals and the EU.

European Council: Provides political direction to the EU. Comprises heads of state or government of the member states and the president of the European Commission.

European Parliament: Comprises Members of the European Parliament (MEPs) who are directly elected for a five-year term of office from each member state, with the number of national MEPs being in proportion to population. The most important area of the European Parliament's influence is its power to amend and adopt legislation via the co-decision procedure, while its approval is also necessary for appointments to the European Commission.

confirmed by the fact that each member state took its turn in chairing the meetings (a duty that rotated every six months). However, as the Treaty of Rome included a provision for decisions to be taken on a qualified majority basis from 1966 (as opposed to just a **unanimity** basis), it would be possible for a nation's interests to be overridden by the views of the majority. And in so far as majority and qualified majority voting were viewed to be of importance in ensuring that the Community's progress could not be hijacked by the views of any one member state, it was a process that contained an element of supranationalism. Moreover, it would provide the pretext for the French President, Charles de Gaulle, to block the Community's proceedings in the second half of 1965 [**Document 19, p. 128**]. Curiously, there were few concerns about this process in the early days of the Community's existence (Marjolin, 1989: 305).

To assist member states with the administrative tasks of the Council meetings, a Committee of Permanent Representatives (Coreper) was created in 1958, although it would not be until the **Merger Treaty** of 1967 that it would obtain the status of a full legal institution of the Community [**Document 18, p. 127**]. The national representatives who were in charge of the **permanent representation** were to play an important role in the functioning of the Community, having the responsibility to provide preparatory briefings to government ministers and to take uncontroversial decisions (Blair, 2001). Yet, while this body served to bolster the interests of the member states, it was the decision taken by the leaders of national governments to meet at summits that cemented the position of member states. The first of these summit meetings took place in Paris in February 1961, with the meetings in due course transforming themselves into the **European Council**.

The third major institution created by the Treaty of Rome was the Parliamentary Assembly which served as a direct replacement for the advisory body that was provided for by the ECSC Treaty. The Parliamentary Assembly – which in 1962 was renamed the **European Parliament** – was provided with a limited number of supervisory powers over the Commission and the Council of Ministers. This included the right to put questions to the Commission, to discharge the annual budget and to censure the Commission (a power that was not used until 1999). The powers entrusted to what became the European Parliament were for the most part of a limited nature and this meant that it exercised little effective control over the European Commission or the Council of Ministers. Individual Commissioners could not be sacked by the Parliament and this institution had little influence over budgetary matters and no ability to force amendments to legislation. This state of affairs continued for the next three decades, with the European Parliament's institutional weakness finally addressed in the 1993 Treaty on

European Union when it obtained a more decisive role in the decision-making process (**co-decision procedure**).

To ensure that the supranational institutions of the Community were kept in check and that the laws of the Community were implemented in a common format, a European Court of Justice was established as the fourth major institution. Based in Luxembourg, the Court consisted of judges appointed upon the recommendation of member states for six-year renewable terms. The Court was given the specific responsibility of handling cases from all three Community treaties and from disputes arising between member states, member states and the Communities, individuals and member states and finally individuals and the Communities. Its decisions were taken by majority voting and were final and have been particularly evident in areas of economic policy, such as the internal market. The very presence of Community law provided an important distinction between the Community and other international organisations through the emergence of a Community legal order, although it was nevertheless the case that Community law existed alongside national legal systems.

So while the Treaty of Rome paid attention to developing supranational structures, a significant degree of influence was retained by the member states through intergovernmental structures. Just as the supranational Commission was entrusted with the responsibility for both initiating and implementing policies, the interests of the member states were reflected in the Council of Ministers which had the primary task of legislating on the basis of the proposals arising from the Commission. Of the remaining institutions, the Parliamentary Assembly's influence was of a limited nature, while the Court of Justice played a more significant role by interpreting EEC decisions. And although this balance between the supranational and intergovernmental would initially tilt in favour of the Commission, as the Community progressed into the second half of the 1960s the institutional battle would favour the member states.

Co-decision procedure: Introduced in the 1993 Treaty on European Union. Increases the powers of the European Parliament by allowing it to prevent a proposal being adopted if its views are not taken into consideration by the Council.

POLICIES AND COMPETENCIES

A central aim of the new organisation was the creation of a customs union and common market to promote free and equal competition between the participating member states, being influenced by two main factors: first, a desire to create higher levels of economic growth; second, an aspiration that member states should not return to a system of national protectionism that had been a dominant feature before the war (George, 1996: 193). Article 2 of the Treaty of Rome stressed that 'The Community shall have as its aim, by establishing a common market and progressively approximating the economic policies of member states, to promote throughout the Community a harmonious development of economic activities, a continuous and balanced expansion, an increase in stability, an accelerated raising of the standard of living and closer relations between its member states' [**Document 14, p. 123**].

The very creation of such a customs union resulted in the member states having to agree to certain common practices and standards that centred on eliminating the distinctions – and borders – between the different national markets. This included the abolition of tariffs and restrictive practices, such as price fixing and the dumping of products. In addition to these internal policies, member states agreed to the creation of a common external tariff to ensure that non-Community countries were presented with a common tariff irrespective of which member state they traded with. In the end, a full customs union was established by 1 July 1968, 18 months ahead of the schedule that had been laid down in the Treaty. But apart from these economic benefits, the federalists also hoped that over a period of time there would take place a gradual shift of decision-making away from member states towards the European institutions. In other words, economic integration would lead to European unity within a wide variety of areas, including social affairs, financial matters and foreign policy.

Of these various areas, economic objectives proved to be the most easily attainable and by the end of the 1960s many of the objectives that had been set in this policy area had been met. The attainment of these objectives was greatly influenced by Walter Hallstein's leadership of the European Commission. At the same time, the 1960s also saw the Court of Justice establish the concepts of 'direct effect' and 'primacy', which are two of the most important concepts of Community law. The concept of direct effect was established in the 1963 ECJ judgment of *van Gend en Loos* where the Court was asked to rule on whether a particular provision of a Community Treaty had to be enforced when there was contradictory national legislation. The outcome was a decision that confirmed the binding nature of Community law, with member states being required to implement the law within their legal system. One year later in 1964 the primacy of Community law over national law was established in ECJ ruling in the case of *Costa v. ENEL*, when the Court ruled that '. . . the law stemming from the Treaty . . . (cannot) be overridden by domestic legal provisions . . .'. While the principle of direct effect and primacy were of notable significance in establishing the effectiveness of Community law, they also established the foundations that were essential for market integration to take place.

Gross domestic product: The total value of the goods and services produced in a country over a period of one year. It excludes foreign-exchange earnings.

In the period between 1958 and 1970, trade among 'the Six' increased by five times, exports to the rest of the world increased by two-and-a-half times and the **gross domestic product** (GDP) of Community member states grew at an annual average of 5 per cent (Young, 1991: 41). By 1962 the EEC was the world's largest single trading power. A combination of economic growth, the creation of united policies based on supranational institutions and the overall size of the combined economies of the Six increased the Community's influence on world affairs. This was evidenced by a desire to improve the access that the Six's former colonies had to the Community: in 1963 the **Yaoundé Convention** was signed between the Community and 18 African states and Madagascar, which would be further extended in 1969 with a second Yaoundé Convention. An awareness of the EEC's important role as a trading organisation led the Community to tackle the issue of market access with other developed countries, as highlighted by the 1967 Kennedy tariff rounds. As a demonstration of the external role being carved out by the EEC, and the recognition attached to it by the outside world, these negotiations reduced tariff barriers between Europe and North America and acted as a further stimulus to economic growth.

Despite these significant economic achievements, by the end of the 1960s the Community had not realised all of its initial objectives. The continuing presence of restrictions on the free movement of capital, goods and people ensured that the commitment in Article 3 of the Treaty of Rome to 'the abolition, as between member states, of obstacles to freedom of movement for persons, services and capital' and ergo the promotion of free and equal competition had not been achieved by 1970 [**Document 14, p. 123**]. The reason for this lack of progress can be attributed partly to the greater desire among policy-makers to eliminate tariff and quota barriers in the early stages of European integration rather than to tackle those policies that would aid the creation of an internal market. Indeed, it would not be until the mid-1980s that plans would be set in motion that resulted in genuine free movement within the Community. Second, although a Social Fund had been created in the Treaty of Rome to assist with tackling unemployment, it was relatively small and it proved difficult to achieve common social, regional and transport policies. A key area where the Six did manage to achieve a common policy was the **common agricultural policy** (CAP). And although the policy was a direct response to the food shortage that existed in post-war Europe, it also represented a classic Community compromise. In return for dismantling the protective **barriers to trade** that protected the French economy from foreign competition, the government in Paris argued for the creation of an agricultural policy to protect its farming interests (in excess of 20 per cent of the French workforce was employed in the agricultural sector of the economy at the time). As such, an important factor in the emergence of the CAP was its ability to satisfy French and German interests (Moravcsik, 1998: 152–58).

But while a common agricultural policy was referred to in the Treaty of Rome, it was not exactly clear how such a policy would operate. The only

Yaoundé Convention: A trade agreement between 'the Six' and the 18 nations of the Associated African States and Madagascar which was signed in 1963 in Yaoundé, Cameroon. Entering into force in 1964, the Convention was renegotiated in 1969 and was superseded by the Lomé Convention.

Common Agricultural Policy (CAP): Established in 1962 to support agricultural production. Today it accounts for approximately 45 per cent of the EU budget.

Barriers to trade: The elimination of tariffs and quotas among member states.

guidance provided was that its aims were to secure the supply of agricultural produce by means of increasing production, stabilising prices and providing farmers with an adequate standard of living. In other words, a particular concern was the absence of concrete information as to how the CAP would be financed and this would, in a short period of time, provide the Community with a crucial crisis. Nonetheless, the CAP proved to be an important development for the Community for both economic and political reasons: in 1955 it accounted for a significant percentage of the share of the labour force and made a notable contribution to national GDP. The respective figures were: France 25.9 per cent of the labour force and 12.3 per cent of GDP, Italy 39.5 per cent and 21.6 per cent, Germany 18.9 per cent and 8.5 per cent, Luxembourg 25 per cent and 9 per cent, the Netherlands 13.7 per cent and 12 per cent, and Belgium 9.3 per cent and 8.1 per cent (Hix, 1999: 255). Co-operation on agricultural policy also demonstrated the willingness of the member states to establish a common policy that Hallstein considered to be 'vital to the future of the Community' (Hallstein, 1962: 54). In practical terms it would necessitate bringing together distinct national systems of agricultural support, the work of which would be taken over by supranational organisations. The first regulations on agricultural matters were introduced in January 1962 and by 1968 a fully effective agricultural policy was in existence. To achieve its goal of plentiful production, the CAP established a rather complex system that provided farmers with subsidies and price guarantees, being administered by a European Agricultural Guidance and Guarantee Fund. (The guidance element focused on matters relating to agricultural structural reform while matters relating to the price mechanism were dealt with by the guarantee element of the fund.)

Yet while there is much truth in the assessment that the CAP was a success because of its efforts in forging closer integration, the CAP has nonetheless been subject to a significant amount of criticism. This has been not least as a result of the sums of money involved (Lindberg and Scheingold, 1970: 41). To encourage agricultural production, the CAP provided farmers with a guaranteed price for their products through the **price support mechanism**. This essentially meant that producers inside the Community were more favourably placed than overseas competitors. Moreover, to place its own market at an advantage, the Community established a system of tariffs and customs duties that protected farmers from lower-cost imports. Such a system encouraged efficient farmers to maximise output and consequently led to significant variance in the level of support provided, whereby large farms benefited over small farms. Apart from putting a question mark over the 'common' nature of the CAP, the structural design of the system encouraged the production of surpluses that the Commission purchased to protect prices and guarantee farm income. This inevitably led to the creation of the

Price support mechanism: The system of agricultural support for farmers that results in higher food prices.

so-called 'wine lakes' and 'butter mountains'. Negative externalities also arose in the form of environmental destruction through intensive farming and the emergence of trade disputes because of the use of quotas and subsidies.

Over-production and a policy of maintaining prices that were often higher than world market levels resulted in the CAP being subjected to intense criticism from within and outside the Community. This included the environmental impact of large-scale industrialised farming that encouraged the use of fertilisers. It was also an extremely expensive policy. The CAP accounted for approximately 50 per cent of the Community budget by the 1990s, and despite a number of attempts at reform it continued to account for in excess of 40 per cent of the budget by 2009. This is because the entrenched interests of the farming community that the CAP favoured (particularly within France) meant that it proved to be a difficult policy to reform and impossible to remove from the Community agenda. This is despite the fact that in contrast to its dominant position in the post-war economy, agriculture no longer accounts for a significant percentage of the national labour force or makes a major contribution to the GDP of most member states.

THE NATIONALIST BACKLASH

Having decided not to take part in the negotiations that led to the EEC, the British government was determined to take the initiative and advance its own ideas for a free trade area that had no supranational elements. The 1956 Suez crisis – in which Britain was forced to withdraw from Egypt as a result of American economic and political pressure – demonstrated that Britain was no longer a world power. Yet while the government advanced the case for a free trade area, 'it failed to draw the logical conclusion that membership of the European Community would be the best place of making British influence felt' (Leonard, 1996: 163). Simply put, the British proposal would involve the Six EEC countries being linked by association to the other OEEC countries in the form of a free trade area. Although aimed at uniting Europe, Britain hoped to have the best of both worlds: to maintain preferential trade arrangements with the Commonwealth and the colonies and at the same time to be linked to the Community. But despite these rather selfish aims, the basic concept of a free trade area received warm support in many of the capitals of the Six. Germany and Italy were broadly in favour, although France was more sceptical and there were notable differences between its views and those of Britain. The British government advocated a free trade area based on a loose set of rules, the maintenance of Commonwealth preferences, a rejection of the need to harmonise a range of policies from tariffs to trade policies, and an unwillingness to include agriculture. The French negotiators adopted a totally contrary stance in all of these matters. All in all, the discussions proved fruitless. The British proposal – which lacked any supranational content – was unattractive to 'the Six' (particularly France) which had acknowledged the need for supranationalism in their acceptance of the Treaty of Rome. More importantly, it is evident that if Britain's free trade idea had been successful, it would have transformed the EEC into a large free trade area that would have had a damaging impact on the process of integration that 'the Six' desired.

By 1958 the process of integration had, in any case, started with the first tariff cuts among EEC countries. And having commenced this course of action, 'the Six' were unwilling to allow members of a free trade area to obtain the benefits of access to EEC markets without accepting the responsibilities of the customs union. Willis reports that the then French Information Minister Jacques Soustelle commented in November 1958 that 'it was clear to France that it was not possible to create the free trade area in the way the British wanted' (Willis, 1968: 280). This remark signalled the death of the negotiations which formally came to an end in December 1958 and which in turn resulted in seven of the remaining 11 members of the OEEC commencing a process of discussions that would eventually lead to the creation of the **European Free Trade Association** (EFTA). The seven non-EEC countries of Austria, Britain, Denmark, Norway, Portugal, Sweden and Switzerland accordingly signed the Stockholm Convention on 4 January 1960, thereby marking the creation of EFTA. It was purely concerned with the achievement of a free trade area – based on intergovernmental cooperation – and contained none of the economic or political integration that its members had found so unwelcome in the Treaty of Rome.

The British government's decision to champion open trading relations through EFTA had been based on a belief that its economic, political and security interests were noticeably different from those held by other European nations. British policy-makers considered that the majority of Britain's trade would continue to focus on the Commonwealth, in particular the English-speaking countries of Australia, Canada and New Zealand. It was a viewpoint that was carved out of Britain's historical past and did not fully reflect the post-war reality of the declining importance of Commonwealth trade and the weakening of its overall influence on world affairs. Yet in a short period of time the British government reversed this stance and concluded that the looser ties of EFTA were of marginal benefit. Faced with a decline in its economic fortunes and global influence, the Conservative government of **Harold Macmillan** announced in July 1961 that Britain would make an application to join the EEC **[Document 15, p. 125]**. In essence, 'the wager which the British government had made in 1950, and repeated in 1957,

European Free Trade Association (EFTA): Created in 1960 to provide a less supranational trading group than the EEC. Its relevance has declined as many EFTA members have joined the EU and at the time of writing its membership is limited to Iceland, Liechtenstein, Norway and Switzerland.

Macmillan, Harold (1894–1986): UK Conservative Prime Minister 1957–63, having succeeded Anthony Eden after the Suez crisis. He advocated membership of the European Community, a policy that failed when de Gaulle vetoed the application in 1963.

Plate 1 The Treaty of Rome which established the European Economic Community (EEC) was signed in Rome on 25 March 1957, and entered into force on 1 January 1958. The Treaty establishing the European Atomic Energy Community (Euratom) was signed at the same time and the two are therefore jointly known as the Treaties of Rome. France's chief negotiator, Robert Marjolin, would later comment that 'I do not believe it's an exaggeration to say that this is one of the great moments of Europe's history'.

Plate 2 The French politician Robert Schuman, who served as foreign minister between 1948 and 1952, is regarded as one of the founding fathers of European integration. In cooperation with Jean Monnet, he authored the Schuman Plan that was published on 9 May 1950. This date is now recognised as the start of European political integration.

Plate 3 Commonly regarded as a founding father of Europe, Jean Monnet was a key figure in the European integration process after 1945. He was instrumental behind the Schuman Plan of 9 May 1950 which advocated the creation of an organisation that would take responsibility for Franco-German coal and steel production. Monnet was appointed the first President of the High Authority of the European Coal and Steel Community when it began operating on 10 August 1952.

Plate 4 Jacques Delors, President of the European Commission from 1985–95, led a major transformation of European integration. During his period of office the Community expanded from ten to fifteen members, while there were significant reforms through the Single European Act and Maastricht Treaty on European Union. His efforts to foster closer political integration ensured that he was the most active President since Walter Hallstein.

Plate 5 **www.CartoonStock.com**

The initial design of the Common Agricultural Policy encouraged farmers to produce surpluses to maximise profits. This led to so-called 'wine lakes' and 'butter mountains'. Although recent decades have witnessed attempts to reform the CAP, agriculture still accounts for in excess of 30% of the total EU budget.

Plate 6 The Berlin Wall was the most prominent feature of the Cold War division between capitalism and communism. The collapse of the Berlin Wall on 9 November 1989 signalled the end of communism in Eastern Europe and resulted in the unification of Germany. This in turn unleashed a momentum for European integration that was marked by enlargement to Central and Eastern Europe and an expansion in the number of policies dealt with at the European level.

Plate 7 At the Maastricht European Council of 9–10 December 1991 not everyone is happy with the outcome, with heads of state and government having endured complex negotiations that eventually resulted in the Treaty on European Union.

Plate 8 © **Morten Morland** / *The Times* 04.12.2005/ nisyndication.com

Successive British Prime Ministers have struggled to adopt a coherent policy towards European integration. Tony Blair was no exception. When he became Prime Minister in 1997 he promised to put Britain at the heart of Europe. But this proved to be short-lived, with the then Chancellor Gordon Brown unwilling to commit Britain to joining the single currency.

had not come off' (Thody, 2000: 176). According to Edward Heath (who managed the 1961 application), '[T]he decision of Harold Macmillan's government to apply for membership of the European Community represented an historic moment in post-war politics. It determined the direction not just of British policy, but also that of Europe and the Atlantic alliance . . . It signalled the end of a glorious era, that of the British Empire, and the beginning of a whole new chapter of British history' (Heath, 1998: 203; **[Document 15, p. 125]**.

This change of strategy was based on economic, political and security grounds, and reflected the increasing attractiveness of the Community to non-member states. Over the years that followed this would result in many countries signing an **association agreement** with the Community as a means of establishing a formal relationship, of which the first agreement was with Greece in 1961. Although each prospective member tended to have specific concerns relating to membership, economic factors were particularly paramount for Britain. As already mentioned, the 1956 Suez crisis highlighted the limitations of British military and political influence. It therefore 'confirmed that Britain was not the force in world affairs that many policy-makers considered it to be, and a direct consequence of this was the re-orientation of Britain's strategic interests towards Europe' (Forster and Blair, 2002: 18). Economic factors were also of considerable importance in influencing the government's decision to seek membership of the Community. Not only was Britain's economic growth flagging behind 'the Six' (who were enjoying the benefits of economic integration and reductions in tariff barriers), but British trade with the countries of Western Europe was increasing at a faster rate than with the Empire and the Commonwealth (Urwin, 1995: 87). 'Over the first three years of its existence, British exports to EFTA countries rose by 33 per cent. Over the same period, British exports to EC countries (now facing escalating tariffs) rose by 55 per cent' (May, 1999: 31). Finally, this reorientation of policy towards Europe reflected the preferences of the US, which was a strong advocate of Britain's entry and had been unsupportive of British plans for a free trade area. US support was influenced by a consideration that Britain's membership would help to defend American interests and dilute the Franco-German relationship. This consequently led Macmillan to conclude that 'the "special relationship" with the US was probably better maintained inside the EEC than outside it' (Lundestad, 1998: 134).

Despite the economic and political arguments for membership, the application was framed within the wider context of continued links to the Commonwealth and the US. Such a position did not find favour from France, who under de Gaulle's leadership was overtly hostile to American influence on NATO via European matters. And as Article 237 of the Treaty of Rome required that the admission of new member states to the Community

Association agreement: An agreement between the EU and non-member countries that fosters a close economic and political relationship.

was dependent on a unanimous vote within the Council of Ministers, Britain's application for membership could be torpedoed by a veto. In the end, this was the policy that de Gaulle used on the grounds that Britain's membership would destabilise the Community. In any event, the negotiations over the membership applications became linked to a wider debate about the future of the Community, as the economic progress that it had achieved led 'the Six' to pay closer attention to matters of a political nature. Yet while most member states thought that the Community should play a greater role in world affairs, some countries, such as France, were of the opinion that this should not be at the expense of national influence. Although de Gaulle wanted a stronger Europe (partly to act as a counter to the influence of the US) and was also aware of the economic benefits that France obtained from membership, he questioned the need for the transfer of too many powers to the supranational institutions of the Community. To resolve this impasse, the leaders of 'the Six' agreed at the 1961 Bonn summit to establish an intergovernmental committee, chaired by the French Ambassador Christian Fouchet, to examine the case for closer political integration. By the end of the year the Fouchet committee had produced a draft treaty that proposed the creation of an intergovernmental organisation outside of the Treaty of Rome to coordinate foreign and defence policy, and in doing so rejected the federal model.

For de Gaulle, a key aspect of the plan was that France's interests would be protected because decisions would be subject to unanimous agreement. Such a strategy reflected France's and de Gaulle's desire to rein back some of the powers which had been granted in the Treaty of Rome. The other members of the Community – particularly Belgium and the Netherlands – did not share this view and argued that the proposals would undermine the supranational design of the existing Community institutions through the separation of economic affairs from those of defence and security. As a consequence it proved impossible to reconcile the gulf between the desire of the majority to maintain the 'Community method' and de Gaulle's vision of 'l'Europe des Patries' (a Europe of nation states). An inability to resolve these differences of opinion resulted in the ending of discussions of the **Fouchet Plan**, which in turn led France to develop a bilateral foreign policy agreement with Germany, as set out in the January 1963 Franco-German Treaty of friendship [**Document 17, p. 127**]. The significance of the Franco-German Treaty – which provided for institutional cooperation between both countries across a broad range of policy areas – lay in the fact that it was the first bilateral relationship in the Community and in this context brought classical 'realpolitik' diplomacy among 'the Six'. The Franco-German Treaty thus further cemented the role of member states as the key determinants about the future of European integration.

Fouchet Plan: A draft Treaty for political union published on 2 November 1961 by a committee chaired by Christopher Fouchet of France. Proposed the creation of a council of Heads of Government or Foreign Ministers where decisions would only be taken by unanimity and the establishment of an international secretariat composed of officials taken from national Foreign Ministries. The plan was opposed by all member states apart from France.

Even though the Fouchet Plan negotiations were not directly linked to Britain's application, the failure of the talks strengthened de Gaulle's uncertainties about the suitability of Britain joining an organisation that he wanted France to control. Thus, when Britain agreed to purchase the Polaris nuclear missile system from the US in December 1962, it provided de Gaulle with the necessary justification to veto Britain's membership application on the basis that Britain would be an American 'Trojan horse' in Europe [**Document 16, p. 126**]. Such was France's concern about American influence over European policy that de Gaulle subsequently withdrew France from the military command structure of NATO in 1966, which in turn brought about the need for NATO headquarters to relocate from Paris to Brussels.

De Gaulle's use of the veto ended any immediate hopes of Britain joining the Community. However, it did not necessarily signal a reorientation of British policy away from Europe. Writing in his diary after the veto, Harold Macmillan noted that 'the great question remains, "What is the alternative?" to the European Community. If we are honest, we must say there is none' (Macmillan, 1973: 374). Many of the other member states had welcomed the prospect of British membership as a means of counterbalancing French influence. Thus, not only did the veto sour relations between London and Paris but also between Paris and the capitals of the five other member states. This tension between de Gaulle's vision of European integration and that of the other member states came to a head in 1965 when the President of the European Commission, Walter Hallstein, put forward a package deal that combined measures to provide a financial basis for CAP with a requirement that the budgetary expenditure should be subject to parliamentary control (a policy advocated by the Netherlands). Hallstein considered these proposals to be necessary because the existing method of financing the relatively small Community budget out of national contributions would be inadequate for the considerable additional resources that the CAP necessitated. De Gaulle reacted to the proposals with considerable hostility as he favoured European integration based on free trade and an absence of supranationalism. He disliked the prospect of adding to the supranational power and independence of the Commission by providing the Community with its own resources from customs duties and agriculture levies, and saw no reason to support the Commission's proposals to augment the European Parliament's influence. But while de Gaulle was prepared to stand firm against the Commission's proposals, a far graver concern for him was the Treaty of Rome's provision to move from unanimity to majority voting in certain areas of the Council of Ministers' work from 1966 onwards. This change in voting procedure represented a strengthening of the supranational design of the Community and would in turn result in a reduction of national control.

Empty chair crisis: A period when the Community was brought to a standstill by France's refusal to participate in meetings of the Council of Ministers between July and December 1965.

Luxembourg Compromise: An informal agreement that was created in January 1966 as a means of overcoming France's boycott of the Community (the so-called 'empty chair' crisis).

An inability to resolve differences of opinion over the Commission's proposals led de Gaulle to prohibit his ministers from attending Council meetings from July to December 1965, a period commonly known as the '**empty chair crisis**'. The crisis was finally resolved in January 1966, with the Hallstein Plan being abandoned in favour of the '**Luxembourg Compromise**': member states agreed to an interim financial regulation for CAP, to limit the powers of the Commission and the European Parliament, and to introduce the procedure of majority voting with the provision that 'where very important interests are at stake the discussion must be continued until unanimous agreement is reached' [**Document 19, p. 128**]. In other words, a member state would be able to use a veto on those policies that it regarded to be at odds with its national interest. It was an outcome which indicated that member states would in future play an increasingly important role that would extend into the area of policy initiation. The Luxembourg Compromise thus signalled an important shift in power away from the Commission towards the national governments of the member states. Until 1965, the responsibility for initiating policy had rested principally with the Commission, which under the leadership of Walter Hallstein had successfully managed to forge ahead with the process of European integration. In the wake of the crisis, the Commission's role of formulating and initiating policy altered to that of a consensus builder that implemented agreements that were acceptable to the member states. And while this state of affairs served the immediate interests of many of the governments, it is widely accepted that the 'empty chair crisis' and the Luxembourg Compromise limited the opportunity for further European integration over the next two decades. In this sense, as a result of the crisis, the Community's future development assumed the structure that it would maintain for the next 20 years. Indeed, it would not be until the 1987 Single European Act that the Community would engage in a process of reform that significantly went beyond the Luxembourg Compromise.

On 1 July 1967 the ECSC, Euratom and the EEC merged so that the three Communities – which remained intact – were served by a single Commission and Council of Ministers [**Document 18, p. 127**]. In practical terms, this referred to the coming together of the *executive* bodies as the three Communities already shared the Assembly (from 1962 the European Parliament) and the Court of Justice. Thus, the two Commissions of the EEC and Euratom, and the ECSC High Authority, merged into a single Commission of the European Communities. In addition to these changes, the Merger Treaty gave legal recognition to the Committee of Permanent Representatives (Coreper) which despite its absence of reference in the Treaty of Rome nonetheless proved to be a vital body in preparing the groundwork for ministerial meetings in the Council of Ministers. Apart from these institutional developments, a full customs union and the completion of CAP were also achieved.

The attainment of these objectives, combined with the Community's post-1965 attachment to intergovernmental methods of decision-making, ensured that the prospect of joining the EEC became increasingly attractive to a number of European countries. The question of **enlargement** reappeared in 1967 when the British Labour government, under the leadership of **Harold Wilson**, put forward a second application to join the Community [**Document 20, p. 129**]. Once again, the United States was supportive of this policy, hoping that Britain's entry would strengthen **Atlanticism** among European nations (Lundestad, 1998: 81). But, as he had done before, de Gaulle vetoed the British application, pointing to the weakness of the British economy and the fact that London did not fully accept the constraints that membership of the Community implied. Observers might have thought that the British government would have withdrawn its application, as it had done in 1963. But this did not happen and the British application was instead 'left on the table' so that it could be reactivated at an appropriate time. In practical terms, this basically meant that Britain's prospects for membership would change only when de Gaulle was no longer in office. This would happen in 1969 when de Gaulle was forced to resign, less than a year after the May 1968 trade union and student unrest in France, and was succeeded by George Pompidou in April of that year.

By this stage French dominance over the Community could no longer be taken for granted: its economy was declining at a time when Germany was economically resurgent. A combination of concern over Germany's growing economic power and increased political assertiveness, as represented by the policy of **Ostpolitik** (rapprochement towards the Soviet bloc, replacing the **Hallstein Doctrine**) carved out by its new Chancellor **Willy Brandt**, proved to be of great influence on French policy. Whereas de Gaulle had opposed the enlargement of the Community, Pompidou realised the potential value of British membership, which combined with France could act as a counterbalance to German influence.

THE SPIRIT OF THE HAGUE

A combination of concerns over Germany and domestic pressures for a positive French initiative towards the Community led French President Georges Pompidou to call a special meeting of the leaders of 'the Six' member states to be held at The Hague in December 1969 in order to 'relaunch' the Community [**Document 21, p. 129**]. In calling the Hague summit,

Enlargement: The preamble of the Treaties of Rome contains reference to the determination 'to lay the foundations of an ever closer union among the peoples of Europe'.

Wilson, Harold (1916–95): UK Labour Prime Minister 1964–70 and 1974–76. Oversaw the UK's second application for EEC membership in 1967 and in 1974 renegotiated the terms of entry that Edward Heath had obtained. In 1975 he held a referendum on Community membership.

Atlanticism: When the interests of a nation state are maximised by a close relationship with the US.

Ostpolitik: The policy towards Eastern Europe that was adopted by the coalition government of Social Democrats and Liberal Free Democrats that came to power in the Federal Republic of Germany (FRG) in 1969. The policy was described as 'change through rapprochement' and replaced the Hallstein Doctrine.

Hallstein Doctrine: Named after Walter Hallstein, this policy stipulated that the Federal Republic of Germany (FRG) was the sole representative of Germany because, in contrast to the government in the German Democratic Republic (GDR), the FRG's government had been democratically elected.

Brandt, Willy (1913–92): Socialist Chancellor of the Federal Republic of Germany from 1969–74; leader of the Social Democratic Party (SDP) from 1964–87; developed an active foreign policy towards Eastern Europe and the Soviet Union (referred to as *Ostpolitik*).

Deepening: The advances made in European integration from the initial customs union to the creation of the eurozone.

Accession: The process by which countries join the EU. The treaties that cover the conclusion of the negotiations between applicant countries and the EU are known as 'Treaties of Accession'.

Own resources: The Community was provided with an ability to raise its own finances in April 1970 rather than being dependent on the financial support of the member states. They have four elements: (1) customs duties based on the imports from non-EU member states; (2) agricultural duties and the sugar and isoglucose levies; (3) the VAT resource based on a portion of the revenue of each member state's VAT; (4) and a percentage of the GNP of a member state.

Third countries: Any state that is not a member of an organisation such as the EU.

Pompidou argued for the strengthening of existing Community competencies, the completion of the financing regimes for the common agricultural policy and the **deepening** of Community competencies in certain areas. Pompidou's desire to directly involve the leaders of the national governments was a deliberate attempt to inject some impetus into the Community, which had not experienced the automatic process of integration that the federalists wished for. Although the Community's experience of such meetings had been limited, 'circumstances pointed to the need for a fresh injection of political will into the process of integration: decisions to bring this about could only come from Heads of Government. If nothing else, the sixties had proved conclusively that the process would not continue automatically and indefinitely. "Spillover" would not of itself lead to a united Europe' (Henig, 2002: 63–4).

With de Gaulle no longer in office, The Hague summit of government leaders and foreign ministers provided an important opportunity to resolve a number of issues, which resulted, according to the Commission, in a 'turning point in its history' and led to 'the spirit of the Hague'. Agreement was reached on the question of enlargement (France had blocked Britain's applications in 1963 and 1967). A reversal of this policy under Pompidou was shaped by a hope that British **accession** would act as a balance to a resurgent Germany and limit the opportunity for the supranational development of the Community. But while Pompidou accepted the principle of enlargement, he refused to set a date for the accession negotiations to commence. He argued that enlargement could take place only once the question of the financing of the CAP – which had dogged the Community since 1965 – had been resolved. To resolve this impasse the other five members of the Community agreed to work out the question of CAP funding in return for France's guaranteed commitment to the commencement of enlargement negotiations.

In getting to the bottom of CAP funding, member states agreed in April 1970 to provide the Community with its own financial resources, a decision that represented a move away from direct national contributions. These **'own resources'** extended beyond the remit of financing the CAP and were designed to ensure the Community had sufficient income to satisfy all the policies that the Commission administered. This funding would be achieved through a combination of agricultural levies charged on the importation of agricultural products from **third countries**, customs duties levied on industrial products imported into the Community, and a small amount of funding that would not exceed 1 per cent of the revenues a member state obtained from value added tax. In providing the Community with this financial base, member states divorced themselves from the process of inspecting expenditure. To remedy this 'accounting deficit', it was agreed to provide the European Parliament with the authority to examine the Community's budget (as the 1965 Hallstein Report had wanted). The implication of these developments was perfectly clear: it enhanced the supranational design of the Community. As Urwin has reflected, 'The importance of all this was that, by enlarging the role of the Commission and Parliament, it increased the supranational possibilities of the EC' (Urwin, 1995: 154).

What this funding agreement meant in practice was that those countries, such as Germany, that imported large quantities of agricultural produce and industrial goods would account for a greater proportion of the contributions to the Community's budget than a country that had fewer imports. But while the resolution of CAP funding paved the way for the future enlargement of the Community, the agreement was devoid of any input from those countries that wished to join the Community. It proved to be a crucial mistake. As a large industrialised economy with a small but efficient agricultural industry, Britain imported a substantial amount of foodstuffs. The 1970 agreement thus meant that Britain faced a requirement on its accession to the Community of having to pay significant sums into the Community budget at a time when its economic fortunes were in decline (which was a key reason for joining). Whereas the British government had hoped it would receive additional financial resources from the Community, it was instead faced with the horrifying prospect of providing a significant amount of its resources. Moreover, as Britain had a large industrial base and the smallest agricultural sector in the Community, it would receive little back in the way of CAP funding. It was a predicament of which Britain's chief negotiator, Anthony Barber, was nonetheless aware and one which the government was prepared to accept to obtain membership (Barker, 1971: 247). All in all, this meant that Britain would become a **net contributor** to the EC and this disparity between Britain's low rate of economic growth and high budgetary contributions laid the groundwork for the subsequent budgetary disagreements that dominated the work of the Community in the late 1970s and early 1980s [**Document 29, p. 136**].

Net contributor: EU member states that obtain less funding out of the EU than they contribute to its budget.

In addition to resolving the CAP funding, The Hague meeting was significant for its agreement to widen the Community's membership (paving the way for subsequent applications from Britain, Denmark, Ireland and Norway) and to deepen the EC's activities with a view to extending cooperation within the economic and political fields. To some observers, the simultaneous objectives of widening and deepening were incompatible: in an enlarged Community there would be less likelihood of achieving agreement on deeper European integration. Two committees were nonetheless established to examine the case for deeper economic and political integration. The premier of Luxembourg, Pierre Werner, was given the responsibility of leading a committee to examine the case for monetary union, while the Belgian diplomat (and future European Commissioner) Viscount **Étienne Davignon**

Davignon, Viscount Etienne (b. 1932): As political director of the Belgian foreign ministry in the 1970s he chaired the committee which devised the report that laid the foundations of European Political Cooperation (EPC). He later served as a European Commissioner from 1977 to 1985.

led the committee which investigated the possibility of achieving closer political integration. The reports of both committees were published in 1970. The October **Werner Report** stressed that 'economic and monetary union is an objective realisable in the course of the present decade' (that is, by 1980) and that this would mean 'that the principal decisions of economic policy will be taken at Community level and therefore that the necessary powers will be transferred from the national plane to the Community plane' [**Document 22, p. 130**]. The significance of this declaration was nonetheless cautioned by the Werner Report emphasising that progress depended on 'the political will of the member states to realise this objective' [**Document 22, p. 130**]. Thus, while the Werner Report provided a blueprint for monetary union that could be attained in stages by 1980 and provided the motivation for member states to create a mechanism for managing and coordinating the different national currencies (the 1971 European currency management system, or the '**Snake in the tunnel**'), the success of these objectives clearly rested on the support of the member states [**Document 24, p. 132**].

Having been instructed by the Hague summit 'to study the best way of achieving progress in the matter of political unification, within the context of enlargement' of the EC, the November 1970 **Davignon Report** recommended that foreign-policy coordination 'should be the object of the first practical endeavours to demonstrate to all that Europe has a political vocation' [**Document 23, p. 131**]. In focusing on foreign policy, the Davignon Report pointed to the need for the EC to develop a stronger European voice in international affairs at a time when there was a notable gulf between the views of the United States and Western Europe on a number of international issues (such as US involvement in Vietnam). To achieve these aims, the Davignon Report recommended that an intergovernmental system of **European Political Cooperation** (EPC) be established to facilitate foreign-policy **harmonisation** and coordination among member states. An emphasis on intergovernmental methods of operation ensured that the EPC sat outside the Community and was devoid of any supranational input (the Davignon Report deliberately avoided the establishment of a Secretariat that would manage foreign-policy coordination). Coordination would be achieved principally through six-monthly meetings of foreign ministers (to be chaired by the Council Presidency), the establishment of a Political Committee (comprising the political directors of the national foreign ministries) and the linking of foreign ministries through a direct telex network (COREU). After the 1973 Copenhagen Report foreign minister meetings increased to four a year and several working groups were established to prepare ministers' consultation (covering such areas as the Mediterranean, the Middle East and Asia).

Reaction to both reports was mixed among 'the Six'. For France, EPC provided an important means of positioning Germany's increasingly active

Werner Report: Published in October 1970, it set out a three-stage process for the creation of monetary union within a period of ten years.

'Snake in the tunnel': A March 1972 agreement that limited the fluctuation of currencies of European nations by means of restricting movement against the US dollar at a rate of 1.25 per cent on either side.

Davignon Report: Published in November 1970, it recommended that closer foreign-policy cooperation among member states should be achieved through the mechanism of European Political Cooperation.

European Political Cooperation (EPC): Cooperation by EC foreign ministers in the field of foreign policy began in 1970 and was replaced with the Common Foreign and Security Policy (CFSP).

Harmonisation: The process of bringing states closer together by the setting of common European standards from which they cannot deviate.

policy of *Ostpolitik* – which sought to establish relations with Eastern Europe – within the framework of the Community. In itself *Ostpolitik* mirrored a broader warming in superpower relations in the 1970s, a period that became known as détente and which provided a highpoint in the European context of the 1975 Helsinki Final Act that established the **Conference on Security and Cooperation in Europe** (CSCE). As was the case with EPC, the CSCE placed little in the way of controls on the national decision-making of national governments. The same could not be said for the Werner Report, which called for the creation of a monetary union over a ten-year period [**Document 22, p. 130**]. Such a process would not just involve the strengthening of economic policy cooperation among the member states. Decisions on interest rates, exchange rates and the management of reserves would be taken at the Community level. Fiscal harmonisation and cooperation on structural and regional policies would also have to take place, while various institutions would have to be created. Most obviously, this would include institutions to take decisions on economic policy and to coordinate the work of the central banks of the member states, while a direct implication of this was to further advance the cause of supranationalism.

Conference on Security and Cooperation in Europe (CSCE): Established in 1975 with 35 members as part of the period of détente to provide a forum for dialogue between the Warsaw Pact and NATO. It was renamed the Organisation for Security and Cooperation in Europe (OSCE) in 1990.

4

The Enlarged Community: 1970–84

After the national backlash that beset the Community in the 1960s, many hoped that the 1970s would produce a more positive approach to European integration given the objectives that had been set at The Hague. This proved not to be the case, with the Community's progress being affected by internal and external factors. This included Britain's renegotiation of its terms of membership, poor leadership from the European Commission and a spike in world oil prices that impacted on industrial competitiveness. In all, the combined difficulties that the Community encountered during the 1970s led to the decade being categorised as a 'dark age' of European integration. This difficult climate continued into the early years of the 1980s, with many commentators concluding that the limit of European integration had been reached.

THE FIRST ENLARGEMENT

The consensus reached at the December 1969 Hague summit on the principle of enlargement was followed by the start of substantive discussions in June 1970 with the four applicant states of Britain, Denmark, Ireland and Norway. By that stage the progress of the Community had been substantial: 1968 marked the completion of the customs union and a fully functioning agricultural policy. And although the integrative process suffered a setback with the 1966 Luxembourg Compromise, the Community's overall economic and political progress was a considerable draw for applicant states. This was particularly true for members of the European Free Trade Association, which was unable to offer an alternative to the economic and political strength of the Community.

Britain, which was now led by the Europhile Conservative Prime Minister **Edward Heath**, had come to the conclusion that neither the Commonwealth nor EFTA offered the advantages of market access and increased status that

Heath, Edward (1916–2005): UK Conservative Prime Minister 1970–74. A committed pro-European, he was in charge of the UK's first application for membership.

the Community did. The Heath government had been greatly influenced by the views of the business and banking community that membership was essential to revitalise Britain's economy (Middlemas, 1995: 74). There had in effect occurred a waning of foreign policy options for Britain as the economic and political arguments for membership became impossible to ignore. 'Taking the years 1960–1970 as a whole, the GNP of "the Six" increased by an average of 4.2 per cent a year, compared with 2.3 per cent in Britain' (May, 1999: 41). Developments within the Community further improved the prospects for Britain joining. The Luxembourg Compromise's weakening of supranationalism **[Document 19, p. 128]** and the Yaoundé Convention's provision of guarantees to former colonies of 'the Six' lessened Britain's concern about the adverse effect of the common external tariff on its preferential trading relations with the Commonwealth. Over and above these factors, it was Heath himself who greatly enhanced the prospects of Britain joining. As Dick Leonard recalls, 'Heath had one inestimable advantage over the authors of the two previous British applications, Macmillan and Wilson. Unlike them, he was no reluctant convert, but a long-term and passionate believer that Britain's destiny lay in Europe' (Leonard, 1996: 168). In practical terms, Heath's election as Prime Minister emphasised the refocusing of Britain's strategic priorities towards Europe. Yet it was a view that was not fully supported by the opposition Labour Party and as such Heath's act of faith in joining the Community did not mean that Britain's long-term commitment to the Community would be particularly straightforward.

Each of the applicants brought specific concerns to the membership negotiations, which in the case of Britain primarily related to Commonwealth trade, the cost of the CAP and the position of sterling (Hannay, 2000). The overriding importance of joining the Community meant that British demands were considerably more modest than they had been in the previous two applications **[Documents 15 and 20, p. 125 and p. 129]**. Heath was a realist who understood that Britain's failure to engage in the ECSC and Treaty of Rome meant that there was a price to be paid for Community membership. This 'price' would take the form of having to make significant contributions to the Community's budget, and the reality of this state of affairs was highlighted in the government White Papers of 1970 and 1971. Nonetheless, the common view among British negotiators at the time was that the impetus provided to the economy through entry to the Community would in part offset this price.

Britain's application was the determining factor that influenced the decision of the other applicants to follow its lead. As Ireland's economy was intrinsically linked to Britain's (approximately 70 per cent of Ireland's imports came from Britain and in excess of half of its exports went to Britain), it had little choice but to follow the British position. Nevertheless, policy-makers in

Dublin hoped that Community membership would in the longer term help Ireland to become less dependent on Britain by developing economic and political links with a wider group of countries. Just as the economic and political benefits of membership were clear for Britain and Ireland, this was also true for Denmark and Norway and their strong economic links with Britain suggested that they should follow Britain's path. A key benefit of membership for Denmark was that it provided an increased market for its highly efficient agricultural sector. But despite the potential benefits of membership, both Denmark and Norway were suspicious of European involvement, having advocated the concept of Nordic unity since the end the Second World War.

All in all, the major issues regarding membership for all four applicant nations were settled within a year, with discussions in the latter half of 1971 focusing on relatively minor issues. And because the Community had already reached agreement on legislation such as EU **decisions** and **directives** that the applicants had to accept as a condition of membership (the so-called **acquis communautaire**), a decision was taken to lessen the burden of implementing EC policies with the granting of a five-year transition period. Of the four applicants, Britain was the only country not to hold a **referendum** on joining the Community: the decision to join was instead taken by Parliamentary vote. A referendum in Ireland produced an overwhelming majority of 83 per cent to 17 per cent in favour of membership, while in Denmark the vote was 63.3 per cent to 36.7 per cent in favour. This pattern would not be repeated in Norway, as its terms of membership were rejected in a popular referendum in September 1972 by 54.5 per cent to 45.5 per cent. Concerns over the necessity of international cooperation and the impact of Community membership on the agricultural industry had been paramount behind the Norwegian 'no' vote.

Although Norway's rejection of membership was a shock to the Community – it was the first time a state had rejected Community membership – it neither impeded the access of the other states nor adversely affected the EC's future. As a consequence, the Community grew to nine (not ten) when Britain, Denmark and Ireland joined on 1 January 1973. The three new member states would add 60 million people to the EC, which in 1973 had a combined population of 250 million – a number broadly equivalent to the populations of the US and Soviet Union at that time. Just as the population of the Community was to increase, so too was its economic influence. The new member states would add to the EC's commercial standing (being broadly equivalent to the US and Japan) and would result in it accounting for one-fifth of world trade. Enlargement did, of course, reduce the membership and importance of EFTA, and with this in mind the applicant nations had emphasised the importance of establishing some form of special trading

Decisions: A form of EU legislation that has direct applicability in member states without the need for additional national enactment. Decisions could be applied to member states, companies and individuals.

Directives: Targeted at member states, requiring them to adopt appropriate legislation, though they are able to decide on the method and form of implementation.

Acquis communautaire: The assortment of legislation, treaties and rulings of the European Court of Justice that constitute the legal identity of the EU. Referred to as simply the 'acquis'.

Referendum: Governments often ask their electorate to register their vote on policies and decisions. In the EU context referendums have sometimes been used when a member state has applied for membership as well as to approve significant changes, such as joining the single currency.

agreement between the EC and EFTA. The end product of these negotiations was a July 1972 agreement on a free trade area that would permit free trade among the nine EC countries and seven EFTA nations.

Even though it was clear that enlargement would enhance the EC's influence on world affairs, the future direction of an enlarged Community was less clear. The response to this question was once again to come from the French President, Georges Pompidou. He decided to convene a summit meeting of heads of state and government in October 1972 in Paris to examine how best to optimise the benefits of enlargement. As with the December 1969 Hague summit, Pompidou looked to the national leaders to map out the future path of European integration and in so doing provided additional evidence that the institutional pendulum had swung from the Commission towards the member states. It moreover confirmed the extent to which the Community had moved from the vision set out by the likes of Monnet, and as such the 'limited gains [of the 1970s] came about primarily not because the Commission initiated policy but because the Council of Ministers willed it' (Middlemas, 1995: 82).

Although they were technically not yet members of the Community, the applicant states took part in the summit meeting, which produced a number of agreements. This included a commitment to achieve the goal of Economic and Monetary Union (EMU) by 1980 (as had been set out in the Werner Report), the need to establish a common external trade policy towards the Soviet Union and Eastern Europe, and the need to make progress on a number of environmental, social and scientific matters. One of the most significant points to come from the meeting was agreement to develop a European Regional and Development Fund (ERDF) to promote economic and social cohesion. The ERDF – a proposal from Pompidou – was designed to provide the British Prime Minister, Edward Heath, with a positive European policy with which he could assuage domestic political criticism of Britain's entry to the Community to offset its minimal payments from the common agricultural policy. Thus, for some member states the ERDF helped to balance out the costs of EC membership. When working, the ERDF would provide financial aid for depressed industrial regions and Heath obviously hoped that such aid would lessen the cost – and reduce the criticism – of Britain's membership of the Community. In short, the Paris summit attempted to resolve potential problems and chart the future progress of the Community, as emphasised in the summit communiqué: 'The member states of the Community, the driving force of European construction, affirm their intention before the end of the present decade to transform the whole complex of their relations into a European Union.'

As the Community approached 1973, its future appeared bright. 'Three years after the Hague summit,' John Young has written, 'the Community seemed on the brink, not merely of a major enlargement but of a leap towards full economic union' (Young, 1991: 46). This was not to happen. The Werner Report's goal of establishing economic and monetary union by 1980 was undermined by instability in the international economy. One reason for this volatility was the US decision to cut interest rates in May 1971 and the decision a few months later on 15 August 1971 to suspend the dollar convertibility. In response to the increasingly precarious international financial system, Community member states attempted to inject a degree of stability into European economies in April 1972 by agreeing to restrict currency fluctuations. It would be achieved by a system of currency cooperation – the 'Snake' – that would restrict the fluctuations of EC currencies within a 2.5 per cent boundary inside a 'tunnel' [**Document 24, p. 132**]. But while the six EC members of the 'Snake' were joined in May 1972 by Britain and Denmark, the new participants' involvement was only temporary: both withdrew one month later, while Italy's membership was terminated in February 1973.

The inability of participants to stay within the 'Snake' was the product of a difficult international economic situation that spawned rising unemployment and high levels of inflation. Economic conditions were made worse by the October 1973 Arab–Israeli War that was immediately followed by soaring oil prices. In an effort to grapple with these developments, a European Monetary Cooperation Fund was set up in 1973 to provide additional support to weak currencies, although it was of limited worth. Concerned about the ongoing economic difficulties, Pompidou yet again called for a meeting of heads of government, to be held this time in Copenhagen in December 1973. Faced with a chronic international economic climate, the leaders of the (now) nine member states failed to reach agreement on how best to respond. The meeting proved worthless, producing no initiatives to assist EC economies, and was immediately followed by the French withdrawal from 'the Snake' on 19 January 1974. And although France rejoined the 'Snake' in July 1975, it was forced to withdraw for a second time in March 1976 and by then the very existence of the 'Snake' looked increasingly precarious. The economic conditions that undermined the 'Snake' also damaged the potential of achieving monetary union. Indeed, as early as 1975 a European Commission report would emphasise that 'Europe is no nearer to EMU than in 1969. In fact, if there has been any movement, it has been backward' (Marjolin et al., 1975: 1). The lack of stability in the international economy meant that European governments 'ignored the prescriptions of the Werner Report for the harmonization of fiscal and monetary policies' (Aldcroft and Oliver, 1998: 149). As a consequence, interest in the 'Snake' lessened and member states buried any hopes of achieving monetary union by 1980.

BRITAIN'S INDECISION

International economic difficulties were one of two main problems that impacted on Community progress in the 1970s. The other concerned Britain, as it appeared that 'the decade that followed the first enlargement lent support to those who had predicted that widening (the Community) would be the enemy of deepening' (Pinder, 1998: 63). In the British general election of February 1974, Harold Wilson's Labour Party defeated the Conservative government and as a result Wilson once again occupied the position of Prime Minister. Labour's victory was achieved partly on the back of a campaign that sought to renegotiate the terms of entry to the Community that Heath had obtained. In truth, however, the commitment to renegotiate was as much influenced by the need to pacify the deep divisions within the Labour Party on European issues as it was by the need to appease the electorate. Scepticism within the Labour Party on European matters had increased in the wake of Wilson's failed application for membership in November 1967. Concerns over threats to sovereignty, the impact on the Commonwealth and fears over higher prices all helped to fuel Labour Party scepticism on European matters.

In the 1974 general election campaign the Labour Party thus declared that if elected they would seek 'a fundamental renegotiation of the terms of entry', after which an election or referendum would be held so as to ensure that the population was consulted on the key issue of European membership. Yet, as Alex May has correctly noted, no provision existed in the Treaty of Rome for a country to renegotiate its terms of entry and 'Britain's European partners would have been within their rights to call Britain's bluff by refusing one' (May, 1999: 59). It did not happen and along with his Foreign Secretary, James Callaghan, Wilson set about the process of renegotiating the terms of entry. As with many other issues, Wilson was pragmatic on the question of Europe and possessed none of the pro-European credentials of Heath. Callaghan, by contrast, was rather more sceptical and was publicly willing to question the value of Britain's membership of the Community.

In making the case for renegotiation, Wilson was aware that his leadership of a minority government could come unstuck over Europe. And although there were notable supporters of European integration within the Labour Party (such as **Roy Jenkins** and David Owen), a significant proportion of the rank and file of the party were sceptical and the renegotiation was thus aimed at reconciling divisions 'between those strongly for continued membership of the Community despite the terms which Heath had negotiated, and those strongly against' (Dell, 1991: 17). The process of renegotiation was thus part of Wilson's strategy to maintain unity within the Labour Party and was regarded by many to be a 'superficial exercise'. The former British

Jenkins, Roy (1920–2003): President of the European Commission 1977–81, having previously served as UK Home Secretary and Chancellor of the Exchequer for the Labour Party. As Commission President he was a keen advocate of the European Monetary System (EMS) and helped to steer the Community out of a period of Eurosclerosis.

Ambassador to Germany, Nicholas Henderson, has written that Wilson '. . . did not seem to see himself in any creative political role. He was quite frank . . . about his main objective, which was to keep all the clashing balls of the Labour Party in the air at the same time' (Henderson, 1994: 72).

Having been entrusted with the responsibility of dealing with the renegotiations, Callaghan managed at his first Council meeting in April 1974 to irritate his fellow foreign ministers by informing them of Britain's demands. Even though the government stressed that the renegotiations hinged on seven points, many were of little relevance. 'Labour's manifesto had promised to retain a zero VAT rate on basic items, but EC rules *did* not obstruct this; neither did the EC prevent Britain from protecting its balance of payments by limiting capital movements with Europe; and the Labour party's criticism of EMU was pointless because EMU was no longer in the realm of practical politics' (Young, 2000: 113). This meant that the renegotiations were dominated by four key issues: extending the Yaoundé Convention to assist Commonwealth and other **third world** exporters; reforming the CAP to lower food prices and help third world producers; ensuring that the Commission would not interfere with Britain's industrial and regional policies; and readjusting Britain's budgetary contributions. Some of the issues were more difficult than others.

Third World: An expression that is used to refer to those less developed countries that are mainly to be found in Africa, Asia and Latin America. Such countries tend to be reliant on producing primary products and generally suffer from poor infrastructure.

Britain's desire to assist Commonwealth and other Third World countries chimed with a general viewpoint that the Community should do more to improve its relations with the third world. It would lead in a matter of months to the February 1975 Lomé Convention which helped to protect the exports of developing countries by exempting them from tariffs and providing them with various guaranteed quotas. Other issues proved more difficult to resolve. Britain's desire to reform the CAP made little headway as the new French President, **Valéry Giscard d'Estaing** (who succeeded Pompidou after his death in May 1974), was unwilling to adjust a policy that favoured French farmers. Discussions over the Community budget were the most difficult and for Britain were not helped by a May 1974 Treasury report which forecasted that by 1980 it would be responsible for 24 per cent of the EC budget despite accounting for only 14 per cent of the Community's gross national product.

Giscard d'Estaing, Valéry (b. 1926): President of France 1974–81. Influential in the institutionalisation of summit meetings of Community heads of state and government and supported the development of the European Monetary System. Chaired the discussions on the Convention on the future of Europe that took place between March 2002 and June 2003.

In the end it would take two summit meetings before agreement could be reached on the terms of Britain's renegotiations at Dublin in March 1975. Prior to that meeting, the Paris summit of December 1974 produced agreement on the exact size of the ERDF: Britain would receive 28 per cent of all funding, while France, Ireland and Italy would also obtain significant support. The ERDF – which Heath had argued for in the accession negotiations – provided Wilson with an opportunity to demonstrate to his critics that Britain was 'getting something back'. The Paris summit was significant for producing agreement on a 'corrective mechanism' which would ensure that

Britain, or for that matter any member state, would not pay too much into the EC budget. The summit also took the opportunity to resolve a number of issues that were unrelated to the renegotiations. These included the principle of direct elections to the European Parliament (the first of which took place in 1979) and the taking of a decision to commission the Belgian Prime Minister, **Leo Tindemans**, to provide a report on European union. When published in December 1975, the Tindemans Report contained little to satisfy those who hoped it would lead to a federal Europe. It focused instead on institutional reform and the further widening of the Community's activities (as in the field of foreign and security policy) and outlined a proposal for the creation of a **two-speed Europe** in which the degree of integration would depend on the willingness and ability of member states to cooperate. Not surprisingly, this was unacceptable to many of the smaller member states and, combined with other concerns over the erosion of sovereignty, led to the Tindemans Report being silenced [**Document 26, p. 134**].

By far the most significant development at Paris was the recognition of the important role that summits had come to play in the Community's progress. Member states thus reached agreement that such summits would in future take the form of a European Council, whose first meeting would take place in Dublin in March 1975. It would comprise heads of government, with the President of the Commission being given the right to attend. In terms of operation, it would meet three times a year (changed to twice a year in 1985) and be led by a member state that would assume the role of the 'Presidency of the European Council', which would rotate among the member states on a six-monthly basis [**Document 25, p. 133**]. But whereas President Giscard d'Estaing thought that the European Council meetings would take the form of intimate conversations among heads of government, 'the European Council was quickly sucked into the political vacuum at the centre of the Community, to take decisions that the Council of Ministers was unable to take' (Pinder, 1998: 37). As a consequence the future of European integration would therefore greatly depend on the decisions taken by heads of government at European Council 'summits' and the nature of relationships among the member states. This particularly applied to the Franco-German axis. After the difficulties of the early 1970s, a particularly close relationship was formed between French President Giscard d'Estaing and the German Chancellor **Helmut Schmidt** (both of whom came to office in 1974), which lasted for the rest of the decade.

Apart from the symbolic nature of the March 1975 Dublin European Council, it was noteworthy for finally producing agreement on the outstanding issues of Britain's renegotiations. This included the nature of the 'corrective mechanism' whereby a rebate would be given to any net contributor state that met a rather complex Commission formula. For this to happen a member state would have to meet certain criteria that related to its balance of payments,

Tindemans, Leo (b. 1922): Prime Minister of Belgium 1974–78 and Foreign Minister 1981–89. Member of the European Parliament 1979–81 and 1989–99. Author of the 1975 Tindemans Report on European Union.

Two-speed Europe: Describes a situation when a group of member states choose to advance at a faster pace of integration than other member states.

Schmidt, Helmut (b. 1918): Chancellor of the Federal Republic of Germany 1974–83. Played an important role in the development of the EEC, being one of the principal advocates of the European Monetary System that was endorsed by the European Council in 1978.

growth rate and share of gross national product (GNP). The exact nature of the rebate would be two-thirds of the difference between its share of GNP and its budget contributions, although not more than its total VAT contributions. In the end, however, the renegotiations did little to assist Britain in building a fruitful relationship with other member states, who regarded it as an 'unreliable partner in Europe' (Henderson, 1994: 66). According to Roy Jenkins, President of the European Commission at the time, the whole process 'produced the minimum results with the maximum ill-will' (Jenkins, 1991: 375). It is a point echoed by Roy Denman, who considered that it produced 'the minimum of gain for the maximum of irritation' (Denman, 1996: 250). Having been a member of the Community for just over a year, the process of renegotiation severely impacted on Britain's status in the Community and raised suspicions within the Community about British membership.

Domestically, the renegotiated terms did little to ease the divisions within the Labour Party. This was despite the fact that the terms received majority support from the Cabinet, which voted 16 to 7 in their favour on 17 March 1975. The House of Commons too offered its support on 9 April by 398 votes to 172 in favour. Thus, having received this endorsement, Wilson started the process of holding a referendum on the renegotiated terms. Yet because the Labour Party – and moreover the Cabinet – was far from united on the question of Europe, Wilson dropped the established practice of collective responsibility and permitted government ministers to exercise their own decision. When the membership referendum eventually took place in June 1975, the terms were supported by approximately 2 to 1 of the voters: 17.3 million people voted in favour and 8.4 million against. Many would be forgiven for thinking that the outcome of the renegotiation and referendum would be to settle once and for all the question of British membership. This was not to happen. Many individuals within the Labour Party continued to argue against EC membership, including withdrawal from the Community (a policy that the party committed itself to in the 1983 general election). At a broader level, the renegotiated terms had failed to rectify fully the level of Britain's budget contributions. This was starkly emphasised by a government calculation that Britain would be the largest net contributor to the Community budget by 1978, despite being ranked fifth in terms of its share of the Community's gross domestic product.

EUROSCLEROSIS

The history of renegotiation, referendum and budgetary dispute did little to enhance Britain's status within the Community. If anything it confirmed its position as 'an awkward partner'. British indecision was, however, not the primary reason for the difficulties that beset the Community in the 1970s.

The progress anticipated at the 1969 Hague summit had been hampered by the unwillingness of member states to support new initiatives at a time of international economic instability. The latter had been principally influenced by the decision of the Organization of Petroleum Exporting Countries (OPEC) to restrict the supply of oil to world markets in 1973 that consequently lead to a dramatic increase in oil prices. Before the decade was over the 1979 Iranian revolution led to a further increase in oil prices. These oil hikes created much disruption to world economic activity, as industry struggled to maintain output. At the same time, the supranational institutions of the Community, particularly the European Commission, appeared unable to deal with the challenges that the Community faced. And although the appointment of Roy Jenkins as President of the European Commission in 1977 – after **François-Zavier Ortoli's** lacklustre presidency – appeared to signal a renewed sense of purpose and dynamism in the Community's activities, for all intents and purposes the Community's fortunes had not been substantially revived by the early 1980s. In part, the Commission's lack of purpose was influenced by the legacy of de Gaulle and his efforts to reduce the influence of the supranational institutions.

Despite the general malaise that dominated a period that was subsequently referred to as one of '**Eurosclerosis**', there were some notable developments, including the creation of a **Court of Auditors** in 1975. One year previously, the Paris summit of 1974 took the decision to establish the European Council and confirm the principle of direct elections to the European Parliament [**Document 25, p. 133**]. Both decisions had a lasting impact on the future progress of the Community. The creation of the European Council, which comprised the heads of state and government of the member states and which was led by a presidency that rotated among the national governments on a six-monthly basis, institutionalised the practice of summitry [**Document 25, p. 133**]. As such, it also emphasised a decline in the importance of the supranational influence of the Commission and an increase in the importance of intergovernmental relations. But while this state of affairs pleased the member states, it also raised the question as to how the Community would be able to deal adequately with future challenges in the absence of strong leadership. This included the prospect of enlargement; applications were received from Greece in 1975 and Portugal and Spain in 1979.

In contrast to the immediate impact that the European Council had on European integration, the European Parliament's influence was not substantially altered in the immediate term by the decision to elect its membership in future by direct election, and as such contributed to the view that the Community suffered from a **democratic deficit**. The European Parliament continued to remain a relatively weak institution in the eyes of both the electorate and the member state governments, as it had little ability to shape the decision-making process. This was because while Parliament had to be

Ortoli, François-Zavier (1925–2007): French President of the Commission 1973–77, continuing to serve as a member of the Commission until 1984. As President he struggled to manage the economic problems that stifled the Community's growth through the 1970s.

Eurosclerosis: A term that is generally used in reference to the 1970s when there was little growth in the pace of European integration.

Court of Auditors: Monitors the management of the finances of the Community.

Democratic deficit: The belief that the EU lacks sufficient democratic and parliamentary supervision. Often used in connection with the desire to increase the powers of the European Parliament.

Consultation procedure: Requires an opinion from the European Parliament before the Council can take a decision.

consulted on decisions as a result of the **consultation procedure**, neither the European Commission or the Council of Ministers was required to take these views into consideration. Linked to this limited involvement in the decision-making process, the Parliament had a low level of recognition among the electorate; in the first election in 1979 Britain had the noteworthy status of having had fewer people vote as a percentage of the population than elsewhere in the EC [**Document 37, p. 145**]. The first direct elections to the European Parliament of 1979 were therefore not part of a wider process of reform and its influence on the decision-making process changed only when the Single European Act and subsequent Treaty on European Union revised the decision-making procedures that had initially been established in the Treaty of Rome.

Just as the holding of direct elections did not immediately transform the Community's fortunes, the same could be said for the decision to establish the **European Monetary System** (EMS) in March 1979 [**Document 27, p. 134**]. On his appointment as President of the European Commission in 1977, Jenkins' desire to inject a fresh sense of purpose in the Community had been emphasised by his wish to re-proclaim 'the goal of monetary union' that had been outlined initially in the October 1970 Werner Report (Jenkins, 1991: 463) [**Document 22, p. 130**]. Under the leadership of Giscard and Schmidt, France and Germany were once again supportive of this goal: they argued in favour of creating a fixed exchange rate that linked European currencies as a means of overcoming the economic difficulties of the 1970s and in particular the instability created by the US devaluation of the dollar. Support for the EMS was to be found among other member states and as such demonstrated a change in the underlying political climate that once again emphasised further integration in this area of policy-making. The EMS, which was made up of a European currency unit (ECU) and an **Exchange Rate Mechanism** (ERM), was regarded as a way of reducing exchange rate instability and as a means of combating the divergent inflation rates that were prevalent in European economies in the late 1970s. Yet while it managed to provide stability by the mid-1980s, its early years of operation were subject to significant instability, with not all member states willing to participate (including Britain).

European Monetary System (EMS): A forerunner of the single currency. Established in 1979 as a 'zone of monetary stability'. It comprised the ERM, which was a parity grid for restricting the fluctuation of currencies, the ECU and the European Monetary Cooperation Fund (EMCF).

Exchange Rate Mechanism (ERM): A central component of the European Monetary System (EMS) that was established in 1979. The ERM acted as a stabilizing mechanism for reducing currency fluctuations among the participating countries whose currencies were given an exchange rate set against the European Currency Unit (ECU).

TRANSATLANTIC DIFFICULTIES

'The EC's external relations', Desmond Dinan has written, 'were every bit as problematical as its internal development in the early 1980s' (Dinan, 2005: 87). This was the result of two linked but distinct factors. First, in the wake of the period of **détente** that had dominated the 1970s, the emergence of a **Second Cold War** in the early 1980s raised serious questions about the ability of the Community to react to the changed international environment through the intergovernmental European Political Cooperation (EPC) framework that had been established in 1970 [**Document 23, p. 131**]. This was because, despite the fact that the intergovernmental nature of EPC reflected the determination of member states to maintain national control over foreign policy, the absence of provision for majority voting and the lack of a permanent secretariat at times led to difficulties in establishing a united policy. Second, **Ronald Reagan** took office as President of the United States in 1981 with the aim of restoring US military and political strength, particularly vis-à-vis the Soviet Union (Weinberger, 1990: 234). Essentially, Reagan wanted to overcome the 'Vietnam syndrome' – a lack of willingness to intervene in the Third World, and the 'Carter syndrome' – a weak stance against the Soviet Union. But EC member states for the most part did not share this view as they were attempting to create a working relationship between themselves and the Soviets. In essence 'where the Europeans saw opportunities for accommodation, the Reagan administration saw the possibility for a more aggressive counter policy against the USSR' (Hyland, 1986: 26–7).

Nowhere was this change in US policy more apparent than in the area of nuclear weapons. The Reagan administration outlined the concept of a Strategic Defence Initiative (SDI) in March 1983 which would protect America from Soviet attack through the development of a system of satellites armed with lasers that could destroy Soviet missiles in flight as well as in their silos. And even though there were questions over the feasibility of this project, it was nevertheless the case that its objective of creating a laser astrodome of defence meant that it would 'overrule or overcome the core principle of deterrence by taking the "mutual" out of mutual assured destruction (MAD), as it removed the threat of Soviet retaliation' (Blair and Curtis, 2009: 90). In addition to its implication on the Cold War balance of power, SDI also had implications for America's allies in NATO as the principle of equal security (and equal vulnerability) which had formed the bed-rock of NATO would have been reduced as the US obtained greater protection than its allies.

Europeans responded angrily: as they saw it, the US was abandoning them and protecting its own interests (Ryan, 2003: 98–99). Helmut Schmidt noted this view when he said that 'today there is a growing tendency in the United States to focus on its own national interests as it perceives them; at present there prevails almost a kind of euphoria about American vigour and strength, which is reflected in current American arms and military policy. And, frankly, these attitudes are disturbing to Europeans' (Schmidt, 1985: 59). As evidence of this divergence of views, in 1982 the United States

Détente: The improvement in relations between the US and the Soviet Union that took place in the 1970s and was associated with a number of measures to limit and contain the spread of nuclear and conventional weapons.

Second Cold War: After the era of détente that dominated much of the 1970s there emerged a period of superpower tension during 1979–85 which became known as the Second Cold War.

Reagan, Ronald (1911–2004): As President of the United States 1981–89 he played a key role in the events that resulted in the end of the Cold War and the collapse of the Soviet Union. Reagan believed that military strength and confidence in US leadership was a prerequisite for peace. He oversaw a dramatic increase in US defence spending and a return to Cold War conflict with the Soviet Union after the era of détente that dominated much of the 1970s.

imposed sanctions on US companies and licence holders involved in the construction of a 3,600-mile Soviet gas pipeline, which was designed to export Soviet gas from the Western Siberian Urengoy gas field to Western Europe. Concerned about the possibility of job losses through a loss of contracts, European governments were angered by the hypocrisy of the Reagan administration which continued to sell grain to the Soviet Union while seeking to block the pipeline.

A combination of the intergovernmental nature of EPC and a divergence of views with the United States resulted in a renewed effort among Community member states to develop stronger forms of foreign-policy cooperation. This included the October 1981 London Report, the 1981 **Genscher-Colombo Plan**, the 1983 Stuttgart **Solemn Declaration** and the 1984 European Parliament's Draft Treaty establishing the European Union (the Spinnelli Plan). At the same time that EC member states wanted to improve the effectiveness of their foreign policy cooperation by further developing EPC, they sought to 'reactivate' the Western European Union as a way of countering the dominance that the US exercised in foreign and security policy and in East–West relations. Thus, as the United States was the dominant force in NATO, EC member states viewed the WEU as an organisation in which they could discuss their differing views from the United States. All in all, these developments demonstrated that there was considerable support among member states to make changes to the institutional design of the Community, not least in the area of foreign policy because of the changed geopolitical environment. But before such changes could take place, the Community would have to resolve the outstanding question of Britain's budget contributions.

Genscher–Colombo Plan: In 1981 the German and Italian foreign ministers, Hans-Dietrich Genscher and Emilio Colombo, set out a plan to extend European Political Co-operation to cover security and defence issues.

Solemn Declaration: At the June 1983 Stuttgart European Council member states agreed to a 'Solemn Declaration' which emphasised the international identity of the Community and noted the desire to develop foreign-policy cooperation beyond European Political Cooperation (EPC).

BRITAIN'S BUDGETARY QUESTION

After the difficulties that had engulfed Britain's membership of the European Community under the Labour governments of the late 1970s, there was a genuine hope within Britain that the election of a Conservative government led by **Margaret Thatcher** in May 1979 would produce a more positive British attitude towards European integration. Such an outlook was influenced by the fact that the Conservatives had consistently been the 'Party of Europe' and that Thatcher had herself supported a continuance of Britain's membership of the Community at the time of the 1975 referendum. It was a false hope. In government Thatcher failed to establish the positive policy that had been expected and instead deployed a combative style of leadership on European issues.

Thatcher, Margaret (b. 1925): UK Conservative Prime Minister from 1979 to 1990. A tough negotiating stance on the budget and her forthright personality accentuated the nation's position as an 'awkward partner'.

Thatcher's support for Europe was based on practical grounds rather than as a result of some form of deep-seated bond. She followed the path taken by the majority of Britain's post-war prime ministers who (apart from Edward Heath) viewed European matters as part of a cost–benefit analysis. She realised the importance that EC membership meant for the British economy in terms of market access and as a means of creating and sustaining employment opportunities through inward investment. The Community's position as the world's largest trading bloc enhanced Britain's international role. At a time of renewed Cold War tension she understood the political role that the Community played in uniting a large number of European countries against the Soviet Union. But despite the evident benefits of membership, she believed that there should be clear limits to the Community's influence and that key decisions should continue to rest with the member states. It was a viewpoint that would in a short period of time create a significant division between Britain and her European partners.

Without doubt the key issue that dominated the early years of the Thatcher government was the British budget question [**Document 29, p. 136**]. Commonly referred to as the 'Bloody British Question' in Brussels, it was an issue that Harold Wilson had been unable to resolve satisfactorily at the time of the 1974 renegotiation of Britain's membership. The 1975 rebate mechanism that derived from the renegotiations failed to overturn Britain's status as one of the main net contributors to the Community budget (the other being Germany) and when combined with the escalating costs of the common agricultural policy ensured that the question of Britain's budget contributions remained a key issue for British negotiators. Britain received little funding from the CAP because British farmers tended to be more efficient than continental farmers, as well as concentrating in such areas as sheep farming that were not as generously subsidized (Thatcher, 1993: 62; Grant, 1997: 72). By the end of the transitional period of adjustment in January 1978, the British Treasury predicted that it would be the largest net contributor to the budget, with a projected deficit of £1 billion for 1979–80, despite Britain's income being less than the EC average (Jenkins, 1991: 493; Thatcher, 1993: 63). In short, Britain was paying too much into the Community budget and receiving too little in return. This contrasted with other member states who were **net recipients**.

Thatcher lost no time in attempting to address the budget imbalance in a number of informal meetings with the French President, German Chancellor and Italian Prime Minister. For the most part, the discussions resulted in little concrete progress and although the German Chancellor, Helmut Schmidt, was broadly sympathetic to Britain's plight given that Germany was the other net contributor, its economic strength nevertheless ensured that the budget contributions did not overly worry Germany. Having not got very far in these

Net recipients: EU member states that obtain more funding out of the EU than they contribute to its budget.

informal meetings, Thatcher managed to put the budget question 'squarely on the [EC] agenda' when, according to her, she 'spelt out the facts' at the June 1979 Strasbourg European Council (Thatcher, 1993: 64). But while Thatcher thought that she 'had made an impression as someone who meant business', the then President of the European Commission, Roy Jenkins, reflected that she 'performed the considerable feat of unnecessarily irritating two big countries, three small ones and the Commission with her opening performance at a European Council' (Thatcher, 1993: 64; Jenkins, 1991: 495). A few months later, in October 1979, Thatcher stressed that Britain could not accept the existing situation on the Community budget because it was 'demonstrably unjust' and it signified a tougher negotiating position on her part. Although Britain's partners were by that stage more willing to acknowledge the presence of a serious problem, they were unwilling to accept the argument that Britain's payments to the budget should be approximately equivalent to what it received from the Community. But instead of producing a diplomatic breakthrough, Thatcher's style of diplomacy served only to cement the position of the other member states which were unwilling to accept the British demands (Tugendhat, 1979: 121; Jenkins, 1989: 529–30).

Thatcher's confrontational approach to EC matters also created concern at home. The Foreign and Commonwealth Office – under Peter Carrington's leadership as Foreign Secretary – favoured a more cautious and less public approach to resolving the budget question. 'Here both European leaders and experienced officials from the Foreign Office', Seldon and Collings have written, 'were surprised, shocked even, by her aggressive and stubborn form of diplomacy. In the past, EC Summits had been at least calm and reasoned on the surface, if fairly Machiavellian beneath' (Seldon and Collings, 2000: 12). Despite these concerns at home and abroad, Thatcher nevertheless stood steadfast in campaigning for a budget rebate because in her eyes 'Britain was asking no more that its due' (Thatcher, 1993: 81). As part of an effort to deflate the argument, the Commission proposed at the Dublin meeting that Britain receive a rebate of £350 million along with the promise that Britain would in future obtain more direct Community funding. But for Thatcher it was an unacceptable offer and the failure to provide the full rebate of £1 billion ensured that the Council meeting broke up without agreement [**Document 29, p. 136**]. This strategy of holding firm ensured that the budget question dominated the Community agenda for some time to come, despite the presence of many other vital issues to which the member states needed to respond. This included domestic economic recession, unemployment and an unstable international environment that was marked by the renewed Cold War conflict and the 1979 Soviet invasion of Afghanistan.

Britain's insistence that it would block any issues until the budget question was resolved antagonised the other member states which contemplated excluding Britain from new EC initiatives as a means of moving beyond the deadlock. But Thatcher was also just as tired with the budgetary battle and had come to the conclusion that the time was drawing near to settle the debate, with a solution finally being reached at the June 1984 Fontainebleau European Council. The agreement provided Britain with an immediate lump-sum payment of 1000 million ECU for 1984, while in subsequent years it would receive a rebate amounting to two-thirds of the difference between what it contributed in VAT and what it received from the Community budget. The settlement also led to Britain agreeing to a general increase in EC revenue from 1 per cent to 1.4 per cent of national VAT receipts in order to remedy a general deficit in budgetary resources. But at what price had Prime Minister Thatcher secured a budget rebate? Even though the financial sums involved were sizeable, they were not considerably more than what had been available in previous months and when put into a national context were even smaller: the entire EC budget was equivalent at that time to the expenditure of a large British department of state and in total accounted for approximately 1 per cent of the national income of member states (Young, 2000: 189). Moreover, the Fontainebleau deal did not settle Britain's concerns over the EC budget once and for all: the agreement could be subject to a future review and it did not prevent the possibility of further increases in the budget. More importantly, while Thatcher presented the budget dispute as a means of defending Britain's national sovereignty, by 1984 Britain was far more closely integrated with the Community than it had been when she was elected Prime Minister in 1979.

In diplomatic terms, Thatcher's attitude towards the Community is often compared with de Gaulle's hostility towards the deepening of integration in the 1960s. But while both leaders rejected the concept of European federalism, it was the case that despite de Gaulle's concerns about the erosion of national sovereignty he was nevertheless committed to the creation of a strong Europe that was independent of the United States. France's underlying commitment to the Community was rarely doubted. The same could not be said for Britain. The budget dispute did little to enhance Britain's position within the Community and if anything the diplomatic methods employed had caused friction with other member states who increasingly viewed it as 'an awkward partner'. As a former member of her Cabinet pointed out, Thatcher's actions 'only united them more firmly than ever' (Prior, 1986: 144).

5

The Transformation of Europe: 1985–93

For much of the 1970s a range of factors hampered the European Community's progress. This included a downturn in the international economy that was exacerbated by the 1973–74 and 1979–80 oil crises and the difficulty of integrating new members (particularly Britain). At the same time, the Community's institutions appeared to be too weak to deal with these challenges. It was therefore hoped that the 1980s would result in a revival of the EC's fortunes by marking an end to the period of Eurosclerosis that had dominated the 1970s. Central to this effort was an awareness of the need to improve economic growth rates within the Community because of the strong competition provided by Japan and the United States. The internal market programme that emerged from this environment prompted an examination of areas of integration that had hitherto rested with member state governments. This included the question of monetary union and the establishment of common policies ranging from social affairs to foreign and security policy. Such debates over the scope and remit of the Community's competence were a key feature of the period, being influenced by the need for the Community to respond to the changed geopolitical European landscape as a result of the break-up of the Soviet-sponsored regimes in Central and Eastern Europe.

CREATING THE INTERNAL MARKET

Although the resolution of the budget dispute was a significant victory for Britain, it is difficult to disagree with John Young's assertion that 'despite Thatcher's confident position at home however, profound changes were afoot in Europe which complicated her position enormously' (Young, 2000: 133). In the early 1980s there was a growing consensus among member states and the EU institutions about the need to foster renewed European integration. A 'Declaration on European Union' was presented at the June 1983 Stuttgart European Council and while it proved to be of little value, it was demonstrative of a climate of change. At the same time, the Community was faced with a decline in its economic competitiveness, which by 1982 had fallen dramatically behind that of Japan and the United States (Moravcsik, 1991: 73). American and Japanese companies had established a dominant position in the new technologies of semiconductors and consumer electronics. This state of affairs prompted the European Commission, member states and business **interest groups** jointly to advocate the implementation of initiatives that would improve the economic competitiveness of the Community. This particularly applied to the creation of an internal market.

Interest groups: Often used in the same context as pressure groups, they are essentially a group of individuals who aim to exert influence on political decisions.

The objective of an internal market could be traced back to the Treaty of Rome: Article 2 stipulated that 'The Community shall have as its aim, by establishing a common market and progressively approximating the economic policies of member states, to promote throughout the Community a harmonious development of economic activities, a continuous and balanced expansion, an increase in stability, an accelerated raising of the standard of living and closer relations between its member states' [**Document 14, p. 123**]. But despite the initial progress that the Community had made in the 1960s, the objective of creating a 'common market' had become bogged down from the late 1960s until the early 1980s. For the majority of that period, member states had faced economic difficulties that led national governments to adopt inward-looking policies that were prompted by a desire to protect domestic jobs from foreign competition.

In practical terms this meant that, although the process of European integration had brought the member states together by, among other factors, increasing the number of cross-border tourist flows within Europe, which increased from 40 million cross-frontier arrivals in 1960 to over 160 million in 1980, there nevertheless remained significant barriers which hindered the Community's competitiveness. In this sense, the concept of an internal market based on the free movement of workers, goods and the **mutual recognition** of products did not exist. It was a point that had in fact been most notably highlighted in the European Court of Justice's (ECJ) 1979 *Cassis de Dijon* ruling which tackled a German ban on the importation of alcoholic beverages from other member states that did not meet minimum German alcohol contents [**Document 28, p. 135**]. In responding to this situation, the Court ruled that 'There is therefore no valid reason why, provided that they have been lawfully produced and marketed in one of the Member States, alcoholic beverages should not be introduced into any other Member State; the sale of such products may not be subject to a legal prohibition on the marketing of beverages with an alcohol content lower than the limit set by

Mutual recognition: The principle that a product sold in one EU member state should be able to be sold in any EU member state.

the national rules' [**Document 28, p. 135**]. While the Court's decision noted the principle of mutual recognition, 'the ruling did not itself impose a policy of mutual recognition of product standards' (Alter, 2001: 226). The ECJ's ability to tackle questions that related to market access was moreover wholly dependent on cases that were lodged and the Court therefore could not be relied upon to make whole-scale change. As a consequence, individual member states continued to exercise their ability to ban the importation of certain goods. France ignored the Court's decision by banning lamb imports in 1980, while ecological concerns prompted Denmark to prohibit the sale of beer and soft drinks unless they were sold in recyclable containers.

Such examples were symptomatic of a broader trend that developed in the 1970s for member states to protect their domestic markets at a time of economic downturn. In a climate of high inflation and soaring unemployment, Community law prohibited member states from protecting their industrial sectors from the competition of other member states through the use of quotas and tariff barriers. Faced with this situation, national governments utilised a plethora of **non-tariff barriers** to trade to protect their domestic markets (Cameron, 1992: 43–44). This included the use of regulations and the granting of subsidies through the use of so-called **state aids**. Yet the use of non-tariff barriers by member states to protect domestic employment levels had a direct impact on the competitiveness of the EC as a whole because the use of subsidies helped to sustain high-cost production as companies were sheltered from wider market competition (Pinder, 1998: 82). Such a course of action arguably represented a retreat from, rather than an advance towards, a common market; there continued to exist a number of barriers that hindered the concept of the free movement of goods, peoples or services among the member states. This state of affairs was moreover reflected in a slowdown in the growth of intra-European trade. As Armstrong and Bulmer have reflected, 'a customs union had been created but a common market had not' (Armstrong and Bulmer, 1998: 16).

The advances that had been made by many of the Community's main trading partners compounded the lack of improvements in the economic competitiveness of EC member states. The Community was faced with increasing levels of imports from the United States and Japan and a number of newly industrialising countries that included Hong Kong and Taiwan. And as the poor competitiveness of the EC limited its number of exports, the Community as a whole experienced large trade deficits (Pelkmans and Winters, 1988: 6). This situation was made worse by evidence that the Community's ability to attract and sustain inward investment, particularly from the United States, was declining. Business groups, which were increasingly organised on a European-wide basis, were particularly concerned about the Community's lack of competitiveness that they rightly perceived to be strongly influenced

Non-tariff barriers: Barriers that hinder trade between countries that take can include rules on product specifications, technical standards, and rules of origin.

State aids: Finance provided by member state governments to companies to support their operations, which can provide them with an unfair advantage vis-à-vis companies in other member states. EU competition law requires such support be subject to scrutiny by the European Commission, with the European Court of Justice being the final arbiter.

by the presence of non-tariff barriers to trade. National governments too were worried about levels of competitiveness, a situation that was strongly influenced by the election of a number of right-of-centre governments in Belgium, Denmark, Italy, the Netherlands and Britain. West Germany's coalition of Free Democrats and Christian Democrats was also supportive of market reform. There was consequently a convergence of national interests, with many Community member states sharing similar goals of free competition. National governments – particularly Britain, Germany and the Netherlands – and business lobby groups were united in their desire to develop an internal market as a means of improving the economic performance of the Community and narrowing the technological gap with the United States and Japan (Sandholtz and Zysman, 1989: 103–6; Cowles, 1995).

In the early 1980s these concerns were reflected in a number of developments, including the communiqués of the European Council and in the work of the European Round Table of Industrialists, which lobbied for the completion of the internal market. The European Round Table, which comprised a mixture of public and private representatives, including the then European Commissioner for Industry, Etienne Davignon, was influential in the establishment in 1982 of the ESPRIT programme for cross-border European cooperation in information technology (Peterson and Sharp, 1998: 70–73). However, it was not until the June 1984 Fontainebleau European Council that significant progress was made towards the creation of an internal market. Having resolved the problem of Britain's budget contributions, the Fontainebleau meeting moved on to the question of institutional reform and the development of the internal market. The first question of institutional reform had been influenced by the European Parliament's approval in February 1984 of the Draft Treaty on European Union which, under the leadership of the Italian Euro-federalist Altiero Spinelli, had called for the negotiation of a new treaty to replace the existing treaties. The second question of the internal market received significant endorsement from the member states, illustrated when the British government tabled a proposal at the Fontainebleau European Council for the creation of a genuine 'common market' in goods and services which signalled a more positive British approach to the EC.

To take some of these matters forward, the Fontainebleau meeting established two ad-hoc committees to examine the future of European integration. One committee was to be chaired by Jim Dooge (an Irish senator), with the remit of focusing on institutional matters, while the other, chaired by Pietro Adonnino (an Italian parliamentarian), would examine the possibility of creating a 'People's Europe'. Of these committees, the Adonnino committee presented a number of proposals for a Citizen's Europe that in the short term proved to have little impact on the Community. The same could not be said for the Dooge committee. Its conclusions, which were presented to the

Brussels European Council of March 1985, recommended a strengthening of Community institutions (including a more effective role for the European Parliament), an end to the use of the national veto in EC decision-making and the creation of a single European market.

Parallel to these developments, a new Commission entered office at the start of 1985 under the presidency of **Jacques Delors** who set out a swift plan of action for reforming the Community with the goal of completing an internal market and therefore eliminating the Community's internal frontiers by the end of 1992. This desire for a grand policy was evocative of Jenkins' pursuance of the European Monetary System; Delors' appointment marked a sea change in the institutional make-up of the Community, with the Commission becoming a 'policy entrepreneur' whereby it acted as a key initiator of policy (Majone, 1996: 74–7; Pollack, 1997). Delors argued that if there were to be a genuine internal market, there would have to be an increase in supranationalism so that national economic interests could not hamper the development of the Community. The Commission's influence in shaping the internal market agenda mirrored neo-functional accounts and contrasted with intergovernmentalist arguments that the internal market was the product of a convergence of member states' policy preferences. In reality, however, various factors interacted, including the Commission's policy leadership role and a convergence of national interests.

The combination of the convergence of member states' views, interest group pressure, Delors' vision and the Dooge committee's findings resulted in EC leaders asking the European Commission at the March 1985 Brussels European Council to establish a plan that would result in the creation of a genuine 'internal market'. This task was given to the British Internal Market Commissioner, **Lord Arthur Cockfield**, and the ensuing White Paper, *Completing the Internal Market*, set out nearly 300 measures that would be necessary to achieve the removal of all internal barriers within the Community to enable the free movement of people, services, capital and goods by 1992 (Cockfield, 1994). But while such a proposal mirrored British interests, it was also true that for it to be effective the Commission would have to set in motion a process of harmonisation of national regulations. At the same time, the Commission would have to take on the responsibility for managing and 'policing' the internal market. The underlying implication of Cockfield's proposals was perfectly clear: it would lead to a dramatic increase in the supranational power of the Commission and lessen the influence of the member states.

In advancing the case for the internal market, the Commission argued that the progress of the Community was hindered by the presence of fiscal, physical and technical barriers. Fiscal barriers related to the different levels of value-added tax that existed among member states, which the Commission

Delors, Jacques (b. 1925): President of the European Commission 1985–95. Played a significant role in developing the EEC, both in terms of widening membership and increasing the scope of the policies it embraced.

Cockfield, Lord Arthur (1916–2007): UK Conservative Secretary of State for Trade from 1982 to 1983. Member of the European Commission with responsibility for the Internal Market 1985–88.

argued was a central factor in influencing the presence of frontier controls. This was because member states used frontier controls to stop the importation of goods – such as cigarettes and alcohol – from a state with a lower tax rate into a state with a higher rate. To remedy this situation, the Commission proposed that value-added tax rates should be harmonised into two rates of 14–20 per cent and 4–9 per cent. In contrast to fiscal barriers, physical barriers related to the custom and immigration controls; the Commission argued that their presence placed a heavy burden on business and therefore proposed that they should be abolished (a policy that was particularly attractive to many Europeans). The final category of technical barriers concerned the technical regulations and standards that differed in each of the member states and as such ensured that it was quite likely for a product that met the requirements of one country to be unacceptable to another. To remedy this state of affairs the Commission proposed a harmonisation of member states' regulations based on the principle of mutual recognition which had been initially highlighted in the 1979 *Cassis de Dijon* case and which would be confirmed in the Single European Act **[Document 30, p. 137]** (Alter and Meunier-Aitsahalia, 1994). In all, the Commission's proposals for the creation of an internal market were clearly of a substantial nature, but for them to be effective it would also be necessary to reform the process of decision-making within the Community.

THE SINGLE EUROPEAN ACT

At the Milan European Council of June 1985 the heads of government of the member states discussed the Commission's White Paper (for completion of the single market by 1992) and the Dooge Report's proposals for institutional reform, the latter of which advocated a reduction in the use of the national veto in Community decision-making. The gathering consensus behind the need for institutional reform was further shaped by the concerns of existing members about the impact of enlarging the EC. Greece had joined in January 1981 and the Community agreed in June 1984 that Portugal and Spain would join in January 1986. The imminent nature of the EC's enlargement raised questions about whether it would be possible to achieve agreement among the national governments in a Community of 12 member states. The prospect of prolonged discussions and unresolved questions thus prompted member states to consider the use of majority voting for the taking of decisions.

The combination of the internal market programme, the Dooge Report on institutional reform and the enlargement of the Community led a number of member states to advocate that to tackle fully these issues a new treaty should be negotiated in an intergovernmental conference (IGC). But as some member states – particularly Britain – did not support the need for holding an IGC, the chairman of the Milan European Council, Italy's Bettino Craxi, took the extraordinary step of calling for a majority vote on the IGC. Of the ten member states, only Britain, Denmark and Greece voted against, having argued that there was no need for institutional reforms. It was, however, a view that was not shared by the majority of member states, which agreed to the holding of the IGC. Such an outcome further complicated the position of Britain, Denmark and Greece because their opposition had failed to stop the Community's development. Faced with this state of affairs, they could, of course, have boycotted the IGC. Yet it was an unrealistic objective because the combined significance of the talks and the importance of the Community to each of their economies meant that they had no option but to participate and be bound by the results. For Thatcher, the situation was all the more galling because the internal market programme had been greatly influenced by her efforts. She later commented, 'I had witnessed a profound shift in how European policy was conducted – and therefore in the kind of Europe that was taking shape. A Franco-German bloc with its own agenda had re-emerged to set the direction of the Community' (Thatcher, 1993: 558–9). But despite this opposition, there was nonetheless a tacit acknowledgement within the British government that the continuing use of the national veto ensured that any member state would have the ability to slow down the internal market programme.

Single European Act (SEA): Played a key role in advancing the internal market programme, widening the scope of the competence of the EC and advancing the cause of Economic and Monetary Union.

The IGC negotiations commenced in September 1985 and culminated in agreement on a **Single European Act** (SEA) at the Luxembourg European Council of December 1985 [**Document 30, p. 137**]. The SEA was the first major revision of the Community since the 1957 Treaty of Rome and was concerned as much with implementing new policies and decision-making procedures as it was with formally recognising policies that had developed since 1957. The latter included the Regional Development Fund and European Political Cooperation. At the same time, the SEA extended the Community's competence into a number of new areas, including environmental, social and technological policies. These developments, such as the provision of a legal base for environmental policy in the SEA, demonstrated both a shift in the focus of the Community's attention to areas of policy that had traditionally rested with member states (with decisions, such as those on environment, to be taken by qualified majority voting) and a strengthening of the Commission's legislative and regulative role within the Community. This would in turn lead the Commission to play a stronger role in many international negotiations. Such activity pointed to the growing role that the Community played as a global actor, having an input on international policy ranging from economics and trade to environmental and development co-operation. The changing nature of the European policy process also meant that the Community became a far more attractive venue for interest groups to engage in lobbying activities that centred on the European Commission.

Apart from these developments, the SEA impacted on the role of the European Parliament which, despite its position as a democratically elected body (since 1979), had played a relatively minor role in the policy-making process. Set against this background, Germany and Italy were two of the most vociferous member states that argued that the European Parliament's powers needed to be strengthened so as to increase the democratic legitimacy of the Community. Britain opposed such a development because it represented a federalist view of European integration. France also opposed increasing the European Parliament's powers. Despite this opposition, an agreement was eventually reached at the December 1985 Luxembourg European Council on the SEA which included an augmentation in the European Parliament's influence. (The SEA only came into effect on 1 July 1987 because of the difficulty of getting it ratified in the member states.) As a result of this agreement, the European Parliament's powers were increased through the introduction of an **assent procedure** and **cooperation procedure** which ensured that it would be fully involved in the legislative process, including the majority of the internal market directives. In addition to these changes to the role of the European Commission and the European Parliament, the other major institutional reform introduced by the SEA concerned the introduction of qualified majority voting within the Council of Ministers. Despite concern among some member states that QMV represented an erosion of national sovereignty, there was nonetheless a genuine acceptance that its introduction was essential so as to ensure that individual member states could not block the future progress of the Community. As such, QMV was applied to a majority of the internal market legislation, with only a few issues, such as the harmonisation of direct taxes, being excluded (primarily because of the insistence of Britain).

Assent procedure: The procedure whereby the European Parliament's assent, by means of an absolute majority of its members, is necessary before certain important decisions can be adopted.

Cooperation procedure: Introduced in the SEA to provide the European Parliament with a greater input to the legislative process so as to reduce the democratic deficit. The Parliament has to be consulted twice before a legislative proposal from the European Commission takes effect.

THE ROAD TO 1992

As part of an attempt to demonstrate the likely economic benefits of the internal market, in 1986 and 1987 the Commission funded a project led by Paolo Cecchini to examine the 'costs on non-Europe' to demonstrate what the costs to the Community would be if the Community were to maintain a fragmented market. Making use of data from the four largest EC states, the Cecchini Report set out the costs to firms of maintaining customs controls and the opportunity costs of lost trade (Cecchini *et al.*, 1988). The Cecchini Report noted that significant economic benefits would accrue to the Community as the remaining barriers to the free movement of goods, capital, labour and services were removed. Specifically the EC could increase its GNP by 6.5 per cent if frontier and custom controls were removed and therefore economies of scale realised. Thus the gap between the Community and the US and Japan would be narrowed. The benefits would essentially come from four sources, namely cost savings for producers who would benefit from large-scale production; the so-called 'X' efficiency gains from enhanced managerial practices; the removal of technical barriers such as those restricting market entry or competition between the member states of the Community and, finally, the removal of physical barriers to trade such as border delays.

Schengen Agreement: Signed in the Luxembourg town of Schengen in 1985 to remove border controls between EU member states. The initial signature countries were Belgium, France, Germany, Luxembourg, the Netherlands, Portugal and Spain. The Agreement was incorporated into it by the Treaty of Amsterdam.

The latter issue influenced the creation of the **Schengen Agreement** on 14 June 1985 whereby West Germany, France and the Benelux countries agreed to the gradual abolition of frontier controls between them.

But despite these benefits, the implementation of the internal market programme was not as quick as many would have liked. One of the problems that arose concerned the claims of the poorer member states (Greece, Ireland, Portugal and Spain) who advocated that, in return for their support for market liberalisation, the Community should provide greater spending on regional and social policy. In response to this situation, the Commission proposed a number of measures which aimed to close the gap between the Community's rich and poor member states (as well as between the rich and poor regions within the member states) by means of establishing a cohesion policy. Its effectiveness rested on the ability to secure a significant increase in the Community budget. Put another way, the richer member states of northern Europe would have to make greater financial contributions to the Community. Britain reacted negatively to this prospect of increasing the Community's budget and France and Germany were unwilling to direct existing Community resources to the poorer member states. One possible solution was to reduce the amount of spending on the common agricultural policy – which accounted for in excess of 50 per cent of the Community budget – as a means of solving the question of cohesion funding. But it was impossible to reach agreement. France and Germany were conscious that any reduction in the substantial subsidies that their farming communities received would have grim electoral consequences. The only option for solving the question of cohesion funding was thus to increase the Community budget. Yet because of the differences between Britain and the rest of the member states no progress was made on this issue throughout 1987 and it therefore appeared that, just as the budget had dominated the Community's agenda at the start of the 1980s, so too it would dominate the agenda at the end of the decade. The prospect of the Community once again becoming bogged down in the minutiae of budget negotiations instead of advancing towards the goal of creating a internal market greatly concerned the German government, which agreed at the Brussels summit of February 1988 to pay the cohesion bill. The decision taken by Germany's Chancellor, **Helmut Kohl**, to accept the burden of the financing of the cohesion policy ensured that the Community was able to proceed with the internal market programme that had been set out in the SEA.

Not only did the SEA establish the objective of an internal market, it also raised the question of **Economic and Monetary Union** (EMU) in two paragraphs of the Preamble and Article 20 of the text. Among the 12 Community member states, France and Germany (to a lesser extent) were supportive of the objective of monetary union, arguing (among other reasons) that it would benefit the EC's competitiveness. This viewpoint had been considerably influenced by a 1987 report which argued that national control over monetary policy and the presence of national exchange rates did not sit with the objectives of free trade and capital mobility that had been set out in the internal market programme (Padoa-Schioppa, 1987). France was additionally attracted to the idea of EMU because it offered it an opportunity to exercise influence over European financial policy which had hitherto been dominated by Germany and the German Deutschmark. In this sense, 'EMU offered France the opportunity to re-establish influence over monetary policy by Europeanising it' (Dyson and Featherstone, 1999: 97).

Among the other member states, the British Prime Minister Margaret Thatcher was by far the most vociferous in her opposition to the goal of EMU and the deeper forms of integration that Delors advocated. In her view, it was unacceptable for European integration to encroach on fundamental aspects of national sovereignty, such as social and monetary policy. She regarded the internal market programme as the pinnacle of European integration and not as the launch pad for further initiatives, with these beliefs being reflected in her famous speech at the College of Europe in Bruges in September 1988 [**Document 32, p. 139**]. Yet these views did not have total support within her government as many senior Cabinet ministers argued that it was impossible to just ignore the fact that the majority of other member states were supportive of the deepening of European integration. This included the belief that a genuine internal market could only ever be achieved by creating a single currency, as the presence of distinct national currencies was a hindrance to the Community's economic development. 'For the internal market's potential to be realised', Ben Rosamond has written, 'pure economic logic would contend that EMU is a necessity to maximise economic efficiency' (Rosamond, 2000: 100). The argument here was that the moves to establish the internal market created a series of 'spillover' effects that impacted on other areas of the Community and which reinforced the neo-functionalist viewpoint that

Kohl, Helmut (b. 1930): Chancellor of the Federal Republic of Germany 1982–98. A key figure in the development of the Community, he enjoyed a strong relationship with President François Mitterrand of France, though his relations with the UK Prime Minister, Margaret Thatcher, were not as positive.

Economic and Monetary Union (EMU): Although a formal commitment to EMU was established in the Maastricht Treaty on European Union, member states had discussed the idea of monetary union since the 1970 Werner Report.

greater economic and political integration was not wholly dependent on the member states (Tranholm-Mikkelsen, 1991).

A growing consensus among member states about the need to investigate the possibility of EMU resulted in the decision being taken at the June 1988 Hanover European Council to create a committee to examine the means by which monetary union would be established. The Committee, which was to be chaired by Jacques Delors, was charged with presenting its proposals so that they could be examined at the June 1989 Madrid European Council. When the Committee published its findings in April 1989, it recommended a three-stage transition to monetary union: first, the completion of the internal market; second, the coordination of national monetary policies through a **European System of Central Banks** (ESCB); and, finally, the irrevocable locking of exchange rates and the transfer of monetary authority to a **European Central Bank** (ECB) **[Document 33, p. 139]**. Reaction among the member states to the Delors Report on EMU was, with the exception of Britain, generally positive, buoyed by the success of the Exchange Rate Mechanism in stabilising currency fluctuations among the participating member states. Apart from these internal factors, the decision of member states to agree at the Strasbourg European Council of December 1989 to establish an intergovernmental conference on EMU as a means of setting a formal path towards the creation of a single currency was influenced by the external events that were marked by the fall of the Berlin wall on 11 November 1989 and the subsequent break-up of the Soviet-controlled governments in Central and Eastern Europe in 1990. In addition to its influence in motivating states to progress towards monetary union, the geo-political changes ensured that the Community's focus quickly shifted towards political as well as economic issues.

European System of Central Banks (ESCB): Responsible for managing the single currency, comprising the European Central Bank and the national banks of all EU member states irrespective of whether they have adopted the euro or not.

European Central Bank (ECB): Based in Frankfurt, it is responsible for the monetary policy of the eurozone. Its main objective is the maintenance of price stability.

Gorbachev, Mikhail (b. 1931): General Secretary of the Soviet Union 1985–91. He was instrumental in the change in Soviet policy that was reflected in the policies of *glasnost* and *perestroika*. Established close relations with the United States and Western Europe.

Glasnost: Mikhail Gorbachev championed 'openness' as a means of advancing reform in the Soviet Union from the mid-1980s onwards.

Perestroika: Just as Mikhail Gorbachev advanced *glasnost* to promote openness, he also championed restructuring through *perestroika*. The process of reform set off a tidal wave of unrest that resulted in the downfall of the Soviet system.

EUROPE'S CHANGING MAP

The European landscape in the post-war period had been influenced by the bipolar division of Europe along East–West lines and shaped by the institutions that underpinned this division. For Western Europe this took the form of NATO and the EC, while for Eastern Europe it took the form of the Warsaw Treaty Organization and the founding of the Council for Mutual Economic Assistance (Comecon). Although the superpower influence of the United States and the Soviet Union had been crucial in underpinning these institutions, the 1985 election of **Mikhail Gorbachev** as General Secretary of the Soviet Union resulted in a change in policy that was emphasised by the introduction of *glasnost* (openness), *perestroika* (restructuring) and *novye myshlenye* (new thinking) (Young and Kent, 2004: 578–88). Central to

Gorbachev's reforms was the pursuit of domestic priorities – particularly economic growth – and the jettisoning of expensive foreign-policy commitments (Dunlop, 1993: 4–5). The latter included the need to engage in a drastic reduction in defence expenditure as the Soviet Union could no longer maintain a 'balance of power' with the United States, and this in turn resulted in a series of superpower summits that led to a 1987 agreement to destroy intermediate-range missiles (Ryan, 2003: 106–08).

Although Moscow's changed foreign-policy priorities were initially marked by a withdrawal from the Third World, it in turn led to a loosening in the Soviet grip on the countries of Central and Eastern Europe. This culminated in Gorbachev's announcement at a Warsaw Pact meeting in the summer of 1989 that 'each people determines the future of its own country. There must be no interference from outside.' Such a statement brought to an end the Brezhnev Doctrine of limiting sovereignty in Central and Eastern Europe. The implication of this was that the Soviet Union would not use force to suppress protests against the Communist governments of Central and Eastern Europe (Archer, 2000: 17; Garthoff, 1994: 607). This became known as the **Sinatra Doctrine**. Poland was the first country to go down the road of reform, marked by the Solidarity labour organisation transforming itself into a political party and its leader, Lech Walesa, becoming President. Elsewhere, the barbed-wire barriers to the West were removed in Hungary (resulting in thousands of people entering Western Europe), Erich Honecker's East German regime was toppled in November 1989 along with the Berlin Wall that graphically illustrated the East–West division, while Communist governments in Czechoslovakia and Bulgaria were also overthrown. The whole process took place without bloodshed – with the exception of Romania, where nearly 1,000 people died. This instalment of democratic governments from Czechoslovakia to Poland was referred to as the 'Velvet Revolution' by the Czech playwright and dissident Vaclav Havel.

Sinatra Doctrine: After the collapse of the Berlin Wall the Soviet Union adopted a policy of non-intervention in Central and Eastern Europe. Known as the Sinatra Doctrine by alluding to the song 'My Way' from the famous American singer Frank Sinatra.

Nowhere more so was this changed landscape apparent than in the case of Germany, which after having been divided into East and West Germany was formally unified in October 1990. Yet the prospect of unification and the emergence of an even stronger Germany at the heart of Europe alarmed a number of European leaders. This was particularly true for Britain and France. At the same time, the United States was concerned that the EC might become insular and pursue its own interests at a time when the threat of Communism was no longer strong enough to hold the NATO alliance together. In other words it would lessen US influence on European affairs (Lundestad, 1998: 114–16).

These events had a profound impact on world politics as they signalled the emergence of a post-Cold War order. The Warsaw Treaty Organization became defunct in early 1991 and the Soviet army retreated home from their bases in Central and Eastern Europe (Clark, 2001: 95). But while Gorbachev's willingness to permit freedom for the Central and Eastern European satellite states marked an end to the Cold War conflict, he was less willing to allow freedom within the 15 republics that comprised the Soviet Union, fearing that this would lead to a break-up of the Soviet Union and an end to the influence of the Communist Party which had ruled since the 1917 revolution. Claims for independence from Moscow nevertheless materialised, particularly from the Baltic states of Estonia, Latvia and Lithuania that had been annexed by Stalin in 1940. Faced with an overwhelming support in the Baltic states for total independence from the Soviet Union, Moscow eventually acceded to their wish, while Gorbachev's resignation in December 1991 (after the August 1991 coup) marked the downfall of the Soviet Union as it split into 15 separate republics. The absence of the Cold War gel that had kept countries together consequently led to a wave of nationalism that redrew the geographical and institutional map of Europe. A particular case in point during the 1990s was the former Yugoslavia, where civil war resulted in it violently breaking up into Bosnia-Herzegovina, Croatia, Kosovo, Macedonia, Montenegro, Serbia and Slovenia. In 1993 the so-called 'Velvet Divorce' saw Czechoslovakia split into the Czech and Slovak Republics. The upshot of these events was that by 2009 Europe had 21 more sovereign states than it did in 1990 (Blair and Curtis, 2009: 300).

The collapse of the Soviet Union was clearly one of the most significant events of the twentieth century and brought with it significant discussion about what the nature of the so-called 'new world order' would be. In the summer of 1989 the US academic Francis Fukuyama argued that the end of the Cold War signalled the end of an ideologically divided world that had dominated history, a view which became known as 'the end of history' (Fukuyama, 1989). A few years later Samuel Huntington argued that the post-Cold War order would be marked by a 'clash of civilizations', whereby the primary source of conflict in the new world order would be cultural divisions rather than the ideological or economic factors that had influenced previous times (Huntingdon, 1993). Despite the value of these approaches in providing a framework of analysis, they were unable to provide a complete account of the post-cold war order. For instance, the 1991 Gulf War that was caused by Iraq's invasion of Kuwait was a conflict that emerged within, rather between civilizations (Blair and Curtis, 2009: 107). What is evident in retrospect is that much of the discussion on the post-Cold War order has been influenced by the fact that there has been little agreement about what the term actually means as it lacked the sense of definition that, for instance, the Cold War had provided.

This changed landscape raised questions over the role of the organisations that had defined the Cold War, in particular NATO and the EC (and to a lesser extent the Western European Union). At the heart of this debate lay two competing visions. First, a 'Europeanist' view that was principally propagated by France, Germany, Belgium and Spain, which emphasised the need for a stronger European Community to include some form of defence identity through the WEU and by consequence a lessening of the reliance on the United States and NATO. Second, an 'Atlanticist' view that was advanced by Britain, Denmark, Portugal and the Netherlands which, despite acknowledging the need for a stronger EC, nevertheless stressed that NATO should remain the primary vehicle for Europe's defence and that a strong link should be maintained with the US (Blair, 1998b).

Faced with this changed security environment, NATO began to stress its potential as a peacekeeping and humanitarian body in the post-Cold War era and at the same time developed close relations with the former members of the Warsaw Treaty Organization through the new forum of the North Atlantic Co-operation Council. By 1994, the reality of Europe's new security environment had resulted in the former Warsaw Treaty Organization members developing even closer relations with NATO through the Partnership for Peace (PfP) programme. Such close relations would lead to Russian forces being deployed in 1996 as part of a NATO-led Implementation Force (IFOR) to secure peace following the civil war in Bosnia-Herzegovina, while a NATO–Russia Council was established in 2002 to provide closer cooperation and respond to common threats such as the struggle against terrorism. At the same time, the decision of the NATO Council in June 1997 to enlarge eastwards meant that its membership increased in 1999 to include the Czech Republic, Hungary and Poland. In 1999 NATO also undertook a bombing campaign to force Serbia to withdraw its forces from Kosovo, where Serbian forces were murdering and displacing the majority ethnic Albanian population. And despite the fact that it took 79 days of intensive bombing to get Serbia to withdraw its forces, NATO's use of force nonetheless demonstrated the significance and importance of the US contribution to Europe's security. This was a point that Washington had made back in November 1990 when the US published the Transatlantic Declaration. It had aimed to assuage concerns on both sides of the Atlantic over any weakening in transatlantic relations by providing a more formal set of links between the US and Europe, which were further reinforced by the 1995 New Transatlantic Agenda. Moreover, it was reflective of an overarching US strategy in the post-1945 era to support European integration on the one hand but on the other to develop methods by which European integration could be contained within an Atlantic framework.

In a climate of change, EC member states were also attempting to map out the future development of the Community, with its views on enlargement being formally set out in the July 1997 document *Agenda 2000*. But before agreement could be reached on the objectives of how to enlarge the Community to include former Soviet-controlled states, the existing members of the Community undertook a dynamic process of reform that significantly accelerated the process of integration. Having established a timetable for the creation of an internal market, the President of the European Commission, Jacques Delors, turned the Commission's attention to Economic and Monetary Union and social-policy integration and in so doing emphasised the Commission's role as a 'policy entrepreneur'. Progress towards EMU demonstrated both a convergence of member state interests and at the same time the spillover effects from the European Monetary System, the internal-market programme and capital-movement liberalisation. A combination of French support and German compliance resulted in a decision being taken at the June 1988 Hanover European Council to establish a committee of experts – under Delors' chairmanship – to examine how monetary union might be achieved. The 'Delors Committee' presented a report in April 1989 which detailed a three-stage route to currency union: the completion of the internal market; the coordination of national monetary policies through a European System of Central Banks; and the irrevocable locking of exchange rates and the transfer of monetary authority to a European Central Bank [**Document 33, p. 139**]. At the Strasbourg European Council of December 1989 member states took the decision to convene an IGC on EMU before the end of 1990. The Strasbourg meeting was also noticeable for producing an agreement on a **Social Charter** (without British support) and for discussing the prospect of German reunification.

The dramatic nature of these events influenced the decision of French President **François Mitterrand** and German Chancellor Helmut Kohl to issue a joint letter on 19 April 1990. It stressed that an IGC on European Political Union should be convened because of the 'far reaching changes in Europe' and the need to 'define and implement a common foreign and security policy'. Apart from defining a foreign and security policy, they sought to strengthen the Community's democratic legitimacy and improve the effectiveness of the EC's institutions. Just as Britain had been against the holding of an IGC on EMU, it was also against the further political development of the Community. The British government did not share the Franco-German argument that an IGC on political union was necessary to deal with the challenges posed by the collapse of Communism and German unity. The British position reflected a preference for EC reform to take place via quiet developments rather than by means of high-profile treaty negotiations. In British eyes the Community was already overburdened by the need to complete the internal market and the impending EMU negotiations. Yet this was a view that was not shared by the other member states, which took

Social Charter: Adopted in December 1989 at the Strasbourg European Council, it was a non-legally binding agreement that emphasised the need to develop a social dimension to the internal market programme.

Mitterrand, François (1916–1996): President of France 1981–85. Played a significant role in the deepening of European integration, including the development of a European single currency. Established a close relationship with the German Chancellor, Helmut Kohl.

a majority decision at the June 1990 Dublin European Council to convene a second IGC that would focus on European political union.

THE MAASTRICHT TREATY

At the Maastricht European Council of December 1991 the heads of government of the member states concluded the work of the IGC negotiations on monetary union and political union that had commenced 12 months before at the December 1990 Rome European Council. Of the two IGCs, the negotiations on monetary union were by far the most straightforward and benefited from them having been subject to detailed reports and analysis prior to the commencement of the talks, and having been conducted by a relatively small group of people, comprising national Treasury ministers and officials and central-bank representatives. The political union negotiations were far from straightforward. This was influenced by the fact that little preparatory work had been undertaken prior to the commencement of the talks and because of the range of topics that they covered. Discussions on political union primarily concentrated on strengthening the role of the European Parliament, establishing a European citizenship, the development of new common policies such as culture and interior affairs, the improvement of existing policies including social policy and the environment, and the creation of a common foreign and security policy (Blair, 1999: 53).

The array of topics that the political union negotiations embraced highlighted the extent to which the Community had changed since its foundations in the 1957 Treaty of Rome. The creation of policies dealing with interior affairs had been prompted by an acknowledgement of the need to tackle common problems such as drug trafficking and illegal immigration through the creation of new forms of cooperation at the EC level. National ministries had traditionally controlled a number of the policies that the IGC dealt with, including those on interior affairs, and as such the IGC negotiations impacted on areas of government that had by custom rested with member states. One consequence of this was to increase the number of national government ministries that were directly affected by the political union negotiations, which ranged from social affairs to the environment. The significance of these developments was fourfold. First, the range of topics and number of people involved increased the complexity of the talks. Second, it highlighted a decline in the role of the national foreign ministry to control and shape a member state's European policy. Third, the expansion in the Community's reach of influence pointed to a **Europeanisation** of national government which was reflective of the impact that European

Europeanisation: The impact that the EU has had on member states, whereby the pressure of common policies and structures forces a degree of uniformity.

integration had on policy-making within the member states. Fourth, it pointed to a strengthening of the regulatory function played by the Commission and signalled in certain policy areas, such as the environment, a strengthening of the Commission's negotiating role on external policy matters.

The scope of topics covered by the political union negotiations led to considerable differences of views among the member states as to the nature of the proposals. This particularly applied to Britain, despite the commitment of Prime Minister **John Major** to be 'at the heart of Europe'. Britain's vision of European integration thus continued to be significantly different from other member states, with the government being unwilling to support moves to deepen European political integration. Such a stance was fuelled by traditional British concerns over the loss of national sovereignty and the need for Prime Minister Major to keep the Conservative Party united by placating Eurosceptic members of the government (Blair, 1998a: 178). The British government was particularly concerned about proposed references to the creation of a 'federal' Europe and the development of a European social policy; it believed the latter would reduce labour-market flexibility and lessen the competitiveness of the economy. Britain was additionally unwilling to be tied into a commitment to accept the single currency and argued that any initiatives in the area of foreign and security policy – including the strengthening of the Western European Union – should not disentangle the United States from Europe or undermine the role of NATO as Europe's security guarantor. The latter point was also shared by Denmark, the Netherlands and Portugal. In the case of Britain, such a conclusion 'was not just based on historic sentiment for the Anglo-American special relationship, but also by the harsh reality of the Gulf War, which indicated that an integrated, separate, European security and defence identity was unlikely to emerge, especially as any concept of unity diminished once it became evident sanctions and diplomatic initiatives would not solve the crisis' (Blair, 1998b: 90). To this end, Britain had been one of the few EC member states that had played (and was able to play) a significant role in the Gulf conflict.

Britain's unwillingness to accept certain policies, and the need for the Treaty to be agreed by the common accord of all member states, ensured that in classic EU fashion the final Treaty design was riddled with compromises. Thus, while such a standpoint added to Britain's perception as an awkward partner, other member states too had '**red lines**' that they were unwilling to cross. Greece, Portugal and Spain demanded extra financial assistance for their support for cooperation on social and monetary integration. France demanded that a deadline be set for the start of the single currency. Germany was particularly eager to ensure that a future monetary union did not include countries with a weak currency, on the basis that it could lead to instability in the system as a whole. Germany therefore advocated the need for

Major, John (b. 1943): UK Conservative Prime Minister 1990–97. His period of office was marked by severe splits over the issue of European integration.

Red lines: In EU negotiations this term emphasises the policy areas that governments are unwilling to compromise on.

economic convergence to precede monetary union and that any EMU text should include such priorities as low inflation. The outcome of the December 1991 Maastricht European Council was a **Treaty on European Union** which confirmed that member states (or rather national governments) were firmly in control of the integration process. The Treaty established a three-stage route to monetary union and confirmed that a single currency would begin no later than 1 January 1999. The irrevocability of this decision led the British government to insist on the insertion of a special Protocol to the treaty that would allow it to opt out from the single currency. The route that was chosen for EMU broadly reflected previous recommendations that included a first stage (1990–93) of strict budgetary discipline. Stage two, which commenced on 1 January 1994, was primarily concerned with the establishment of a European Monetary Institute that would strengthen the level of coordination between member states. This included the need for national governments to adhere to strict requirements relating to public spending and price stability. In this context, the emphasis attached to sound economic policies meant that the single currency project would help to ensure that member states pursued stable economic policies, thereby being somewhat reflective of Alan Milward's thesis that the process of European integration had been central to the 'rescue of the nation state' (Milward, 1992).

For a member state to be eligible to proceed to the third stage of EMU – and thereby participate in the single currency – it would have to satisfy four **convergence criteria [Document 34, p. 140]**. These were an average rate of inflation of not more than 1.5 per cent higher than that of the three best-performing member states; a budget deficit of not more than 3 per cent of gross domestic product and a public debt ratio not to exceed 60 per cent of GDP; participation in the 2.25 per cent narrow bands of the ERM for two years without severe tension or devaluation; and an interest rate which during the previous year should not have been more than 2 per cent higher than that of the three best-performing member states. The European Council would take the decision over which states had met the convergence criteria, and although the Treaty included a provision that EMU could start in 1997 if a majority of member states had met the criteria, this proved to be impossible because of a difficult economic climate. In 1996 only Ireland and Italy were certain to meet the convergence criteria, while Italy's public debt of 124 per cent of GDP ensured that it was way off the target (Blair, 2002: 198). Concerned about the economic costs of the single-currency commitment, the less-developed member states of Greece, Ireland, Portugal and Spain secured additional financial support via the creation of a **cohesion fund** that was designed to assist environmental and infrastructure projects in those countries to ensure that they met the convergence criteria requirements of the single currency.

Treaty on European Union (TEU): Signed in 1992, it came into effect in 1993 and is otherwise known as the Maastricht Treaty. Among other measures it increased the powers of the European Parliament, established the pillar framework and set a deadline for monetary union.

Convergence criteria: The economic conditions that member states have to meet before they can participate in the single currency. The criteria are: (1) an average rate of inflation of not more than 1.5 per cent higher than that of the three best performers; (2) a budget deficit of not more than 3 per cent of GDP and a public debt ratio not exceeding 60 per cent of GDP; (3) participation in the narrow bands of the ERM for two years without severe tension or devaluation; (4) average nominal long-term interest rate not more than 2 per cent higher than that of the three best-performing states.

Cohesion fund: Introduced in the Treaty on European Union to provide financial assistance to poorer member states.

Common Foreign and Security Policy (CFSP): Although the 1993 Treaty on European Union established a commitment to develop the foreign and security capacity of the EU, subsequent years demonstrated the difficulty of the EU member states being able to operate as a cohesive group. This became known as the 'capability-expectations gap'.

Justice and Home Affairs (JHA): Introduced in the TEU to increase cooperation among member states on matters of asylum policy, the crossing of the external borders of member states, immigration policy, combating drugs, combating international fraud, judicial cooperation in civil and criminal matters, customs cooperation and police cooperation.

Pillar framework: The Treaty on European Union introduced a three-pillar structure that reflected a Greek temple, with the EU sitting astride each pillar. Pillar one consisted of the European Community which included the EEC, the ECSC and Euratom. Pillar two consisted of the Common Foreign and Security Policy (CFSP) and pillar three Justice and Home Affairs (JHA). Cooperation in pillars two and three was based on intergovernmental methods that did not include the supranational cooperation of the first pillar.

In contrast to the finality of the monetary union negotiations to establish a single currency, the political union negotiations produced a series of compromise agreements that failed to reflect all the interests of the most pro-integrationist member states. Britain's unwillingness to support the aim of a 'federal goal' ensured that the final treaty made reference to the EU as 'a new stage in the process of creating an ever closer union among the peoples of Europe'. British intransigence extended to the question of social policy, where the government's unwillingness to accept the setting of social-policy legislation at the Community level resulted in a separate Social Protocol being secured outside of the Treaty. This in effect meant that the social policy measures agreed to by the other 11 member states would be implemented by intergovernmental cooperation rather than by EC law. But while such an outcome pleased the British government, the decision would not stop the Commission from initiating legislation that was applicable to all member states under the health and safety provisions that had been introduced in the Single European Act, thereby resulting in John Major's government subsequently challenging the introduction of regulations on working hours.

Elsewhere, the Treaty continued the practice established in the SEA of widening the number of policy areas covered by qualified majority voting. The Treaty also extended the Community's competences in more than a dozen areas. This included the acceptance of the notion of European citizenship and the extension of the Community's powers in the areas of consumer protection, culture, education, environment, health, industry, research and technological development, social policy and vocational training. Agreement was also reached on the establishment of a **common foreign and security policy** (CFSP) that was a compromise between the Franco-German 'Europeanist' vision and the British-led preference for the maintenance of the 'Atlanticist' link. Thus, while the agreement allowed for the establishment of common positions and joint actions on foreign policy, the WEU was kept separate from the EC and NATO's remit as Europe's security guarantor was confirmed. Decisions on CFSP and **justice and home affairs** (JHA) were moreover set with an intergovernmental '**pillar framework**' and as such the supranational impact of the Community did not extend to these policies. This outcome favoured the views of those member states which wanted to ensure that national governments would remain the key decision-makers on foreign policy and judicial cooperation.

To account for this intergovernmental method of cooperation, the institutional arrangements of the Community were based on a new pillar structure. The first pillar comprised the EC and contained common policies and actions that involved the supranational institutions of the Community. This included the European Parliament, which was given the right to approve (or not) the European Commission, while a new co-decision procedure with the Council ensured that the European Parliament would be able to block or amend EC legislation by majority vote. This therefore ensured that the European Parliament could 'no longer be accused of lacking teeth' (Corbett, 1994: 210). It would moreover lead Simon Hix to conclude that the EU contained a 'classic two chamber legislature: in which the Council represents the states and the European Parliament represents the citizens' (Hix, 1999: 56). An enhancement of the European Parliament's influence necessitated the European Commission and member states reassessing their approach to policy-making, which had hitherto essentially bypassed the European Parliament. Thus, because the European Parliament was given the ability to block legislation via the co-decision procedure, both the European Commission and the member states had to pay greater attention to the views of the Parliament in the legislative process (Blair, 2001: 144; Judge and Earnshaw, 2003: 52). Other changes that the Treaty introduced included the establishment of a new **Committee of the Regions** and the insertion of the **subsidiarity** provision which stressed that decisions should be taken closest to the citizen at the lowest level of institutional authority. Pillars two and three dealt with CFSP and JHA respectively, with cooperation taking place on an intergovernmental basis and not involving the Community's supranational institutions, while the **European Union** encompassed all of these elements.

Although the Maastricht Treaty on European Union was signed in February 1992, it did not formally enter into force until 1 November 1993. The delay was caused by difficulties over its ratification by the member state governments which had been significantly influenced by Denmark's rejection of the Treaty in a referendum in June 1992 by 50.7 to 49.3 per cent, or some 42,000 votes. The Danes, who had wanted to be the first to ratify the Treaty, consequently sparked a ratification crisis that was followed by the French electorate accepting the Treaty by the slimmest of margins in September 2002: 51.05 to 48.95 per cent. And while the Treaty was in the end passed in a second referendum in Denmark in May 1993, albeit only after its government obtained an **opt-out** on defence policy and a further clarification of its opt-out from the single currency, the whole process weakened the level of confidence in the EU's future development. Increasing scepticism about the stability of the EU's fortunes was not helped by a crisis in the Exchange Rate Mechanism from July 1992 until August 1993, during which time Britain and Italy were forced to leave the system (Blair, 2002: 160–83). These events lessened the support for the EU among an electorate that concluded the Maastricht Treaty to be 'a Treaty too far' and this in turn impacted on the scope and success of future treaty reform.

Committee of the Regions (CoR): Comprises representatives of local and regional authorities who are appointed by national governments and not directly by any regional authority.

Subsidiarity: The concept that decisions should be taken at the lowest level of government. If that is not possible then the decision should be passed up to the next, or most appropriate, level of government.

European Union (EU): An economic and political union of member states (presently 27). The EU was form established by the Treaty on European Union and covers a wide range of policies from internal market to the single currency. The origins of the EU can be traced back to the European Coal and Steel Community (ECSC).

Opt-out: A situation when it has been decided that a member state does not want to join others in a specific EU policy area.

6

Building a New Europe: 1994–2010

Observers could have been forgiven for thinking that the difficulties surrounding the ratification of the Maastricht Treaty would have led to a period of stock-taking on the part of the member states and EU institutions. This proved not to be the case. Barely eight months after the Maastricht Treaty entered force on 1 November 1993, EU member states took the decision in June 1994 to convene a Reflection Group with a view to holding yet another intergovernmental conference (IGC) negotiation that would result in treaty reform. Why was this the case? The answer to this question was that while the Maastricht Treaty had made a number of reforms to the decision-making procedures and created new policies such as the single currency, there was a belief that the institutional and decision-making structures did not reflect the pressures that the EU faced. These pressures took various forms, ranging from the need for the EU to have a stronger and more effective foreign and security policy, to the need for the EU to be able to respond to the challenges of a globalisation. As the years progressed these discussions became more complicated by the very fact that the EU was itself changing as a result of enlargement; the number of member states increased from 12 member states in 1994 to 27 member states by 2007 [**Document 35, p. 142**].

ENLARGING THE EU

The changing nature of European integration in the late 1980s and early 1990s brought a number of European Free Trade Association countries to conclude that they were disadvantaged through being outside of the then EC. The response of the Community was in the first instance to propose the creation of a new form of EC–EFTA association as a means of preventing an immediate enlargement at a time when the Community's energies were focused on the single-market programme. To this end, a 1992 EC–EFTA agreement was signed to create a **European Economic Area** (EEA) that was intended to lead to full EU membership. The EEA, which came into existence in January 1994, was designed to provide for the free movement of capital, goods, services and workers.

European Economic Area (EEA): Permits the free movement of goods, capital, services and workers between the EU and the countries of the European Free Trade Association (EFTA).

Far from forestalling an immediate EU enlargement, the EEA negotiations spurred on the desire of Austria, Finland, Norway and Sweden to join the Union. (Switzerland had initially shown a willingness to join the EU, but dropped its application in the wake of a negative 1992 EEA vote.) As with previous enlargements, the negotiations were focused on those policy areas that were most sensitive to national interests. For Austria, Finland and Sweden, this included the question of whether their neutrality would hinder their ability to participate in the EU's CFSP that included a commitment to the 'eventual framing of a common defence'. But it proved to be a relatively uncontroversial issue, with the Austrian, Finnish and Swedish governments being prepared to accept the CFSP in a post-Cold War environment. More controversial issues included the question of EU environment policy, as standards were for the most part higher in the applicant countries. Other troublesome questions included energy and fisheries policy, primarily as a result of Norway's refusal to surrender control to the EU. Disputes over these and other issues were nevertheless resolved, not least because of their desire 'to be at the top table when major political, security and economic issues were being discussed and decided' (Cameron, 2004a: 5). As a result, the four applicants signed treaties of accession in January 2004 that would in turn have to be ratified at the national level. But as Norway had held a referendum in November 1994 in which 52 per cent of the country's voters had decided against membership, only Austria, Finland and Sweden joined the EU on 1 January 1995.

Although the 1995 'northern' enlargement had been an uncomplicated process – all three countries were net contributors to the EU budget, had experience of intergovernmental cooperation in EFTA and had the necessary administrative and judicial structures to implement policies in the form of the *acquis communitaire* – it brought to the fore questions relating to the institutional design and the policies embraced by the EU. This was particularly relevant because of the prospect of future enlargement to Central and Eastern European states. Applications for membership had already been received from Cyprus, Malta and Turkey, when in June 1993 the Copenhagen European Council offered the prospect of membership to the countries of Central and Eastern Europe if the applicants were able to 'assume the obligations of membership by satisfying the economic and political conditions required'. For this to happen, the Council set out the exact tests that the applicants would have to pass for them to join the EU, the so-called 'Copenhagen

Europe Agreements:
Agreements that have been concluded between the EU and Central and Eastern European countries since 1991.

criteria' [**Document 35, p. 142**]. As a result of the Copenhagen decision, applications for EU membership were received from Hungary and Poland in 1994; Bulgaria, Estonia, Latvia, Lithuania, Romania and the Slovak Republic in 1995; and the Czech Republic and Slovenia in 1996. These applications had been aided by the support that had been provided to them since the collapse of Communism, most notably in the form of '**Europe Agreements**' which enabled them to participate in the economic, political and trading aspects of European integration.

Whereas the 1995 enlargement did not result in a wholesale reassessment of the institutional design of the EU, it was clear that the accession of more countries could not simply follow the practice of working within the parameters of existing institutional structures. In 1995, the College of Commissioners had simply increased in size from 17 to 20 to accommodate the three new members. Reform of the Commission – including the practice whereby the larger member states had two Commissioners – would therefore be a necessity prior to any future enlargement so as to avoid it becoming an unwieldy body. At the same time there was a need to extend the use of QMV – to avoid policies being blocked by the use of the national veto – and the need to examine the distribution of votes in the Council of Ministers.

Structural funds: Promotes cohesion between EU member states. Structural funds are the European Social Fund, the European Regional and Development Fund and the guidance section of the European Agricultural Guidance and Guarantee Fund.

Outside these questions of institutional reform, the prospect of future enlargement motivated member states to discuss other issues. This included the prospect of large-scale migration from the accession countries, the reform of the Common Agricultural Policy and the cohesion and **structural funds**, which together accounted for approximately 80 per cent of the EU budget. Of these issues, the unwillingness of some member states (particularly France) to decrease the financial burden of the CAP had in the past limited the opportunity for reform, with the CAP continuing to account for approximately 50 per cent of the Community budget in the early 1990s. The prospect of EU enlargement to include countries with large agricultural sectors, which accounted for approximately 20 per cent of employment in Central and Eastern Europe (four times the EU level), meant that there was a need to reassess the principle of subsidising farmers on the basis of production and guaranteed prices. As one commentator has noted, 'if all farmers were to receive the level of agricultural subsidies received by existing member states, the EU budget would skyrocket' (Friis, 2003: 189–91). Pressure to reform the CAP was also influenced by the external climate of criticism in World Trade Organization talks that EU support for its farmers was an anti-competitive practice.

Agenda 2000: The plans that were set out by the European Commission in 1997 in response to the enlargement of the EU Central and Eastern Europe. This included proposals for the reform of the CAP and cohesion policy.

Chirac, Jacques (b. 1932): Gaullist politician and President of France 1995–2007. Previously Prime Minister 1974–76 and 1986–88.

Such viewpoints influenced the Commission to set out in its 1997 policy on enlarging the EU, **Agenda 2000,** to decouple the support for farmers from production and to link support to social and environmental objectives. But France, which since 1995 had been led by President **Jacques Chirac**, refused to accept this proposal and as a consequence the scope of the reforms was severely limited. Thus, even though member states understood the implications that enlargement would have on the EU's institutions and policy areas, there was nevertheless reluctance by existing member states to fundamentally alter the 'cost–benefit balance sheet'. This was not least because of domestic political pressures that were compounded by the difficult economic conditions of the early 1990s, whereby unemployment in the existing 12 member states reached 17 million by early 1994. This difficult economic situation was made worse by governments having to make unpopular cuts in public expenditure to ensure that they met the convergence criteria requirements of the single currency [**Document 34, p. 140**].

TREATY OF AMSTERDAM

Member states were mindful of questions relating to institutional reform when they took the decision at the June 1994 Corfu European Council to convene a Reflection Group, under the chairmanship of the Spanish Diplomat Carlos Westendorp, to make preparations for the holding of yet another IGC. Despite the Treaty of Maastricht having come into force on 1 November 1993, there was a commitment in Article N of that treaty to hold another IGC before the end of 1996. The Commission, Council and European Parliament were entrusted with the task of drawing up reports that would guide the work of the Reflection Group. The reports, which were presented in early 1995, emphasised a number of common themes. These included the effectiveness of the decision-making procedures, particularly with regard to the two intergovernmental pillars. Other themes were the need for greater openness, legitimacy, **transparency** and the simplification of procedures.

In focusing on these issues, the reports were mindful of the institutional implications that would result from further EU enlargement. A number of member states also welcomed the opportunity to review the extent of the effectiveness of the Maastricht reforms. This particularly applied to the CFSP, whereby the reality of the EU's experience in the former Yugoslavia had pointed to a number of shortcomings in the effectiveness of EU cooperation. A number of member states – chiefly Belgium, France, Germany, Italy, Luxembourg and the Netherlands – consequently viewed the IGC negotiations as an important opportunity to deepen European integration. This was, however, an assessment that was not shared by Denmark and Britain, both of which had been badly scarred by the crisis surrounding the ratification of the Maastricht Treaty. In Britain, this had assisted the cause of the Eurosceptic wing of the Conservative Party, which in turn limited the ability of the

Transparency: The degree of openness within the EU institutions. Includes ensuring that there is access to information and documents, and that information is easy to read. Questions about transparency often reflect a view that the EU decision-making is remote and inaccessible.

Blair, Anthony (b. 1953): UK Labour Prime Minister 1997–2007. A committed pro-European, he attempted to raise the UK's profile in Europe, although his premiership was overshadowed by his support for the US-led invasions of Afghanistan in 2001 and Iraq in 2003.

Treaty of Amsterdam: Signed in 1997, it came into effect in 1999. It widened the scope of the co-decision procedure, increased the use of qualified majority voting, improved the effectiveness of foreign policy co-operation, incorporated the Schengen Agreement into the Community and established an employment chapter.

Santer, Jacques (b. 1937): President of the European Commission 1995–99, having previously served as Prime Minister of Luxembourg from 1984–95. His period as Commission President was tarnished by a March 1999 fraud report by a Committee of Independent Experts which criticised the operation of the Commission.

Prodi, Romano (b. 1939): Italian President of the European Commission 1999–2004. Served as Prime Minister of Italy 1996–98 and 2006–08. His period as Commission President was not as dynamic in reforming the EU policy-making process as many would have liked.

government to orchestrate a positive European policy (George, 1999: 264–74; Forster and Blair, 2002: 91–116). British hostility was therefore a common feature of the IGC negotiations which had commenced in March 1996, and it was only the election of the Labour government in May 1997 under the leadership of **Tony Blair** that created the possibility for the negotiations to conclude at the June 1997 Amsterdam European Council.

The product of the IGC negotiations was a **Treaty of Amsterdam** that made a number of minor amendments to the EU, but which lacked the sense of possessing a 'grand theme' (as the Maastricht Treaty had). The question of institutional reform – to prepare the EU to meet the challenge of enlargement – was largely avoided: the Treaty failed to tackle key issues such as the size of the Commission and the reweighting of a member state's votes in the Council of Ministers. The Treaty did, nevertheless, extend the scope of QMV to an additional 16 policy areas, while it also enhanced the role of the European Parliament by extending the co-decision procedure to embrace existing policies and new areas of responsibility. The effect of this was to ensure that the co-decision procedure would apply to more than 80 per cent of Council decisions. The Parliament was also given the power to confirm or refuse a nominated Commission President, with this augmentation in the Parliament's influence over the Commission being illustrated with the resignation of the European Commission in the early hours of 16 March 1999. The Commission, which had been led by President **Jacques Santer**, resigned as a result of the threat from the leaders of two of the four largest groups in the European Parliament to resign or face dismissal after the publication of a fraud report which found instances 'where commissioners, or the Commission as a whole, bear responsibility for instances of fraud, irregularity or mismanagement in their services or areas of special responsibility'. Yet, in true European style, the Commission continued in office until **Romano Prodi** assumed the responsibility of President in 2000.

Concern over the ability of an enlarged EU to progress at a common pace resulted in the insertion of a number of **flexibility** clauses in the Treaty that would enable some countries to progress at a quicker pace of integration than others by means of **enhanced cooperation**, albeit with the provision that member states would be able to block decisions in the Council as to whether flexibility should be used (Stubb, 2002). But while such changes inevitably resulted in concerns about the implications of the possibility of a **multi-speed Europe**, there already existed numerous examples of different levels of cooperation among member states, of which relevant examples included Schengen, the ERM and monetary union. Other notable changes included the incorporation of the Social Protocol into the EU proper (which John Major had opposed at the Maastricht European Council), made possible by the election of the British Labour government in May 1997. Improvements were also made to the CFSP as a result of European embarrassment to orchestrate a coordinated and effective response to the crises in the Balkans (White, 2001: 150). Efforts were therefore made in the Treaty of Amsterdam to strengthen the cohesiveness of the CFSP through the appointment of a High Representative (to be combined with the post of Secretary-General of the Council). In the summer of 1999 EU member states agreed to the appointment of the former Spanish foreign minister and at the time serving Secretary General of NATO, **Javier Solana**, to the post of High Representative. An effort to strengthen the EU's nascent foreign policy also resulted in a decision to create a policy-planning unit to advise the High Representative.

One of the most significant areas of change concerned the agreement to establish an **area of freedom, security and justice**, and resulted in a number of aspects of the JHA provisions of the third pillar being incorporated in the regular first pillar provisions of the EU. This specifically applied to those matters that related to the free movement of people, including matters relating to asylum, immigration and visas. The Schengen agreement on the free movement of persons between member states was also incorporated into the first pillar provision of the EU. The effect of these changes was that the third pillar was renamed 'Police and Judicial Cooperation in Criminal Matters'. This emphasis on the need for common action in police and judicial cooperation among member states was the product of the growing threats posed to member states from organised crime, including illegal immigration and money laundering. Terrorist threats were additionally an important factor, particularly in the wake of the 11 September 2001 attacks on the United States.

It is evident from the changes introduced by the Treaty of Amsterdam that they did not contain a central theme as the SEA or Maastricht negotiations had, and nor were they meant to: 'the Amsterdam IGC was not convened with the intention of launching a major economic project, but was planned as a follow-up conference, with a mandate to amend provisions in the Maastricht Treaty' (Weiner and Neunreither, 2000: 1–2). The negotiations were therefore aimed at reviewing events since Maastricht, during which time the EU's energies were focused on the progression towards the single currency.

Overall, the Treaty of Amsterdam therefore produced a series of reforms that reflected incremental rather than whole-scale change. Improved co-operation on JHA and the extension of the co-decision procedure has to be set against the failure of the Treaty to fully prepare the EU for enlargement. Questions relating to the composition of the European Commission and the weighting of votes in the Council, which were central to the future enlargement plans, were avoided. Member states were also unable to agree on a reduction in the number of policy areas in which they maintained a right of

Flexibility: A concept that is used to highlight a situation whereby all member states are not committed to a specific EU policy, such as the single currency.

Enhanced cooperation: Permits those member states that wish to develop deeper forms of integration than others.

Multi-speed Europe: When there are variations in the pace of European integration between member states.

Solana, Javier (b. 1942): Served as Secretary-General of the Council of the European Union, Secretary-General of the Western European Union and the EU's High Representative for the Common Foreign and Security Policy 1999–2009. A former Spanish Minister for Foreign Affairs (1992–95), he also served as Secretary General of NATO 1995–99.

Area of Freedom, Security and Justice (AFSJ): The Treaty of Amsterdam brought the Schengen agreements into the European Community. This provided for the abolition of frontier controls, the free movement of people and cooperation between judicial and police authorities to combat cross-border crime.

veto. A lack of consensus among member states on a number of core issues ensured that the negotiations produced a Treaty that represented the lowest common denominator position where agreement could be produced among the member states. The reality of this need to achieve agreement over and above all else consequently led the member states to postpone the more complex issues for a future IGC, with the Treaty containing a Protocol which required that a further IGC be convened to carry out a review of the institutional provisions at least one year before EU membership exceeded 20 member states.

Beyond the parameters of the Amsterdam negotiations, the EU played an important role in the negotiations that resulted in the 1997 Kyoto Protocol on climate change, which represented a non-binding agreement by a majority of the world's nations to reduce their carbon emissions. In 1998 EU member states went one step further and agreed to reduce their carbon emissions to 8 per cent below 1990 levels by the year 2012. Also in 1998 member states agreed to further develop the capabilities of the CFSP with a view to the creation of a European Security and Defence Policy (ESDP), with this being influenced by the EU's inability to respond sufficiently quickly to the Kosovo crisis. Movement in this policy area had been aided by the convergence of the views of Britain (Atlanticist) and France (Europeanist), which led to a meeting between Prime Minister Blair and President Chirac in the French port of St Malo on 4 December 1998. The meeting produced a Letter of Intent on defence cooperation and a joint declaration on European defence in which both countries emphasised that while NATO would retain the main security responsibility for Europe, European member states would nevertheless increase their institutional arrangements for collaborative action in those areas that did not necessitate US involvement, such as peacekeeping. This agreement provided towards the decision taken at the December 1999 Helsinki European Council to create an ESDP based on the establishment of a multinational corps of 50,000 to 60,000 forces by 2003, with the capability of mounting an autonomous European mission if NATO declined to get involved in a crisis situation. Apart from progress on CFSP/ESDP matters, member states also made headway on the single currency. Here it was noticeable that whereas British input had been crucial to the CFSP/ESDP discussions, the government in London nevertheless continued to remain adrift from monetary union. Thus, the single currency came into existence in January 1999 as a result of 11 member states having met the convergence criteria requirements. Greece would later meet the criteria in January 2001 and as a result of the then 15 member states, only Denmark, Sweden and Britain remained outside of what became known as the **eurozone** when the changeover to the use of euro banknotes and coins commenced in January 2002.

Eurozone: Consists of the member states which have adopted the euro as the single currency.

TREATY OF NICE

Even though the Treaty of Amsterdam contained a Protocol commitment to carry out a further examination of EU reform, member states had concluded the necessity of institutional reform throughout 1998 and came to an agreement at the June 1999 Cologne European Council (only a month after the Treaty of Amsterdam came into force) to hold an IGC in 2000 that would address the issues that had been irresolvable at Amsterdam. The key issues included the size and composition of the Commission, the weighting of votes in the Council and the possibility of extending the use of qualified majority voting in the Council. The decision to hold yet another IGC negotiation had been influenced by the decision in 1999 to widen the accession negotiations to include all 13 countries (Bulgaria, Cyprus, Czech Republic, Estonia, Hungary, Latvia, Lithuania, Malta, Poland, Romania, the Slovak Republic, Slovenia and Turkey). This was instead of limiting the discussions to the six countries which had been engaged in accession talks since December 1997 (Cyprus, the Czech Republic, Estonia, Hungary, Poland and Slovenia). The opening up of the accession negotiations to all 13 countries increased the likelihood of a large-scale enlargement which therefore added further urgency to the need to address the institutional questions which the Treaty of Amsterdam had been unable to resolve.

The IGC negotiations commenced in February 2000 under the presidency of Portugal with a limited agenda that reflected the desire of the member states to focus specifically on the institutional matters that had been left over from the Treaty of Amsterdam so as to prepare the EU for enlargement. By the time of the June 2000 Feira European Council, the IGC agenda had been widened to include the question of 'closer cooperation', by which member states would be able to cooperate more closely with other member states in individual areas. A widening of the IGC did not, however, suggest that differences between the member states on institutional matters had been resolved. A divergence of views was particularly apparent at the October 2000 Biarritz European Council (which was the last meeting of heads of state and government before the December Nice summit). Key areas of divergence included the future shape of the European Commission, whereby the larger member states' suggestion of a smaller Commission based on a rotation system was criticised by the smaller member states.

A lack of consensus between member states continued to the December 2000 Nice European Council, with agreement on a new treaty that provided the green light for enlargement being achieved only after four days of negotiations. The lengthy nature of these negotiations reflected the desire of member states to achieve some form of agreement rather than no agreement. Discussions over institutional reform were among the most problematic.

These included the questions of QMV and the reform of the Commission. Although most member states were aware of the need for greater use of QMV in an enlarged EU, some governments nevertheless wanted to ensure that certain policies would continue to be governed by the national veto. Britain stressed that defence, social security and taxation could not be subject to QMV. Ireland and Luxembourg shared Britain's concerns about taxation, while Germany was unwilling to extend QMV to asylum and immigration policy. As befitting its status as one of the main benefactors of EU funding, Spain obtained an agreement that the use of the national veto would continue until 2007 for any agreements to provide financial assistance to poorer countries. In the end, the **Treaty of Nice**, which was signed on 26 February 2001 and came into force on 1 February 2003, resulted in an agreement to extend QMV to nearly 40 additional treaty provisions, while the number of votes distributed among the member states was altered to take account of the EU's increased population [**Document 36, p. 144**]. It was, however, not a whole-scale adjustment of votes, as small states continued to be over-represented and Germany's status as having the largest population did not transcend into more votes. This was primarily because of French concern about allowing Germany to have more votes than the other large member states. To this end, questions relating to the power and influence of the member states in the EU were a key feature of the IGC negotiations. The QMV agreement was also extremely complex, comprising three elements: first, the support of in excess of 70 per cent of the member states' weighted votes; second, the support of a majority of the member states; and, finally, the necessity that those states in favour of the decision comprised not just 70 per cent of the weighted votes but also represented at least 62 per cent of the EU population.

In terms of the size and composition of the Commission, it was apparent that existing arrangements whereby the number of Commissioners simply increased with each enlargement would in the end produce an unwieldy body. This was because, when compared with the six countries that signed the Treaty of Rome, the EU's membership would have increased four-fold with the accession of ten additional member states. In practical terms, the EU would comprise too many countries for it to work in an effective manner based on existing methods of decision-making. For this reason there was a need to revise the practice whereby the largest member states of Britain, France, Germany, Italy and Spain had two Commissioners and the remaining member states one Commissioner. In the end, agreement was reached at Nice that from 1 January 2005 there would be one Commissioner per member state, thereby resulting in the five largest member states having to give up their right to have two Commissioners. It was also agreed that the

Treaty of Nice: Signed in 2001, it came into effect in 2003. It attempted to reform the EU to take account of enlargement. Notable changes included reform to the European Commission and the weighting of votes in the Council for decisions by a qualified majority.

total number of Commissioners would in future not exceed 26 members and therefore if the EU were to grow to more than 27 members, the total number of Commissioners would be less than the number of member states. So as to ensure that all members would be treated fairly in an EU of 27 or more member states, the Treaty introduced a commitment to a principle of a rotation system. The treaty also provided for a redistribution of votes in the European Parliament, which both set a total limit of 732 MEPs (the Amsterdam Treaty had set a ceiling of 700 MEPs) and sought to provide a more equitable distribution of seats among the member states [**Document 37, p. 145**]. The treaty also extended the application of the co-decision procedure to seven treaty articles, including judicial cooperation in civil matters (apart from family law).

THE FIFTH ENLARGEMENT AND CONSTITUTIONAL REFORM

Notwithstanding the fact that the exclusive focus of the Treaty of Nice on institutional matters ensured that its remit was not as wide as that of the SEA, Maastricht or Amsterdam Treaties, member states acknowledged that the final Treaty did not provide an optimal outcome. As such, a Declaration was annexed which stressed that yet another IGC would be convened to examine the institutional arrangements necessary for enlargement. To fully discuss these issues, at the December 2001 Laeken European Council, member states adopted the Laeken declaration on the Future of Europe which identified the need for the EU to improve its internal workings and to ensure that it was capable of playing a full and active role in world affairs. The latter point had been further clarified by the September 2001 terrorist attacks on the US. In terms of the enlargement negotiations, the Laeken meeting also noted that negotiations with ten applicant states – namely Cyprus, Estonia, Hungary, Latvia, Lithuania, Malta, Poland, the Slovak Republic, the Czech Republic and Slovenia – should be concluded by the end of 2002. To further examine the issues that were raised at Laeken, member states took a decision to convene a **Convention on the Future of Europe** that would undertake the preparatory work for the IGC.

The Convention, which was chaired by former French President Valéry Giscard d'Estaing, met between March 2002 and June 2003 and discussed a number of proposals that reflected a desire to improve the quality of leadership offered by the EU, streamline its institutional structures and ensure that its range of policies reflected the challenges that the EU faced. Such points

Convention on the Future of Europe: Established in 2002, chaired by former French President Valéry Giscard d'Estaing. A draft Constitutional Treaty was published in June 2003 which set out possible routes for future European integration in light of the 2004 enlargement of the EU.

Constitutional Treaty:
Emerging out of the work
of the Convention on
the Future of Europe,
member states reached
agreement on a Con-
stitutional Treaty in June
2004 that attempted to
provide a clearer struc-
ture to the EU by con-
solidating all previous
Treaties into a single
document. Reaction to
the Treaty was mixed,
with many being con-
cerned about the cre-
ation of a 'European
Constitution' and this
eventually resulted in
the Treaty being rejected
in referendum votes in
France and the Nether-
lands in June 2005.

were set out in a series of recommendations that were presented in the form
of a draft **Constitutional Treaty** in June 2003 and which in turn served as
the basis for the IGC negotiations that commenced a few months later, in
October, and concluded at the Brussels summit of 18 June 2004. By that time
the European Union had enlarged to 25 member states with the accession of
Cyprus, Estonia, Hungary, Latvia, Lithuania, Malta, Poland, the Slovak Republic,
the Czech Republic and Slovenia on 1 May 2004 and in so doing increased
the EU population by more than 100 million people.

The final outcome of the IGC negotiations was agreement at the Brussels
European Council of June 2004 on a new Constitutional Treaty that con-
solidated all the previous treaties into one single document to provide the EU
with a simpler and more accessible set of rules. This effort to add clarity to
the EU and improve many of its procedures had led some observers to incor-
rectly conclude that the Treaty was merely a 'tidying up' exercise. Instead, the
Treaty made a number of important reforms that aimed to improve the
EU's ability to respond to the challenges posed by enlargement. One of
the most difficult issues to resolve in the negotiations concerned the system
of majority voting in the Council of Ministers that had been agreed to in the
Treaty of Nice. Criticism of the Nice agreement rested on two arguments:
first, that the three-stage QMV procedure was far too complex; second, that
the distribution of votes was unfair. Thus, Germany and other member states
argued that it was unjust to provide Poland and Spain with nearly as many
votes as the larger EU countries. For Germany this was a particularly important argument. It posed the legitimate question as to why it should have only
a few more votes than member states which not only had approximately half
of its population but which made either no or merely minimal contributions
to the EU budget while Germany's financial contribution accounted for
between 25 and 30 per cent of the total EU budget.

Having increased their influence in the Nice Treaty, Poland and Spain
were predictably unwilling to contemplate a change to a system that favoured
their interests. The upshot of this was that it proved impossible to broker a
suitable agreement at the Brussels summit of December 2003. This state of
affairs would continue until the election of a new Spanish government in
March 2004 that brought with it a stronger willingness to resolve Spain's differences in the discussions over the Constitutional Treaty. As a result, member states reached agreement in June 2004 on a new simplified 'two-stage'
procedure, whereby an agreement would be reached if it was supported by
55 per cent of the member states as long as this reflected 65 per cent of
the EU population. Such an outcome reinforced the influence of the larger
member states that represented the majority of the EU population. In addition to altering the voting threshold, member states took the decision to

extend majority voting to 44 new policy areas. This included the area of justice and home affairs that had previously been governed primarily by intergovernmental methods of decision-making. Such an initiative reflected the need for member states to work more effectively in their efforts to tackle matters relating to illegal migration, terrorism and cross-border crime. Nevertheless, concerns over the maintenance of national interest resulted in the introduction of a new 'emergency break' formula in some of the policy areas that are now subject to majority voting. The new procedure, which would be applied to social security and criminal procedural law, ensured that where a member state is in disagreement with a majority vote decision it is able to refer the matter back to the Council (at which stage the Council can either accept the proposal on a unanimity basis or ask the Commission for a new proposal).

One of the most significant developments concerned the creation of a post of EU President, to be elected by heads of government for a term of two-and-a-half years. Such a change was prompted by concerns that the previous system of a six-monthly rotation of the President among all member states hindered the continuity of EU policies and created confusion for non-member states. Concern over the EU's international identity led to the creation of an EU Minister for Foreign Affairs that will combine the existing positions of the Council's High Representative for foreign policy and the European Commissioner for external relations. In short, the new post will provide a single spokesperson who will be able to provide a clearer co-ordination of EU foreign policy, which ranges from diplomatic negotiations to the distribution of foreign aid. Linked to this issue of foreign policy, the Treaty strengthened EU defence policy by permitting a core group of countries to enhance their cooperation on military matters if such a move is approved in the Council by majority vote. Thus, those member states that are more willing (and more able) will take a stronger role in EU military operations. A final notable change was the incorporation of the Charter of Fundamental Rights into the Treaty, thereby demonstrating the support of all member states to a range of rights that are applicable to EU citizens.

Despite the fact that many agreed that these changes were necessary to improve the EU's mode of operation, there was serious concern among the EU electorate that the Constitutional Treaty represented a significant erosion of national sovereignty. These concerns led to a ratification crisis for the Treaty in 2005, with it being rejected in referendum votes in France (with a 'no' vote of 54.5 per cent) and the Netherlands (with a 'no' vote of 61.6 per cent). This resulted in the Constitutional Treaty grinding to a halt to provide a period of reflection.

LISBON AND BEYOND

After a necessary period of reflection and contemplation about the implications of the failure of the Constitutional Treaty to be ratified, member states reached agreement at the June 2007 European Council to further examine developments with a view to the adoption of a new 'Reform Treaty'. By that stage the EU had undergone another enlargement with the accession of Bulgaria and Romania on 1 January 2007. Some member states were additionally heavily involved in fighting the war on terror, through armed forces deployment in Afghanistan and Iraq in response to the terrorist attacks on the US that took place in September 2001. In the period since 2001 there had at times been a lack of consensus among member states as to the degree of response, with Britain for instance being at the forefront of the US-led coalition. This lack of cohesiveness among EU member states on foreign-policy issues was one of the reasons why many argued that the new Treaty was important in enhancing the EU's abilities. With this in mind, the new Treaty was signed by the leaders of the EU's 27 member states at the December 2007 Lisbon European Council and as such it has become known as the **Treaty of Lisbon**.

Critics of the Lisbon Treaty have argued that it is the Constitutional Treaty in all but name as it contains many of the changes that it attempted to introduce. One crucial change is that whereas the Constitutional Treaty sought, as its name suggests, to set down in a single document the rules, policies and procedures that govern the EU, the Lisbon Treaty by contrast amends the Treaties that already exist. In this sense, it follows the path taken by previous Treaty reforms. Such an approach was obviously deemed to be more palatable to the European electorate given the debacle surrounding the ratification of the Constitutional Treaty. At its heart, however, The Lisbon Treaty has the same objective of attempting to change the working structures, practices and policies of the EU so as to ensure that an EU of 27 member states can work effectively. Inevitably, this still results in many people arguing that the Lisbon Treaty is part of a broader plot to further curtail the sovereignty of the member states.

This is a point that is somewhat laced with truth, not least because the Lisbon Treaty does mirror the approach of the Constitutional Treaty. For instance, it contains the same provision for a full-time post of **President of the European Council** that would be appointed for a period of two-and-a-half years by EU member state governments. As with the Constitutional Treaty, the argument is that in replacing the existing six-monthly rotating Presidency of the European Council, the EU would be served with a more stable source of political direction. This particularly applies to matters of international affairs. In a similar vein, the Lisbon Treaty establishes the

Treaty of Lisbon: After the failure of the Constitutional Treaty, member states agreed to a Treaty of Lisbon on 13 December 2007 which entered into force on 1 December 2009. Key provisions of the Treaty include the creation of the post of President of the European Council, the new position of High Representative, a redistribution of weighting of votes among member states and a removal of national vetoes in a number of policy areas, the creation of a smaller European Commission and the strengthening in the powers of the European Parliament.

President of the European Council: Introduced in the Treaty of Lisbon, the President is elected for a period of two and a half years, thereby replacing the previous system whereby the Presidency rotated between among EU member states on a six-monthly basis.

position of **High Representative for Foreign Affairs and Security Policy** to be appointed by the European Council with the agreement of the President of the European Commission. This will result in the amalgamation of the offices of the EU Commissioners for External Relations with the High Representative as part of an effort to provide the EU with a greater clarity and coherence of its external relations policy.

As part of a desire to streamline and improve the decision-making procedure, the Lisbon Treaty also extends the use of QMV on such issues as climate change, energy policy and humanitarian aid. But while member states agreed to this extension, they also decided that unanimity should continue to be applied to foreign policy, defence policy, social security and tax. Linked to the extension in the use of QMV, agreement was also reached on the introduction of a new system of Double Majority Voting (DMV). This means that for EU legislation to be enacted, a vote in favour will require a minimum of 55 per cent of the member states who in turn represent 65 per cent of the population. The plan is that this method will come into force in 2014, with there being a transition period until 2017 when a member state can ask for legislation to be enacted in accordance with the provisions set out in the Treaty of Nice. Although such changes are, of course, rather technical, the guiding principle behind the new system is to ensure that the method of voting takes into consideration the population size of member states.

As part of a need to remedy the EU's continuing democratic deficit, the new Treaty enables national parliaments to be directly involved in the EU legislation process. Such a change is to be welcomed as it has often been the case that governments with large electoral majorities have been able to basically ignore domestic parliaments from the business of scrutinising EU policy. As such, national parliaments under the Lisbon Treaty will directly receive proposals for new EU legislation so as to be asked if the proposal reflects the requirements of subsidiarity. If one-third of national parliaments consider that it does not conform to such a requirement, then the proposal gets sent back to the Commission. Moreover, if the Commission proposal is objected to by a majority of national parliaments but nonetheless supported by national governments or MEPs, then the parliaments can strike down the proposal. In many ways such a tactic mirrors the co-decision procedure that involves the European Parliament and Council of Ministers, and consequently assists in closing one element of the democratic deficit by bringing national parliaments into the decision-making process. As with previous treaties, Lisbon continues the practice of extending the use of the co-decision procedure.

One of the most contentious issues in the Constitutional Treaty was the incorporation of the Charter of Fundamental Rights as a number of member states, including Britain, objected to this development on the grounds that it

High Representative for Foreign Affairs and Security Policy: Introduced in the Treaty of Lisbon, this new post combines the previous jobs of High Representative and the European Commissioner for External Affairs. The High Representative is responsible for conducting the EU common foreign and security policy, including presiding over the Foreign Affairs Council and having responsibility for the EU External Action Service and EU delegations in third countries and international organisations.

undermined domestic Courts. So as to appease these concerns Britain was granted a protocol with a view to ensuring that the Charter could not be used by the European Court of Justice to make adjustments to British labour law, or laws that impact on social rights. But while such a viewpoint reflected the tendency of successive British governments to challenge policies that infringed on business competitiveness, it has nevertheless been the case that the history of European integration has demonstrated that such Protocols are not always that effective in defending the national position. For instance, Britain's opt-out from the Social Chapter of the Maastricht Treaty, so as to ensure that British companies were not burdened by what they regarded as uncompetitive EU legislation, was in many ways circumvented by the Working Time Directive that subsequently resulted in the European Court of Justice ruling that it was applicable in Britain. Moreover, at the Amsterdam European Council in June 2007 the newly elected Labour government accepted that the Social Chapter should be applied to Britain.

The argument behind these latest changes has been that there is a need to improve the ability of the EU to respond to the challenges that it faces as well as to ensure that the means of operation take into consideration the implications of enlargement. In recent years this has resulted in a streamlining in the number of European Commissioners and MEPs. To an extent this trend has continued with the Lisbon Treaty. Thus, although there was a desire to reduce the number of Commissioners to move away from the practice of allocating a Commissioner to each member state, many national governments rightly baulked at the idea of being 'Commissionerless'. To appease these concerns, agreement was reached in 2008 that every member state will have a Commissioner. In contrast to the inability of the Lisbon Treaty to set a limit on the number of Commissioners, agreement was reached on limiting the European Parliament to having no more than 751 MEPs with the number of MEPs in any member state set at a maximum of 99 and a minimum of 6. At present the EU 27 has a grand total of 736 MEPs and it is therefore evident that any significant enlargement of the EU would result in reductions being made to the number of MEPs per member state so as to ensure that the figure of 751 is not breached [**Document 36, p. 144**].

Decisions such as those on the number of Commissioners and MEPs reflect the beauty and the beast of the EU. On the one hand, there is a logic that it is just not sensible to maintain a system of allowing each member state to have a member of the European Commission. But in practical terms, it is already the case that some Commissioners have more important portfolios than others, as is the case with the allocation of roles in domestic governments. In reality, then, it could be argued that there is more to be lost than gained by limiting the number of Commissioners, while such compromises do help to ensure that national governments are able to get treaties such as

Lisbon ratified. This was certainly uppermost in the minds of EU policy-makers when 54 per cent of the Irish electorate rejected the Lisbon Treaty on 12 June 2008. And although it said something that Ireland was the only member state that committed itself to a referendum, the 'No' vote resulted in member states and the Commission going into overdrive to provide 'legal guarantees' that would assuage the concerns raised by the Irish electorate. These ranged from family issues such as abortion and gay marriage to taxation. The outcome of this was a deal that satisfied the Irish government and which in the end resulted in the Irish electorate voting 'Yes' by a margin of 67.1 per cent in favour and 32.9 per cent against in a vote taken on 2 October 2009.

In light of these events, EU policy chiefs might be forgiven for breathing a sigh of relief for navigating through the potential hurdle of the Irish referendums. The reality of the outcome did, however, appear to be less dictated by the concessions negotiated by the Irish government and more by the fact that many voters did not really understand what the issues were during the first vote. This is a classic problem of referendums. And although a considerable effort was invested by the Irish government in campaigning for a 'Yes' vote, the outcome was in fact influenced more by the impact of the global economic meltdown that took hold in 2008 and which had a harsh impact on countries such as Ireland with strong financial services sectors of their economy. In an effort to tackle the economic situation, Ireland followed a strategy taken by other governments of using taxpayer's money to prop up banks by increasing the amount of government debt. In Ireland, as in other countries, a knock-on effect of these decisions was that governments were basically held in contempt by an electorate for presiding over the financial crisis. The referendum vote that took place in the middle of the economic maelstrom consequently meant that the electorate were presented with a stark choice of registering a vote of protest against their government and the fear that a 'No' vote would damage Ireland's position in an EU, whose membership helped to provide a degree of cushioning to the Irish economy. The history of the Lisbon Treaty therefore provides a valuable lesson to everyone of the importance of the electorate being able to make informed judgments.

The successful outcome of the second Irish referendum provided the green light for the conclusion to the Lisbon Treaty. This eventually took place on 1 December 2009 when the Treaty entered into force after the Czech Republic and Poland also agreed to the Treaty, albeit with some adjustments to take into consideration national concerns about the impact of sovereignty. By 1 December 2009 the EU heads of state and government had agreed that the former Belgian Prime Minister, **Herman Van Rompuy**, would serve as the first permanent president of the EU, and that the British EU Trade Commissioner **Catherine Ashton**, would be the EU's High Representative for

Van Rompuy, Herman (b. 1947): On 19 November 2009 he was elected the first President of the European Council, a position that he will occupy for two and half years. Prior to his appointment he had served as Prime Minister of Belgium since December 2008.

Ashton, Catherine (b. 1956): Since 1 December 2009 has served as EU High Representative for Foreign Affairs and Security Policy and vice-president of the European Commission.

Foreign Affairs and Security Policy. As could be expected from a game of chess that involves 27 member states, negotiations over who would occupy each of these positions followed a path of complicated manoeuvring. At one point the former British Prime Minister Tony Blair appeared to be the front-runner to be EU President. However, many member states were against this given his involvement in the Iraq war and in the end it appears that the heads of state and government have appointed individuals two compromise candidates who are relatively unknown to the wider world. This might be a deliberate policy of ensuring that member states retain a key voice on these important issues.

Part 3

ASSESSMENT

7

The Future of European Integration

The European Union has changed dramatically over the last half century. Today the citizens of the EU enjoy the ability to easily travel and work across some 27 nations, with the EU having brought peace and prosperity to approximately half a billion people. That is not to say that the EU is without challenges, of which it is arguable that the most serious is the level of public disengagement with the European integration process. The most recent European Parliament elections held in 2009 recorded the lowest ever level of voter turnout averaged across the member states. Moreover, since direct elections to the European Parliament commenced in 1979, voter turnout has declined in each of the subsequent seven Parliamentary elections [Document 37, p. 145]. Many observers rightly ask why this situation has come about and the answer is more complicated than voter turnout having a tendency to decline over time. For evidence of public disquiet over European integration it is possible to refer to the various 'no votes' that have been cast in national referendums on EU issues. And although referendums can act as a platform for the electorate to register discontent with domestic governments on non-European policy issues, it is nonetheless the case that there is a consensus that there has been a general decline in popular support for European integration, with this in turn raising questions about the overall legitimacy of the EU.

Why has this situation occurred? It is apparent that while European integration has brought considerable benefits to many of Europe's citizens, such as through improvements in standards of living, many others have fared less well. Whereas over 70 per cent of people thought that their country's membership of the EU was a 'good thing' in the early 1990s, by 2009 this figure had declined to 53 per cent. As far as member state comparison is concerned, in 2009 the highest percentage of individuals who thought that EU membership was a good thing was to be found in Luxembourg (72 per cent), Spain (71 per cent) and Ireland (69 per cent). This is hardly surprising given that virtually everyone in Luxembourg gains some degree of direct benefit of EU membership given the presence of EU institutions in a country with a population of just over 400,000 people. Spain and Ireland have also benefited hugely from massive European investment that has transformed the economic and political landscape of these countries. Nevertheless, all is not rosy even in these countries; Spain continues to have one of the highest unemployment rates in Europe (in excess of 17 per cent in 2009) and Ireland has of course twice rejected EU Treaties in referendum votes. At the opposite end of the scale, Latvia has the most sceptical population. In 2009 just 25 per cent of individuals considered EU membership to be a 'good thing'. This figure is closely followed by Britain (28 per cent) and Hungary (32 per cent). Of these three member states, Britain is well acknowledged to be a sceptical member state and many observers might be surprised that two recent applicants are also sceptical. After all, EU membership is supposed to bring benefits.

Apart from the distinction between member states, there is also a significant gulf between employment and gender groups. In 2009, across the EU more men (57 per cent) than women (49 per cent) thought EU membership to be a 'good thing'. A more telling statistic is that whereas 66 per cent of the most educated citizens – those who have stayed in education until age 20 – consider EU integration to be a 'good thing', only 40 per cent of those who left school at the age of 15 or younger share this view. Of course, many people might not be overly surprised by these statistics, but they do show a troubling polarisation in views that national governments, political parties and EU institutions do not appear to be fully addressing. Thus, while some sections of society, such as managers, view European integration to be a good thing because it creates increased opportunities for travel and employment, the same is not true for less-skilled workers who are often not economically mobile and have traditionally bore the brunt of restructuring brought about by the challenge of operating in a global marketplace.

Many of these issues have come to a head in recent years as result of the 2004 and 2007 enlargements that added 12 member states. But while enlargement increased the EU's size, scope and presence, it also brought significant challenges for the new and existing member states. The new member states went through a process of economic restructuring to get them 'fit' for membership that often eroded traditional communities and employment opportunities, while at the same time the existing member states were faced with having to deal with the challenge of responding to a situation where the economic costs of employing workers tended to be significantly lower in the new member states.

The end result is that it has become harder for people to fully ascertain what the EU stands for. Is the European project about economic integration?

Or is it about achieving peace and security? In truth, the answer is 'yes' to each of these questions. But each question brings with it a different set of implications and this is a situation that has not been helped by the fact that European issues are often the source of conflict within and between political parties at the national level. In practical terms this 'makes it difficult to have a frank and realistic debate about the costs and benefits of European integration and places a premium on simplifying the issues' (Forster and Blair, 2002: 112). As a result, governments often portray the outcome of European negotiations in a way that suggests that they have somehow returned victorious from battle. Yet the fact of the matter is that few European issues tend to be set in stone as a result of the outcome of a decision taken at a meeting. Rather, the history of European integration has shown that the European project has been characterised by a process of evolution. The relative paucity of debate on these issues has not been helped by the fact that twenty-first century Europe has largely failed to deliver heavyweight politicians that have been able to move the European integration process forward. The reality of this state of affairs has meant that electorates are confused when they find out that the decision which protected their national interests a few years ago has somehow changed. Such a point extends to the manner by which governments regularly fail to properly highlight the way such concepts as national sovereignty exist in an international economic setting. It was also a point that was starkly made during the 2008 economic crisis, which created the worst economic situation since the 1920s.

In addition to the absence of frank discussion on European issues, it is also evident that while the EU has brought together former enemies and created the largest integrated market in the world, it regularly fails to live up to its expectations. Back in the early 1990s Christopher Hill referred to a 'capabilities–expectations gap' in noting the contradiction between the desire of EU member states to play an important world role and the limitations incurred by the maintenance of intergovernmental decision-making structures (Hill, 1993). The closing of this gap through more integrated methods of decision-taking and the establishment of relevant administrative structures does not, however, remove the disequilibrium between the EU's total wealth and size, and its collective ability to undertake tasks that are reflective of its position. At the time of writing, the EU's economy has a gross national product of some £11 trillion, a figure that is slightly larger than the US and four times greater than China. Foreign and defence policy provides a useful illustrative example of how the EU's combined population of some half a billion people is subservient to the US. The 27 EU member states can only muster six aircraft carriers: Britain has three, Italy has two, and France has one. This compares with the US which has 11 aircraft carriers. The contrast becomes even starker when the size of the aircraft carriers is compared. The largest European carrier is the Charles de Gaulle of France at some 42,000 tons, with Britain and Italy having what are known as 'light aircraft carriers'. By contrast, 10 of the 11 US carriers are in excess of 100,000 tons.

Such points led Fraser Cameron to come to the conclusion in 2004 that the EU has 'failed to match the US in economic growth, connect with its citizens and punch its weight in the world' (Cameron, 2004b: 149). There is certainly plenty of evidence that can be drawn out to support this view. But it is also potentially a harsh criticism. The US is, of course, a united country with a central taxation policy and it is able to muster its financial resources into policies that reflect its size and scale. By contrast, despite the progress that has been made in European integration, the EU is still a collection of independent states, each with their own cultures, governments, and economic and political policies. Moreover, although the total EU budget is large – about €116 billion for 2009 – this is a tiny figure when put into the context of the member states GNP. Indeed, the total EU budget is just over 1 per cent of the GNP of the EU member states. Nonetheless, the collective efforts of the member states do result in the EU being an important world player. This is reflected in it being the largest contributor to the UN budget and the world's largest provider of development assistance. The EU is also the single largest trading bloc in the world, accounting for in excess of 20 per cent of all global imports and exports. It is a point that is even more impressive when we consider that the 27 EU member states account for just 7 per cent of the world's population.

Where then does this leave us? The first point to make is that the EU has reached a state of integration which makes it impossible to offer comparisons with other international organisations such as the Association of Southeast Asian Nations (ASEAN) or the African Union (AU). The EU enjoys trappings of statehood, in that it has its own currency with an independent central bank that sets interest rates in the eurozone, and exercises a diplomatic presence in overseas missions. It also has its own elected Parliament and an independent Court. As a result of these developments a great deal of discussion has been devoted in the academic literature about the degree to which the EU's influence is comparable to nation states. For some scholars, the EU is more powerful and influential than many nation states, yet for others it is not. The latter view is not just because the EU comprises different national communities, because the fact of the matter is that there are very few states in the world that neatly match national boundaries. Many more states do, in fact, spread across multiple national boundaries, as is the case with Britain. Moreover, while some scholars might point to the fact that the common identity of the EU is hampered by the presence of multiple languages (McCormick, 2008: 32), this is a state of affairs that is common for many other countries that span large geographical areas. Notable examples include India and China, while the US has essentially become a bilingual country through the prevalence of Spanish.

BOUNDARIES OF EUROPE

At the heart of concerns that dominate the EU at the turn of the twenty-first century is a question about where the boundaries of European integration lie. This debate came to a head with the rejection of the Constitutional Treaty. And even though there were some merits in the attempts to create a more united EU position, such as in the field of foreign policy, the fact of the matter is that many individuals considered such developments to go beyond the limits of where European integration should extend. Put bluntly, the pitfalls of membership had begun to outweigh the benefits. Such a viewpoint often comes down to how people view policies. In the case of the Constitutional Treaty, it was evident that the electorates of some member states found the notion of a constitution easier to accept than others. In Britain, for instance, the absence of a written constitution such as that to be found in Germany, meant that many people had little or no knowledge of what a constitution meant in this context. This was despite the fact that a great number of individuals would have come across constitutions in their local sports and social clubs that, in the same context of the Constitutional Treaty, sought to formally set out rules and procedures.

It is certainly the case that despite the evidence of public disquiet over European integration, the EU continues to serve as a magnetic pull for non-member states that regard membership as being central to their nation's foreign policy. At the time of writing, Croatia, Turkey and the Former Yugoslav Republic of Macedonia are formal applicant members and are being subjected to the necessary checks to examine their readiness for membership. There are in addition a number of other countries waiting in the wings that are potential members, with the decision taken by Iceland in 2009 to seek EU membership being the most recent example of this trend.

A cursory glance at the countries that are in the frame for EU membership provides a powerful image of the way in which the EU's geographical map could alter in the future. Of these potential members, Turkey is the most long-standing applicant and is also a country that raises the most debate among EU member states, where there has traditionally been a concern from member states such as France and Germany over the implications of Turkey's membership joining the EU. Such an argument is often couched in terms relating to economic and political factors, including Turkey's human-rights record. Yet, below this argument has been a concern about the implications of extending the EU's geographical reach into Asia (and a quieter concern about Turkey being a Muslim state). This, in other words, reflects a view that Turkey is not a 'European state', even though of course Turkey has been a member of NATO since 1952, with this being the very organisation that was established to defend Europe. Such arguments are often rooted in particular national interests, including the political make-up of the countries concerned rather than an impartial point of view. As such there is therefore much truth in the conclusion that in the case of Turkey 'perceptions about cultural affinity have played a role in the enlargement process' (Lundgreen, 2006: 140). Indeed, from an impartial standpoint, countries such as Turkey have much to offer the EU, not least the presence of a youthful population to offset the ageing populations that threaten the economic competitiveness of many EU member states. A more strategic argument would also extend to saying that the accession of Turkey is of extreme geopolitical importance considering its proximity to many of the world's trouble spots, notably the Middle East.

NATURE OF MEMBERSHIP

Any debate about what countries could become members of the EU inevitably extends to a deeper discussion about the nature of membership. Today, it is apparent that national governments continue to hold a dominant position in the EU and the manner by which the EU has evolved has primarily been a consequence of the decisions taken by the governments rather than the EU institutions. Thus, while such factors as the end of the Cold War, the leadership capacity of the European Commission and the decisions of the European Court of Justice have been influential in shaping the direction of European integration, for all intents and purposes it has been the decisions of the member state governments that have ultimately determined the path of European integration. The expansion in the number of policies that the EU embraces, from the relatively limited areas of coal and steel to matters relating to the environment and key aspects of economic policy, have been shaped by the decisions taken by the member states. Key treaty reforms, including the Single European Act and the Maastricht Treaty on European Union, which enhanced the powers of EU institutions (particularly the European Parliament), have also been the product of the agreements of member state governments.

Many of these changes have been the result of necessity, whereby collaboration has been the only means by which it has been possible to tackle key matters of public policy and to ensure a degree of harmonisation of standards across all member states. To take an example, the development of EU environmental policy was influenced by the reality that environmental pollution extends beyond member state boundaries and that individual member state government action to tackle such problems would be futile. It was also evident that member state governments with strict environmental standards did not want the competitiveness of their companies to be lessened by companies in other member states with inferior standards charging lower prices. But whereas some governments took the development of EU environment policy seriously, it was a view not shared by all. Indeed, in the case of Britain, a change in the traditional unwillingness of governments to accept the importance of EU environment policy in the 1970s and 1980s only came about when there was a domestic political need to address the issue. This was particularly evident in the case of the Bathing Water Directive, when Britain's reluctance to accept this proposal – the government wanted to maintain the practice of pumping raw sewage into the sea – was changed in the 1980s by a dawning that investor confidence in the planned privatisation of the Regional Water Authorities could be undermined by an appearance in the European Court of Justice (Jordan, 2002: 122–23). The end product of these developments has meant that while the motivations for the harmonisation of environmental standards might have differed among member states, the creation of a coordinated environment policy has enabled the EU to have a stronger influence in international environmental negotiations such as the Kyoto Protocol on climate change.

The EU's involvement in such a wide range of policies has been an influential factor in shaping the views of those individuals who argue that it would be better to solve problems at national and sub-national levels. In response to such criticism, greater emphasis has been attached to the principle of subsidiarity, which advocates the taking of decisions at the lowest possible level, including the member state. Yet in the face of this criticism of EU interference, it is evident that the tackling of issues at the EU level is in many instances the only possible option. Moreover, because of the expansion in the number of member states and the increased potential for competing views, it has also been necessary for more decisions to be taken on the basis of majority voting whereby an individual or group of member states can be outvoted. This change in decision-making has, however, occurred out of necessity: in an enlarged grouping of member states progress can only really be achieved through the use of majority voting so as to overcome the threat of a national veto [**Document 36, p. 144**].

And just as there has occurred a lack of distinction between domestic and EU policies, the role of the EU institutions has also changed. A question over the democratic basis of the EU has resulted in the European Parliament (whose members are directly elected) gaining greater influence in every treaty reform. The need to ensure that member states and companies conform to European standards has seen a concurrent increase in the workload of the European Court of Justice, which has been called on to offer rulings on a whole range of topics, from working hours to the free movement of goods [**Document 28, p. 135**]. The necessity to establish commonality within the EU has, at the same time, required the European Commission to take an active role in 'policing' the implementation of directives and regulations which has, in turn, led to discussion over the extent to which the EU has become a 'regulatory state'.

With this in mind, many Eurosceptics and business groups argue that member states are overburdened by what they regard as an avalanche of EU legislation. Yet, the interests of business groups and citizens are not always the same; the focus by business groups on competitiveness often contrasts with a citizen's desire to protect health and safety. Thus, there are often good reasons for regulation to take place. Moreover, it is also evident that were a country to leave the EU it would not somehow result in business facing an absence of regulation. In fact, many of the regulations that infringe on businesses (and everyday activities) originate at a national level. Nevertheless, it is evident that some member states do appear to be better Europeans than others when it comes to implementing legislation and some also go as far as to over-implement, a policy that is known as 'gold-plating'.

What is true, however, is that any attempt to produce a 'figure' about how much of an individual member state's legislation has arisen from EU legislation is fraught with difficulty. One could even go so far as to say it would be a largely hypothetical exercise. Even if it could be possible to establish a definite figure, it is sometimes the case that national legislation already meets EU requirements. This inevitably complicates matters as it emphasises the crucial point that a great deal of legislation would exist were a country to be a member of the EU or not, and as such the impact of EU regulations are harder to pass judgment on. It is also apparent that legislation that has come about because of a EU decision might have occurred in any case. Thus, to apportion the source as the EU does not reflect the likelihood of the necessity of a national response. Moreover, there can also be instances where national legislation is adjusted for domestic rather than EU reasons, but which nonetheless results in the amended legislation incorporating some elements that take into consideration an EU influence. Taken in the round it is therefore extremely difficult to reach a definitive judgement about the extent to which a country could be 'freed' from what are sometimes regarded as excessive EU meddling were the country to withdraw from the EU. This is because it is more than likely that a member state would have implemented a fair number of the legislative acts through national decisions that would have otherwise been shaped by EU decisions.

THE LIMIT OF EUROPEAN INTEGRATION

It should be apparent from the above points that while 'unity' has been a significant feature of European integration, it is also true that there is considerable diversity. In the first instance, divisions exist between member states over the future direction that the EU should take, and not all governments are participants in all EU policies. To take one example, on 1 January 2002, 12 out of a total of 15 EU member states started the process of replacing their distinct national currencies with euro banknotes and coins, while by 2009 there were some 16 out of 27 member states using the euro [**Document 34, p. 140**]. Second, EU legislation, such as that relating to the internal market, is not implemented at the same speed in all member states [**Document 31, p. 137**]. Third, there are notable distinctions in the process, structure and conduct of the governance of member states. Not all governments operate similar welfare state models, with the comprehensive approach provided by Scandinavian countries not being mirrored in the Mediterranean countries of Greece, Portugal and Spain. Fourth, there remain significant differences in the internal labour markets of EU member states, with some countries, such as Britain, being typified by a more flexible labour market with a higher proportion of part-time employees. The study of the EU therefore directs our attention to both the factors that promote unity and the identification of those points that illustrate continuing diversity. Observers would be wrong to conclude that these are a weakness of the EU. Instead, the ability for groups of countries to work together on specific policies is an essential strength of the European integration process. It is clearly impossible for a grouping of at least 27 member states to reach agreement on every policy initiative. Each member state brings specific resources to the EU and moreover has particular interests that it wishes to advance.

What, then, is the likely future direction of European integration? The first point to note is that after two decades of treaty reforms, the appetite among member state governments (and the European public) for big set-piece intergovernmental conference (IGC) negotiations has significantly declined. This was evidenced by the failure of the Constitutional Treaty and it should be expected that there will be few if any grand projects to deepen European integration in the years ahead after the entering into force of the Lisbon Treaty on 1 December 2009.

The outcome of the Irish referendum leads to my second point relating to the support for European integration among the member states. As has been already indicated, there are considerable differences between member states as to whether the EU is perceived as a 'good thing'. But while it is unlikely that there will be significant change to the situation where just over 50 per cent of all Europeans consider the EU to be a 'good thing', the economic crisis that beset the global economy in 2008 further emphasised the reality that the fortunes of nations are intrinsically linked together. In the case of the EU, what this has meant is that whether people are extremely enthusiastic or not about European integration, there is a growing reality that there is a necessity for membership. Nevertheless, there is much than can be done by governments and the EU institutions to ensure that the public are fully aware of the implications of EU membership.

Linked to this, the third point to note is that it should be expected that there will be further enlargement of the EU. This may not happen in the short term, but in the medium to long term it is likely that the EU will expand. The reasons for this include security, political and economic factors, but the end product is that the EU will become a noticeably different organisation. Even today, everyone accepts that it is not possible that all member states could (or should) proceed at the same speed of integration and this point will only be reinforced by future enlargement. Thus, Britain is likely to maintain its own currency in the near future. In essence, member states are likely to adopt a 'pick 'n' mix' approach that will result in them engaging in specific policies that represent their interests. This has already had implications for the way in which alliances are formed between member states and has seen a decline in the importance of the Franco-German relationship that traditionally acted as the driving force behind European integration.

My fourth and final point is that it is likely that European integration will be determined by how the EU responds to the external and internal challenges that will come its way in the years ahead. Much of this focus is likely to be on external issues, especially the challenges of global warming. And although there are differences in the scenarios for predicting the implications of global warming, a general consensus points to a rise in sea levels with many countries being uninhabitable because of their low-lying position. Other countries will also become too hot to live in. At first sight, the majority of the countries directly affected will be outside the EU, although the Mediterranean countries are likely to witness desertification. The greater challenge for the EU is likely to be the impact of migration into Europe as a result of population displacement and the impact of resource wars. The latter is a particularly difficult issue, and one that we already see with regard to countries attempting to secure access to energy, food and water resources.

It should therefore be evident that the EU faces both a stable and a turbulent landscape ahead. On the one hand, it has helped to deliver peace and security to a region that was the source of two world wars. Yet at the same time, there is a realisation that the twenty-first century will see considerable changes, ranging from the emergence of China as a dominant superpower to the need to tackle climate change. But while these issues will necessitate the EU acting as a collective group, it is unlikely that this will result in a lessening of the influence of national governments.

Part 4

DOCUMENTS

Document 1   THE BRIAND MEMORANDUM, 1 MAY 1930

The French Foreign Minister, Aristide Briand, set out his aims for the organisa-tion of a system of European Federal Union.

Compelled by their geographical position to live together, the peoples of Europe, if they are to enjoy security and prosperity, must establish a perman-ent regime of joint responsibility for the rational organization of Europe . . .

   The entente between European nations must be realized on the plane of their absolute sovereignty and complete political independence. Moreover, it would be impossible to associate the idea of political domination with any organization which (like the present one) is deliberately placed under the control of the League of Nations . . .

   . . . Never has the time been so propitious and so pressing for the begin-ning of constructive work in Europe. By the settlement of the principal moral and material problems arising out of the war Europe will soon be freed from heavy burdens, spiritual and economic. The new Europe will be ready for a positive effort, answering to the new order. It is the decisive hour for Europe to listen and choose her own fate. To unite, in order to live and prosper: that is the necessity which confronts European nations today. The peoples seem to have made their feelings clear. The governments must now accept their responsibilities. Otherwise the grouping of material and moral forces for the common benefit which it is their collective task to control will be abandoned to the dangers and chances of uncoordinated individual initiatives.

Source: Leiden University Historical Institute website: http://www.let.leidenuniv.nl/history/rtg/res1/briand.htm.

Document 2   WINSTON CHURCHILL'S SPEECH AT WESTMINSTER COLLEGE, FULTON, MISSOURI, 5 MARCH 1946

Winston Churchill highlighted the growing threat of Communism and argued the need for non-Communist countries to unite and for a close association to develop between the United States and Britain.

From Stettin in the Baltic to Trieste in the Adriatic, an iron curtain has descended across the continent. Behind that line lie all the capitals of the ancient states of Central and Eastern Europe. Warsaw, Berlin, Prague, Vienna, Budapest, Belgrade, Bucharest and Sofia, all these famous cities and the popu-lations around them lie in the Soviet sphere and all are subject in one form or another, not only to Soviet influence but to a very high and increasing measure of control from Moscow. Athens alone, with its immortal glories, is free to decide its future at an election under British, French and American observation . . .

. . . If the population of the English-speaking Commonwealths be added to that of the United States, with all that such cooperation implies in the air, on the sea and in science and industry, there will be no quivering, precarious balance of power to offer its temptation to ambition or adventure. On the contrary, there will be an overwhelming assurance of security.

Source: Robert Rhodes James (ed.) (1974) *Winston S. Churchill: His Complete Speeches 1897–1963, Vol. VII, 1943–49* (Langhorne: Chelsea House), pp. 7285–93.

WINSTON CHURCHILL'S SPEECH AT ZURICH UNIVERSITY ON THE SUBJECT OF A UNITED STATES OF EUROPE, 19 SEPTEMBER 1946   **Document 3**

In this extract, Churchill calls for an immediate start to be made to bringing European states closer together. The underlying theme was that Britain would be 'with Europe' but not 'of Europe'.

And what is the plight to which Europe has been reduced? Some of the smaller States have indeed made a good recovery, but over wide areas a vast, quivering mass of tormented, hungry, care-worn and bewildered human beings gape at the ruins of their cities and homes, and scan the dark horizons for the approach of some new peril, tyranny or terror . . .

Yet all the while there is a remedy which, if it were generally and spontaneously adopted, would as if by miracle transform the whole scene and would in a few years make all Europe, or the greater part of it, as free and as happy as Switzerland is today. What is this sovereign remedy? It is to recreate the European family, or as much of it as we can, and provide it with a structure under which it can dwell in peace, in safety and in freedom. We must build a kind of United States of Europe . . .

. . . The first step in the re-creation of the European family must be a partnership between France and Germany. In this way only can France recover the moral leadership of Europe. There can be no revival of Europe without a spiritually great France and spiritually great Germany. The structure of the United States of Europe, if well and truly built, will be such as to make the material strength of a single state less important. Small nations will count as much as large ones and gain their honour by their contribution to the common cause . . .

. . . In all this urgent work, France and Germany must take the lead together. Great Britain, the British Commonwealth of Nations, mighty America and I trust Soviet Russia – for then indeed all would be well – must be the friends and sponsors of the new Europe and must champion its right to live and shine.

Source: Randolph S. Churchill (ed.) (1948) *The Sinews of Peace. Post-War Speeches by Winston S. Churchill* (London: Cassell), pp. 198–202.

Document 4   THE MARSHALL PLAN. SPEECH BY THE US SECRETARY OF STATE GENERAL GEORGE MARSHALL AT HARVARD UNIVERSITY, 5 JUNE 1947

The Marshall Plan provided the framework for over $13 billion of financial assistance from the United States.

. . . The truth of the matter is that Europe's requirements for the next three or four years of foreign food and other essential products – principally from America – are so much greater than her present ability to pay that she must have substantial additional help or face economic, social and political deterioration of a very grave character . . .

   . . . It is logical that the United States should do whatever it is able to do to assist in the return of normal economic health in the world, without which there can be no political stability and no assured peace. Our policy is not directed against any country or doctrine but against hunger, poverty, desperation and chaos. Its purpose should be the revival of a working economy in the world so as to permit the emergence of political and social conditions in which free institutions can exist . . .

Source: Department of State Bulletin, 15 June 1947, pp. 1159–60.

Document 5   THE BEVIN SPEECH ON WESTERN UNION. EXTRACT FROM AN ADDRESS BY BRITISH FOREIGN SECRETARY ERNEST BEVIN, HOUSE OF COMMONS, 22 JANUARY 1948

This document demonstrates the desire of the British government to find a suitable post-war foreign policy. British policy-makers considered the nation's position was best served by close association with the US.

It must be recognised that the Soviet Government has formed a solid political and economic block behind a line running from the Baltic along the Oder, through Trieste to the Black Sea . . .

   I believe therefore that we should seek to form with the backing of the Americans and the Dominions a Western democratic system comprising, if

possible, Scandinavia, the Low Countries, France, Portugal, Italy and Greece
. . . I believe therefore that the moment is ripe for a consolidation of Western
Europe. This need not take the shape of a formal alliance, though we have
an alliance with France and may conclude one with other countries. It
does, however, mean close consultation with each of the Western European
countries, beginning with economic questions. We in Britain can no longer
stand outside Europe and insist that our problems and position are quite
separate from those of our European neighbours . . .

Provided we can organise a Western European system such as I have
outlined above, backed by the power and resources of the Commonwealth
and of the Americas, it should be possible to develop our own power and
influence to equal that of the United States and the USSR. We have the material resources in the Colonial Empire, if we develop them, and by giving a
spiritual lead now we should be able to carry out our task in a way which
will show clearly that we are not subservient to the United States of America
or to the Soviet Union.

Source: 'The first aim of British foreign policy', Cabinet Memorandum by the Secretary
of State for Foreign Affairs, Ernest Bevin, 4 January 1948, CAB 129/23, Public Record
Office.

TREATY OF ECONOMIC, SOCIAL AND CULTURAL COLLABORATION AND   **Document 6**
COLLECTIVE SELF-DEFENCE BETWEEN THE UNITED KINGDOM OF GREAT
BRITAIN AND NORTHERN IRELAND, BELGIUM, FRANCE, LUXEMBOURG AND
THE NETHERLANDS (THE BRUSSELS TREATY), BRUSSELS, 17 MARCH 1948

*The Brussels Treaty committed Britain, France and the Benelux countries to a
common defence system and to strengthen their relationship with each other so
that they would be able to overcome threats to their security, including those
of an ideological, political or military nature.*

Article IV
If any of the High Contracting Parties should be the object of an armed attack
in Europe, the other High Contracting Parties will, in accordance with the
provisions of Article 51 of the Charter of the United Nations, afford the Party
so attacked all the military and other aid and assistance in their power.

Source: http://www.nato.int/docu/basictxt/b480317a.htm.

Document 7   THE NORTH ATLANTIC TREATY, WASHINGTON DC, 4 APRIL 1949

A desire to establish a common defence system had been set out in the 1948 Brussels Treaty, although the start of the Berlin blockade in the summer of 1948 accelerated the momentum. The Treaty entered into force in August 1949, with the commitment to collective defence being embodied in Article 5.

Article 5

The Parties agree that an armed attack against one or more of them in Europe or North America shall be considered an attack against them all and consequently they agree that, if such an attack occurs, each of them, in exercise of the right of individual or collective self-defence recognised by Article 51 of the Charter of the United Nations, will assist the Party or Parties so attacked by taking forthwith, individually and in concert with the other Parties, such action as it deems necessary, including the use of armed force, to restore and maintain the security of the North Atlantic area.

Source: http://www.nato.int/docu/basictxt/treaty.htm.

Document 8   THE STATUTE OF THE COUNCIL OF EUROPE, 5 MAY 1949

The Council of Europe was established on an intergovernmental principle for the purpose of building peace.

Article 1

(a)   The aim of the Council of Europe is to achieve a greater unity between its Members for the purpose of safeguarding and realising the ideals and principles which are their common heritage and facilitating their economic and social progress.

(b)   This aim shall be pursued through the organs of the Council by discussion of questions of common concern and by agreements and common action in economic, social, cultural, scientific, legal and administrative matters and in the maintenance and further realisation of human rights and fundamental freedoms.

(c)   Participation in the Council of Europe shall not affect the collaboration of its members in the work of the United Nations and of other international organisations or unions to which they are parties.

(d)   Matters relating to national defence do not fall within the scope of the Council of Europe.

Source: The Statute of the Council of Europe, 5 May 1949, http://conventions.coe.int/treaty/en/treaties/html/001.htm, Council of Europe.

THE SCHUMAN DECLARATION. STATEMENT BY THE FRENCH FOREIGN
MINISTER ROBERT SCHUMAN ON POOLING THE PRODUCTION OF COAL
AND STEEL IN EUROPE, PARIS, 9 MAY 1950

Document 9

*Robert Schuman's plan provided the basis for the establishment of the European
Coal and Steel Community (ECSC).*

The French Government proposes that Franco-German production of coal
and steel be placed under a common 'high authority', within an organisation
open to the participation of the other European nations.

The pooling of coal and steel production will immediately ensure the
establishment of common bases for economic development as a first step in
the federation of Europe, and will change the destinies of those regions
which have long been devoted to the manufacture of arms, to which they
themselves were the constant victims.

The common production thus established will make it plain that any war
between France and Germany becomes not only unthinkable but materially
impossible. The establishment of this powerful entity, open to all countries
willing to take part, and eventually capable of making available on equal
terms the fundamental elements of industrial production, will give a real
foundation to their economic unification . . .

By pooling basic production and by creating a new high authority whose
decisions will be binding on France, Germany and the other countries that may
subsequently join, these proposals will lay the first concrete foundation for a
European Federation which is so indispensable to the preservation of peace . . .

Source: The Schuman Declaration, http://ec.europa.eu, © European Union, 1995–2010.

THE PLEVEN PLAN. STATEMENT BY THE FRENCH PRIME MINISTER, RENÉ
PLEVEN, AT THE FRENCH NATIONAL ASSEMBLY ON THE CREATION OF A
EUROPEAN ARMY, 24 OCTOBER 1950

Document 10

*The Pleven Plan's proposal for a European Defence Community (EDC) created
some controversy because it noted that a rearmed Germany could contribute
units to a defence force.*

The French Government believed that, if the coal and steel plan succeeded,
people would become more used to the idea of a European Community
before the extremely delicate issue of common defence was approached. World
events leave it no option. Therefore, confident as it is that Europe's destiny
lies in peace and convinced that all the peoples of Europe need a sense of
collective security, the French Government proposes to resolve this issue by
the same methods and in the same spirit.

. . .

We hope that the signature of the coal and steel plan will very soon seal the agreement of the six participating countries, which will give all the peoples of Europe a guarantee that Western European coal and steel industries cannot be used for aggressive purposes.

As soon as the Plan has been signed, the French Government wants to see a solution to the question of Germany's contribution to the creation of a European force that takes heed of the cruel lessons of the past and looks forward to the kind of future that so many Europeans from all countries hope to see in Europe.

It proposes the creation, for the purposes of common defence, of a European army tied to the political institutions of a united Europe.

. . .

A European army cannot be created simply placing national military units side by side, since, in practice, this would merely mask a coalition of the old sort. Tasks that can be tackled only in common must be matched by common institutions. A united European army, made up of forces from the various European nations must, as far as possible, pool all of its human and material components under a single political and military European authority.

The Member Governments would appoint a Minister for Defence who would be accountable, in a manner yet to be determined, to those appointing him and to a European Assembly. . . .

The contingents provided by the participating countries would be incorporated in the European army, at the level of the smallest possible unit.

The European army would be financed from a common budget. The European Minister for Defence would be tasked with implementing existing international undertakings and negotiating and implementing new international undertakings on the basis of directives from the Council of Ministers. The European armaments and equipment programme would be adopted and conducted under his authority.

Participant states that already have national forces would retain their authority over those of their existing forces that were not incorporated into the European army.

The European Minister for Defence would be responsible for ensuring that the member countries of the European Community furnish this common army with the contingents, equipment, materials and supplies that they are required to supply.

Source: Déclaration du Gouverneur Français René Pleven le 24 Octobre 1950, *Journal Officiel de la République Française*, 10, pp. 7118–19 (1950), Translated by the CVCE. http://www.ena.lu/statement_rene_pleven_establishment_european_army_24_october_ 1950–2-30110 © Translation Centre Virtuel de la Connaissance sur l'Europe (CVCE).

———————◄◉►———————

TREATY ESTABLISHING THE EUROPEAN COAL AND STEEL COMMUNITY, **Document 11**
PARIS, 18 APRIL 1951 (TREATY OF PARIS)

The Treaty of Paris signified the first crucial step on the path to European economic and political integration.

Preamble
THE PRESIDENT OF THE FEDERAL REPUBLIC OF GERMANY, HIS ROYAL HIGHNESS THE PRINCE ROYAL OF BELGIUM, THE PRESIDENT OF THE FRENCH REPUBLIC, THE PRESIDENT OF THE ITALIAN REPUBLIC, HER ROYAL HIGHNESS THE GRAND DUCHESS OF LUXEMBOURG, HER MAJESTY THE QUEEN OF THE NETHERLANDS,

CONSIDERING that world peace can be safeguarded only by creative efforts commensurate with the dangers that threaten it,

CONVINCED that the contribution which an organised and vital Europe can make to civilisation is indispensable to the maintenance of peaceful relations,

RECOGNISING that Europe can be built only through practical achievements which will first of all create real solidarity, and through the establishment of common bases for economic development,

ANXIOUS to help, by expanding their basic production, to raise the standard of living and further the works of peace,

RESOLVED to substitute for age-old rivalries the merging of their essential interests; to create, by establishing an economic community, the basis for a broader and deeper community among peoples long divided by bloody conflicts; and to lay the foundations for institutions which will give direction to a destiny henceforward shared,

HAVE DECIDED to create a European Coal and Steel Community . . .

Source: Treaty of Paris, http://ec.europa.eu, © European Union, 1995–2010.

THE EUROPEAN DEFENCE COMMUNITY TREATY, PARIS, 27 MAY 1952 **Document 12**

The European Defence Community Treaty was an ambitious plan that sought to establish a defence commitment at a time when no progress had been made in establishing the political institutional framework that such a commitment would require.

Article 1
The High Contracting Parties, by the Present Treaty, set up among themselves a European Defence Community, supranational in character, comprising common institutions, common Armed Forces, and a common budget.

Article 2

1.   The objectives of the Community are exclusively defensive.

2.   Consequently, under the conditions set forth in this Treaty, it shall ensure the security of member states against any aggression by taking part in Western defence within the framework of the North Atlantic Treaty; by integrating the defence forces of the member states; and by the rational and economical employment of their resources.

3.   Any armed attack against any of the member states in Europe or against the Europe Defence Forces shall be considered an armed attack on all member states.

The member states and the European Defence Forces shall afford to the State or forces so attacked all the military aid in their power.

Source: http://www.ena.lu/treaty_instituting_european_defence_community_paris_27_1952-2-793 (translated).

Document 13   THE MESSINA DECLARATION. RESOLUTION ADOPTED BY THE MINISTERS OF FOREIGN AFFAIRS OF THE MEMBER STATES OF THE ECSC, MESSINA, 1–2 JUNE 1955

The Messina conference established an intergovernmental committee under the chairmanship of Paul-Henri Spaak, the report of which provided the basis for the two Treaties establishing the European Economic Community (EEC) and the European Atomic Energy Community (Euratom).

The Governments of the Federal Republic of Germany, Belgium, France, Italy, Luxembourg and the Netherlands believe the time has come to make a fresh advance towards the building of Europe. They are of the opinion that this must be achieved, first of all, in the economic field.

They consider that it is necessary to work for the establishment of a united Europe by the development of common institutions, the progressive fusion of national economies, the creation of a common market and the progressive harmonisation of their social policies.

I

To these ends, the six Ministers have agreed on the following objectives:

A.   1.   The expansion of trade and the freedom of movement call for the joint development of the major channels of communication.

A joint study will accordingly be undertaken of development plans based on the establishment of a European network of canals, motor highways, electrified railways, and on a standardisation of equipment, as well as a study of possible means of achieving a better coordination of air transport . . .

2. The development of atomic energy for peaceful purposes will in the near future open up the prospect of a new industrial revolution out of all proportion to that which has taken place over the last hundred years. The six signatory States consider that it is necessary to study the creation of a common organisation to be entrusted with the responsibility and the means for ensuring the peaceful development of atomic energy, while taking into account the special arrangements made by certain Governments with third countries . . .

B. The six governments recognise that the establishment of a European market, free from all customs duties and all quantitative restrictions, is the objective of their action in the field of economic policy . . .

C. The creation of a European Investment Fund will be studied. The objective of this fund would be the joint development of European economic potentialities and in particular the development of the less developed regions of the participating states.

D. As regards the social field, the six governments consider it essential to study the progressive harmonisation of the regulations in force in the different countries, notably those which concern working hours, overtime rates (night work, Sunday work and public holidays) and the length and rates of pay for holidays . . .

Source: S. Patijn (ed.) (1970) *Landmarks in European Unity: 22 Texts on European Integration* (Leiden: A.W. Sijthoff), pp. 93–9.

THE TREATY OF ROME ESTABLISHING THE EUROPEAN ECONOMIC COMMUNITY, ROME, 25 MARCH 1957 **Document 14**

The EEC Treaty set out the main principles of the common market, established a customs union and a common external tariff, as well as a range of other Community policies, such as agriculture, transport and competition.

Article 2
The Community shall have as its aim, by establishing a common market and progressively approximating the economic policies of member states, to promote throughout the Community a harmonious development of economic activities, a continuous and balanced expansion, an increase in stability, an

accelerated raising of the standard of living and closer relations between its member states.

Article 3

For the purposes set out in Article 2, the activities of the Community shall include, as provided in this Treaty and in accordance with the timetable set out therein:

(a) the elimination, as between member states, of customs duties and of quantitative restrictions on the import and export of goods, and of all other measures having equivalent effect;

(b) the establishment of a common customs tariff and of a common commercial policy towards third countries;

(c) the abolition, as between member states, of obstacles to freedom of movement for persons, services and capital;

(d) the adoption of a common agricultural policy;

(e) the adoption of a common transport policy;

(f) the establishment of a system ensuring that competition in the common market is not distorted;

(g) the application of procedures by which the economic policies of member states can be coordinated and disequilibria in their balances of payments remedied;

(h) the approximation of the laws of member states to the extent required for the proper functioning of the common market;

(i) the creation of a European Social Fund in order to improve employment opportunities for workers and to contribute to the raising of their standard of living;

(j) the establishment of a European Investment Bank to facilitate the economic expansion of the Community by opening up fresh resources;

(k) the association of the overseas countries and territories in order to increase trade and to promote economic and social development.

Article 9

1. The Community shall be based upon a customs union which shall cover all trade in goods and which shall involve the prohibition between member states of customs duties on imports and exports and of all charges having equivalent effect, and the adoption of a common customs tariff in their relations with third countries . . .

Article 38

1. The common market shall extend to agriculture and trade in agricultural products . . .

4.   The operation and development of the common market for agricultural products must be accompanied by the establishment of a common agricultural policy among the member states.

Article 48

1.   Freedom of movement for workers shall be secured within the Community by the end of the transitional period at the latest.

Article 92

1.   Save as otherwise provided in this Treaty, any aid granted by a Member State or through State resources in any form whatsoever which distorts or threatens to distort competition by favouring certain enterprises or the production of certain goods shall, insofar as it affects trade between member states, be incompatible with the common market . . .

Article 237

Any European State may apply to become a member of the Community. It shall address its application to the Council, which shall act unanimously after consulting the Commission . . .

Source: The Treaty of Rome, http://ec.europa.eu, © European Union, 1995–2010.

BRITAIN'S FIRST APPLICATION FOR EEC MEMBERSHIP   **Document 15**

The British government set out a series of conditions that had to be met if it was to enter the Community (a), and in so doing marked a shift in focus away from the Commonwealth and Empire towards Europe (b).

(a)

. . . No British Government could join the European Economic Community without prior negotiation with a view to meeting the needs of the Commonwealth countries, of our European Free Trade Association partners, and of British agriculture . . .

During the past nine months, we have had useful and frank discussions with the European Economic Community Governments. We have now reached the stage where we cannot make further progress without entering into formal negotiations . . .

Therefore, after long and earnest consideration, Her Majesty's Government have come to the conclusion that it would be right for Britain to make a formal application under Article 237 of the Treaty negotiations with a view to joining the Community if satisfactory arrangements can be made to meet the special needs of the United Kingdom, of the Commonwealth and of the European Free Trade Association . . .

Source: Extracted from statement by Harold Macmillan on the first British application to the European Economic Community, *Parliamentary Debates* (Hansard), House of Commons, Fifth Series, Vol. 645, pp. 928–31.

(b)

The decision of Harold Macmillan's government to apply for membership of the European Community represented an historic moment in post-war politics. . . . It signalled the end of a glorious era, that of the British Empire, and the beginning of a whole new chapter of British history. The 'three circles' concept, to which Anthony Eden devoted his speech at the Conservative Party conference at Margate in 1953, and which had been the mainstay of British foreign policy since the war, was no longer valid. Eden described Britain then as being at the centre of three circles: the United States, the Commonwealth and Europe. Theoretically, this gave Britain an all-powerful position in world affairs. In actual fact, even by that time this was no longer justifiable. . .

Source: Edward Heath (1998) *The Course of My Life* (London: Hodder & Stoughton), p. 203.

Document 16　FRANCE'S REJECTION OF UK EEC MEMBERSHIP. PRESS STATEMENT BY FRENCH PRESIDENT CHARLES DE GAULLE, 14 JANUARY 1963

This is an extract of General de Gaulle's speech which cast a veto against the UK's first application for EEC membership.

. . . England is, in effect, insular, maritime, linked through its trade, markets, and food supply to very diverse and often very distant countries. Its activities are essentially industrial and commercial, and only slightly agricultural. It has, throughout its work, very marked and original customs and traditions. In short, the nature, structure, and economic context of England differ profoundly from those of the other States of the Continent . . .

It is foreseeable that the cohesion of all its members, who would be very numerous and very diverse, would not hold for long and that in the end there would appear a colossal Atlantic Community dependent on the US and under American leadership which would soon completely swallow up the European Community.

Source: Charles de Gaulle (1970) *Discours et Messages, Pour l'effort Août 1962 – Décembre 1965* (Paris: Librairie Plon), pp. 66–70 (translated).

THE FRANCO-GERMAN TREATY OF FRIENDSHIP, PARIS, 22 JANUARY 1963 **Document 17**

The Franco-German Treaty focuses on three main areas: the holding of regular summits and meetings of foreign ministers, cooperation within the realm of defence and security (which was for many years of a limited nature) and education.

II PROGRAMME

A. *Foreign Affairs*

1. The two Governments shall consult each other, prior to any decision, on all important questions of foreign policy, and particularly on questions of mutual interest, with a view to achieving as far as possible an analogous position. Such consultations shall cover, *inter alia*, the following subjects:
    - Problems concerning the European communities and European political cooperation;
    - East–West relations, in both the political and the economic fields;
    - Matters dealt with in the North Atlantic Treaty Organisation and the various international organisations which are of interest to the two Governments, particularly in the Council of Europe, the Western European Union, the Organisation for Economic Co-operation and Development, the United Nations and its specialised agencies.

Source: 1963: A Retrospective of the Political Year in Europe (Paris: WEU Assembly, 1964).

THE MERGER TREATY. TREATY ESTABLISHING A SINGLE COUNCIL AND A SINGLE COMMISSION OF THE EUROPEAN COMMUNITIES, BRUSSELS, 8 APRIL 1965 **Document 18**

The desire to establish a common Council of Ministers and a Commission that served all three Communities was regarded as an essential step towards European integration. The Treaty came into force on 1 July 1967.

THE COUNCIL OF THE EUROPEAN COMMUNITIES

Article 1

A Council of the European Communities (hereinafter called the 'Council') is hereby established. This Council shall take the place of the Special Council of Ministers of the European Coal and Steel Community, the Council of the European Economic Community and the Council of the Atomic Energy Community.

It shall exercise the powers and jurisdiction conferred on those institutions in accordance with the provisions of the Treaties establishing the European Coal and Steel Community, the European Economic Community and the European Atomic Energy Community, and of this Treaty.

THE COMMISSION OF THE EUROPEAN COMMUNITIES

Article 9

A Commission of the European Communities (hereinafter called the 'Commission') is hereby established. The Commission shall take the place of the High Authority of the European Coal and Steel Community, the Commission of the European Economic Community and the Commission of the European Atomic Energy Community.

It shall exercise the powers and the jurisdiction on those institutions in accordance with the provisions of the Treaties establishing the European Coal and Steel Community, the European Economic Community and the European Atomic Energy Community, and of this Treaty.

Source: The Merger Treaty, http://ec.europa.eu, © European Union, 1995–2010.

Document 19   THE LUXEMBOURG COMPROMISE. AGREEMENT ON DECISION-MAKING REACHED AT THE EXTRAORDINARY SESSION OF THE LUXEMBOURG EEC COUNCIL, 28–29 JANUARY 1966

This is an extract from the Luxembourg Compromise which resolved the 1965 'empty chair crisis'.

Majority voting procedure

I.   Where, in the case of decisions which may be taken by a majority vote on a proposal of the Commission, very important interests of one or more partners are at stake, the Members of the Council will endeavour, within a reasonable time, to reach solutions which can be adopted by all the Members of the Council while respecting their mutual interests and those of the Community, in accordance with Article 2 of the Treaty.

II. With regard to the preceding paragraph, the French delegation considers that where very important interests are at stake the discussion must be continued until unanimous agreement is reached.

Source: Bulletin of the European Economic Community, No. 3, pp. 8–9 (1966), © European Union 1966.

UK SECOND APPLICATION FOR EEC MEMBERSHIP. STATEMENT BY PRIME MINISTER HAROLD WILSON ON THE SECOND APPLICATION FOR MEMBERSHIP OF THE EUROPEAN ECONOMIC COMMUNITY, HOUSE OF COMMONS, LONDON, 2 MAY 1967 **Document 20**

The second UK application reflected a general feeling that another failure could not be risked, not least because its economic fortunes had declined throughout the 1960s.

First, there are the problems associated with the operation of the common agricultural policy of the Community – the problems of its potential effects on the cost of living and on the structure and well-being of British agriculture; problems of the budgetary and balance of payments implications of its system of financing; and certain Commonwealth problems with which I will deal in a moment . . .

There are also highly important Commonwealth interests, mainly in the field of agriculture, for which it is our duty to seek safeguards in the negotiations. These include, in particular, the special problems of New Zealand and of Commonwealth sugar-producing countries, whose needs are at present safeguarded by the Commonwealth Sugar Agreement . . .

We do not see European unity as something narrow or inward-looking. Britain has her own vital links through the Commonwealth, and in other ways, with other continents. So have other European countries. . . .

Source: Parliamentary Debates (Hansard), House of Commons, Fifth Series, Vol. 746, pp. 310–14.

THE HAGUE SUMMIT. FINAL COMMUNIQUÉ OF THE MEETING OF HEADS OF STATE AND GOVERNMENT OF THE EC COUNTRIES, THE HAGUE, 2 DECEMBER 1969 **Document 21**

The Hague summit had the triple objective of completion, consolidation and enlargement of the communities. Two important reports emanated from the meeting, one on monetary union (Werner Report) and the other on political union (Davignon Report).

8. They have reaffirmed their readiness to expedite the further action needed to strengthen the Community and promote its development into an economic union. They are of the opinion that the integration process should result in a Community of stability and growth. To this end they agreed that, within the Council, on the basis of the memorandum

presented by the Commission on 12 February 1969, and in close collaboration with the latter, a plan in stages will be worked out during 1970 with a view to the creation of an economic and monetary union.

13. They reaffirmed their agreement on the principle of enlargement of the Community, in accordance with Article 237 of the Treaty of Rome.

In so far as the applicant States accept the Treaties and their political aims, the decisions taken since the entry into force of the Treaties and the options adopted in the sphere of development, the Heads of State or Government have indicated their agreement to the opening of negotiations between the Community on the one hand and the applicant States on the other.

15. They instructed the Ministers for Foreign Affairs to study the best way of achieving progress in the matter of political unification, within the context of enlargement. The Ministers are to make proposals to this effect by the end of July 1970 . . .

Source: Bulletin of the European Economic Community, No. 1, pp. 11–16 (1970), © European Union 1970.

Document 22   THE WERNER REPORT. CONCLUSIONS FROM THE REPORT OF THE AD HOC COMMITTEE HEADED BY PIERRE WERNER ON THE REALISATION BY STAGES OF ECONOMIC AND MONETARY UNION IN THE COMMUNITY, LUXEMBOURG, OCTOBER 1970

The October 1970 Werner Report outlined a three-stage process for the creation of a monetary union by 1980. The report helped to inspire initiatives such as the 1971 European currency management system (the 'Snake').

A. Economic and monetary union is an objective realisable in the course of the present decade provided only that the political will of the member states to realise this objective, as solemnly declared at the Conference at The Hague, is present . . .

B. Economic and monetary union means that the principal decisions of economic policy will be taken at Community level and therefore that the necessary powers will be transferred from the national plane to the Community plane. These transfers of responsibility and the creation of the corresponding Community institutions represent a process of fundamental political significance which entails the progressive development of political cooperation . . .

C. A monetary union implies, internally, the total and irreversibly convertibility of currencies, the elimination of margins of fluctuation in rates of exchange, the irrevocable fixing of parity ratios and the total liberation of movements of capital . . .

D. On the institutional plane, in the final stage, two Community organs are indispensable: a centre of decision for economic policy and a Community system for the central banks . . .

E. . . . the development of monetary unification will have to be combined with parallel progress towards the harmonisation and finally the unification of economic policies.

F. At this stage the laying down of a precise and concrete timetable for the whole of the plane by stages does not seem feasible . . . Particular emphasis should therefore be placed on the first stage, for which a package of concrete measures is presented. The decisions on the details of the final stages and the future timetable will have to be taken at the end of the first stage.

G. The first stage will commence on 1 January 1971 and will cover a period of three years . . .

Source: Bulletin of the European Economic Community, Supplement 11, pp. 26–9 (1970), © European Union 1970.

THE DAVIGNON REPORT. REPORT ON THE PROBLEMS OF POLITICAL   **Document 23**
UNIFICATION PREPARED BY THE DAVIGNON COMMITTEE AND ADOPTED
BY THE FOREIGN MINISTERS OF THE EC MEMBER STATES, LUXEMBOURG,
27 OCTOBER 1970

The Davignon Report recommended the establishment of a European Political Co-operation (EPC) arrangement to facilitate foreign policy harmonisation and co-ordination among member states.

PART ONE

1. The Foreign Ministers of the member states of the European Communities were instructed by the Heads of State or Government meeting at The Hague on 1 and 2 December 1969 'to study the best way of achieving progress in the matter of political unification, within the context of enlargement' of the European Communities . . .

7. The first fact is that, in line with the spirit of the Preambles of the Treaties of Paris and Rome, tangible form should be given to the will for a political union, which has always been a force for the progress of the European Communities.

8. The second fact is that the implementation of the common policies being introduced or already in force requires corresponding developments in the specifically political sphere, so as to bring nearer the day

when Europeans can speak with one voice. Hence the importance of Europe being built by successive stages and the gradual development of the method and instruments best calculated to allow a common political course of action.

9. The third and final fact is that Europe must prepare itself to discharge the imperative world duties entailed by its greater cohesion and increasing role.

10. Current developments in the European Communities make it necessary for the member states to step up their political cooperation and, in the initial stage, to provide themselves with ways and means of harmonising their views in the field of international politics.

The Ministers therefore felt that foreign-policy concentration should be the object of the first practical endeavours to demonstrate to all that Europe has a political vocation . . .

Source: Bulletin of the European Economic Community, No. 11, pp. 9–12 (1970), © European Union 1970.

———◀●▶———

Document 24   EUROPEAN MONETARY COOPERATION: THE SNAKE. RESOLUTION OF THE COUNCIL OF MINISTERS, BRUSSELS, 21 MARCH 1972

This was an agreement by member states to narrow the margin of fluctuation of their currencies against the US dollar by 1.25 per cent on either side, with the tunnel being the limit to which currencies could fluctuate while the 'Snake' referred to the line that currencies created as they increased and decreased.

1. As a first step towards the establishment of a distinct monetary zone within the framework of the international system, the Council urges the Central Banks of the member states to reduce progressively, while making full use of the fluctuation margins allowed by the IMF on a world plane, the gap existing at any given moment between the exchange rates of the strongest and the weakest currencies of the member states.

   To this end, for a period during which these procedures will be tested, the Central Banks are asked to intervene on their respective foreign-exchange markets in accordance with the following principles:

   (a) As from a date to be fixed by the Governors of the Central Banks, interventions shall be effected in Community currencies, on the basis of the margins recorded on the market at that date;

   (b) As these limits converge the margins mentioned under (a) above shall be narrowed down and shall no longer be widened;

(c)   By 1st July 1972 at the latest, the gap existing at any given time between the currencies of two member states may not exceed 2.25 per cent.

Source: Bulletin of the European Communities, No. 4, pp. 43–4 (1972), © European Union 1972.

————◄●►————

ESTABLISHING THE EUROPEAN COUNCIL. FINAL COMMUNIQUÉ OF THE MEETING OF HEADS OF GOVERNMENT OF THE COMMUNITY (PARIS, 9 AND 10 DECEMBER 1974)   **Document 25**

The 1974 Paris summit established a European Council comprising Heads of State or Government of the member states (assisted by their Foreign Minister) and the President of the European Commission.

Communiqué (extracts)

1.   The Heads of Government of the nine States of the Community, the Ministers of Foreign Affairs and the President of the Commission, meeting in Paris at the invitation of the French President, examined the various problems confronting Europe. They took note of the reports drawn up by the Ministers of Foreign Affairs and recorded the agreement reached by these Ministers on various points raised in the reports.
2.   Recognizing the need for an overall approach to the internal problems involved in achieving European unity and the external problems facing Europe, the Heads of Government consider it essential to ensure progress and overall consistency in the activities of the Communities and in the work on political co-operation.
3.   The Heads of Government have therefore decided to meet, accompanied by the Ministers of Foreign Affairs, three times a year and, whenever necessary, in the Council of the Communities and in the context of political co-operation.

The administrative secretariat will be provided for in an appropriate manner with due regard for existing practices and procedures.

In order to ensure consistency in Community activities and continuity of work, the Ministers of Foreign Affairs, meeting in the Council of the Community, will act as initiators and co-ordinators. They may hold political cooperation meetings at the same time. . . .

Source: Bulletin of the European Communities, No. 12, © European Communities, 1974.

————◄●►————

Document 26   THE TINDEMANS REPORT ON EUROPEAN UNION. EXTRACTS FROM
BELGIAN PRIME MINISTER LEO TINDEMAN'S LETTER TO HIS EUROPEAN
COLLEAGUES, BRUSSELS, 29 DECEMBER 1975

*The Tindemans Report analysed the ways in which a more integrated Europe
could be achieved that was also closer to the citizen. This included proposals
to reduce the number of Commissioners and a move away from unanimity voting to qualified majority voting.*

For me, European Union is a new phase in the history of the unification of
Europe, which can only be achieved by a continuous process. Consequently,
it is difficult to lay down, at this stage, the date of completion of the European
Union. It will only achieve its objectives by means of institutions which have
been strengthened and improved that the Union will be able to give increasing
expression to its own dynamism. In this respect, the role of a directly-elected
European Parliament will be decisive in the development of the Union.
Finally, I am convinced of the need, in 1980, to assess what we have already
achieved so as to open up new prospects and make further progress . . .

Source: *Bulletin of the European Communities*, Supplement No. 1, pp. 14–22 (1976)
© European Union, 1976.

Document 27   ESTABLISHMENT OF THE EUROPEAN MONETARY SYSTEM. RESOLUTION OF
THE EUROPEAN COUNCIL ON THE ESTABLISHMENT OF THE EMS, BREMEN,
5 DECEMBER 1978

*This document sets out the decision of member states to establish a European
Monetary System (EMS).*

1.2   Today, after careful examination of the preparatory work done by the
Council and other Community bodies, we are agreed as follows:
A European Monetary System (EMS) will be set up on 1 January 1979.

1.3   We are firmly resolved to ensure the lasting success of the EMS by policies conducive to greater stability at home and abroad for both deficit
and surplus countries.

2.1   A European currency unit (ECU) will be at the centre of the EMS. The
value and composition of the ECU will be identical with the value of
the EUA at the outset of the system.

2.2   The ECU will be used:

(a)   as the denominator (numeraire) for the exchange rate mechanism;

(b)   as the basis for a divergence indicator;

(c)   as the denominator for operations in both the intervention and
the credit mechanisms;

(d)   as a means of settlement between monetary authorities of the European Community.

3.1   Each country will have an ECU-related central rate. These central rates will be used to establish a grid of bilateral exchange rates.

Around these exchange rate fluctuation margins of +/−2.25 per cent will be established. EEC countries with presently floating currencies may opt for wider margins up to +/−6 per cent at the outset of the EMS: these margins should be gradually reduced as soon as economic conditions permit.

A Member State which does not participate in the exchange rate mechanism at the outset may participate at a later date . . .

3.4   Intervention in the participating countries is compulsory when the intervention points defined by the fluctuation margins are reached.

Source: © ECSC – EEC – EAEC, Brussels-Luxembourg, 1979, source: Compendium of Community Monetary Texts, 1979.

THE EEC COURT OF JUSTICE AND THE FREE MOVEMENT OF GOODS. THE CASSIS DE DIJON DECISION, LUXEMBOURG, 20 FEBRUARY 1979   **Document 28**

The European Court of Justice ruled that it was not possible for restrictions to be imposed on a product lawfully manufactured and on sale in one member state when it was imported into another member state so long as basic health and safety standards were met.

14.   It is clear from the foregoing that the requirements relating to the minimum alcohol content of alcoholic beverages do not serve a purpose which is in the general interest and such as to take precedence over the requirements of the free movement of goods, which constitutes one of the fundamental rules of the Community.

. . . There is therefore no valid reason why, provided that they have been lawfully produced and marketed in one of the member states, alcoholic beverages should not be introduced into any other Member State; the sale of such products may not be subject to a legal prohibition on the marketing of beverages with an alcohol content lower than the limit set by the national rules.

Source: *Report of Cases before the Court*, Part 1, case 120/78, pp. 660–5 (judgement of the Court of 20 February 1979), © European Union, http://eur-lex.europa.eu/.

Document 29   BRITISH BUDGET PROBLEM

These documents reflect on the British budget question which Margaret Thatcher's government sought to resolve (a). Thatcher regularly approached this issue in a combative style (b). A suitable agreement was finally reached at the Fontainebleau European Council of 25–26 June 1984.

(a)

In spite of North Sea oil, by 1979 Britain had become one of the least prosperous members of the Community, with only the seventh highest GDP per head of population among the member states. Yet we were expected shortly to become the largest net contributor.

So from the first my policy was to seek to limit the damage and distortions caused by the CAP and to bring financial realities to bear on Community spending.

Source: Margaret Thatcher (1993) *The Downing Street Years* (London: HarperCollins), p. 63.

(b)

The Council started at 3.40 . . . There was a certain amount of routine stuff . . . Then into the budget question about 6 o'clock, introduced briefly by me. Mrs. Thatcher did quite well for once, a bit shrill as usual, but not excessively so. There was quite a good initial response . . . Then towards the end Mrs. Thatcher got the question bogged down by being far too demanding. Her mistake, which fed on itself subsequently at dinner and indeed the next morning, arose out of her having only one of the three necessary qualities of a great advocate. She has nerve and determination to win, but she certainly does not have a good understanding of the case against her (which was based on the own-resources theory, of theology if you like), which means that the constantly reiterated cry of 'It's my money I want back' strikes an insistently jarring note . . . She also lacks the third quality, which is that of not boring the judge or jury, and she bored everybody endlessly by only understanding about four of the fourteen or so points on the British side and repeating each of them twenty-seven times.

Source: Roy Jenkins (1989) *European Diary*, 1977–1981 (London: Collins), pp. 528–9.

THE SINGLE EUROPEAN ACT **Document 30**

The Single European Act provided for several areas of reform including the creation of an internal market (a) Britain expressed concerns over plans to increase the powers of the Commission and extend the scope of Community policy-making (b).

(a)
'Article 8A

The Community shall adopt measures with the aim of progressively establishing the internal market over a period expiring on 31 December 1992, . . .

The internal market shall comprise an area without internal frontiers in which the free movement of goods, persons, services and capital is ensured in accordance with the provisions of this Treaty.'

Source: Single European Act, http://ec.europa.eu, © European Union, 1995–2010.

(b)

The fruits of what would be called the Single European Act were good for Britain. At last, I felt, we were going to get the Community back on course, concentrating on its role as a huge market, with all the opportunities that would bring to our industries . . . The trouble was . . . that the new powers the Commission received only seemed to whet its appetite.

Source: Margaret Thatcher (1993) *The Downing Street Years* (London: HarperCollins), p. 556.

COMPLETING THE INTERNAL MARKET **Document 31**

The scope and degree of implementation of internal-market legislation in member states is not wholly complete.

Member state implementation deficits of internal market laws as at 11 May 2009

Country	Ranking	Transposition deficit (%)	Number of Directives not transposed
Denmark	1	0.2	3
Malta	2	0.2	3
Bulgaria	2	0.3	5
Romania	2	0.3	5
Finland	5	0.4	6
Lithuania	6	0.4	7
Slovenia	7	0.4	7
Slovakia	7	0.4	7
Netherlands	9	0.6	9
Hungary	9	0.6	10
Sweden	11	0.6	10
Latvia	12	0.7	12
Germany	12	0.8	13
Ireland	12	0.8	13
Spain	12	0.8	13
France	16	0.8	13
Austria	17	0.9	15
Cyprus	17	1.0	16
UK	17	1.1	18
Belgium	20	1.2	20
Estonia	20	1.4	23
Luxembourg	22	1.7	27
Italy	23	1.7	28
Czech Republic	23	1.9	30
Portugal	25	2.0	32
Poland	26	2.1	33
Greece	27	2.1	34
EU average		1.0	

Source: *International Market Scoreboard*, Edition 19 (July 2009), http://ec.europa.eu, © European Union, 1995–2010.

SPEECH GIVEN BY THE BRITISH PRIME MINISTER, MARGARET THATCHER,   **Document 32**
AT THE COLLEGE OF EUROPE, BRUGES, 20 SEPTEMBER 1988

Britain's Prime Minister Margaret Thatcher was hostile to the European Commission's desire to put in place too many rules and regulations that impacted on member states.

. . . And let me be quite clear. Britain does not dream of some cosy, isolated existence on the fringes of the European Community. Our destiny is in Europe, as part of the Community . . .

. . . My first guiding principle is this: willing and active cooperation between independent sovereign states is the best way to build a successful European Community. To try to suppress nationhood and concentrate power at the centre of a European conglomerate would be highly damaging and would jeopardise the objectives we seek to achieve. Europe will be stronger precisely because it has France as France, Spain as Spain, Britain as Britain, each with its own customs, traditions and identity. It would be folly to try to fit them into some sort of Identikit European personality . . .

. . . working more closely together does not require power to be centralised in Brussels or decisions to be taken by an appointed bureaucracy . . . We have not successfully rolled back the frontiers of the state in Britain only to see them re-imposed at a European level, with a European super-state exercising a new dominance from Brussels.

Certainly we want to see Europe more united with a greater sense of common purpose. But it must be in a way which preserves the different traditions, Parliamentary powers and sense of national pride in one's own country; for these have been the source of Europe's vitality through the centuries.

Source: Margaret Thatcher (1997) *The Collected Speeches* (London: HarperCollins), pp. 315–25.

THE DELORS REPORT ON MONETARY UNION   **Document 33**

The Delors Report set out a three-stage transition to monetary union that would culminate in a single currency and a European Central Bank. In this document, the British Prime Minister Margaret Thatcher sets out her hostility towards the Delors Report.

. . . When the Delors Report finally appeared in April 1989 it confirmed our worst fears. From the beginning there had been discussion of a 'three-stage' approach, which might at least have allowed us to slow the pace and refuse to 'advance' further than the first or second stage. But the report now insisted that by embarking on the first stage the Community committed itself irrevocably to the eventual achievement of full economic and monetary union. There was a requirement for a new treaty and for work on it to start immediately. There was also plenty of material in the treaty about regional and social policy – costly, Delorism socialism on a continental scale. None of these was acceptable to me.

Source: Margaret Thatcher (1993) *The Downing Street Years* (London: HarperCollins), p. 708.

Document 34   CREATING THE SINGLE CURRENCY

To ensure member states were fit enough to participate in a single currency, a set of convergence criteria were detailed in the Treaty on European Union (a). The Protocol attached to the Treaty stated that member states should have a budget deficit not exceeding 3 per cent of GDP and a public debt not exceeding 60 per cent of GDP (b). The December 1996 Dublin European Council set out conditions of a Stability and Growth Pact that required member states to adhere to detailed fiscal and budgetary measures (c). By 2009 some 16 member states had adopted the 'euro' (d).

(a)
Article 104 (ex Article 104c)
1. Member states shall avoid excessive government deficits.
2. The Commission shall monitor the development of the budgetary situation and of the stock of government debt in the member states with a view to identifying gross errors. In particular it shall examine compliance with budgetary discipline on the basis of the following two criteria:
    a. whether the ratio of the planned or actual government deficit to gross domestic product exceeds a reference value, unless:
        •   either the ratio has declined substantially and continuously and reached a level that comes close to the reference value;
        •   or, alternatively, the excess over the reference value is only exceptional and temporary and the ratio remains close to the reference value;
    b. whether the ratio of government debt to gross domestic product exceeds a reference value, unless the ratio is sufficiently diminishing and approaching the reference value at a satisfactory pace.

The reference values are specified in the Protocol on the excessive deficit procedure annexed to this Treaty . . .

Source: The Excessive Deficit Procedure, http://eur-lex.europa.eu/, © European Union, 1998–2010. Only European Union legislation printed in the paper edition of the Official Journal of the European Union is deemed authentic.

(b)

Article 1

The reference values referred to in Article 104c(2) of this Treaty are:

- 3 per cent for the ratio of the planned or actual government deficit to gross domestic product at market prices;
- 60 per cent for the ratio of government debt to gross domestic product at market prices.

Source: Protocol (No. 5) on the Excessive Deficit Procedure, © European Union, http://eur-lex.europa.eu/.

(c)

II. Ensuring budgetary discipline in Stage 3 of EMU (Stability and Growth Pact)

18. The Treaty imposes on member states in Stage 3 of EMU an obligation to avoid excessive deficits . . .
19. To that end, the Council proposes to adopt regulations on the strengthening of surveillance and budgetary discipline and on speeding up and clarifying the excessive deficit procedure. These regulations, combined with a European Council Resolution, will constitute a Stability and Growth Pact . . . Euro area member states will be obliged to submit stability programmes and will be subject to agreed sanctions for failure to act effectively on excessive deficits.

Stability and Growth Pact: At the December 1996 Dublin European Council agreement was reached on a set of conditions that necessitated members to adhere to strict budget and fiscal policies to ensure that they could participate in the single currency.

Excessive deficit procedure

26. Adherence to the objective of sound budgetary positions close to balance or in surplus will allow a Member State to deal with normal cyclical fluctuations while keeping its government deficit within the 3 per cent reference value . . . Once it has decided that an excessive deficit persists, and as long as a Member State has failed to comply with a decision under Treaty Article (EC)104c(9), the Council will, in accordance with paragraph 11 of that Article, impose sanctions on a prescribed scale.
27. An excess of a government deficit over the 3 per cent reference value shall be considered exceptional when resulting from an unusual event outside the control of the relevant Member State and which has a major impact on the financial position of general government, or when resulting from a severe economic downturn.

Source: Stability and Growth Pact, Annex to Presidency Conclusions, Dublin European Council, 13–14 December 1996, http://www.consilium.europa.eu/, © European Union, 1996.

(d)

Countries that have adopted the euro

Year	Country
1999	Belgium, Germany, Ireland, Spain, France, Italy, Luxembourg, the Netherlands, Austria, Portugal and Finland
2001	Greece
2007	Slovenia
2008	Cyprus, Malta
2009	Slovakia

Document 35   ENLARGING THE EUROPEAN UNION

Countries wishing to join the EU have to meet certain criteria that were set out in the Copenhagen European Council of June 1993 (a). At the December 1997 Luxembourg European Council, member states further clarified what the process of enlargement would entail (b). The Community has grown from six to 27 member states, with there being three applicant states and six potential applicant states (c). The process of enlargement has resulted in the EU having a population of approximately half a billion people by 2009 (d).

(a)

Membership requires that the candidate country has achieved stability of institutions guaranteeing democracy, the rule of law, human rights and respect for and protection of minorities, the existence of a functioning market economy as well as the capacity to cope with competitive pressure and market forces within the Union. Membership presupposes the candidate's ability to take on the obligations of membership, including adherence to the aims of political, economic and monetary union.

Source: Presidency Conclusions, Copenhagen European Council, 21–22 June 1993, http://www.consilium.europa.eu/, © European Union, 1993.

(b)

10.   The European Council has considered the current situation in each of the eleven applicant States on the basis of the Commission's opinions and the Presidency's report to the Council. In the light of its discussions, it has decided to launch an accession process comprising the ten Central and East European applicant States and Cyprus. This accession process will form part of the implementation of Article 0 of the Treaty on European Union. The European Council points out that all these States are destined to join the European Union on the basis of the same

criteria and that they are participating in the accession process on an equal footing . . .

Source: Presidency Conclusions, Luxembourg European Council, December 1997, http://www.consilium.europa.eu/, © European Union, 1997.

(c)

The Six	The Nine	The Ten	The 12	The 15	The 25	The 27	Applicant countries	Potential Applicant countries
1957	1973	1981	1986	1995	2004	2007		
Belgium	Britain	Greece	Portugal	Austria	Cyprus	Bulgaria	Croatia	Albania
France	Denmark		Spain	Finland	Czech Republic	Romania	Former Yugoslav Republic of Macedonia	Bosnia and Herzegovina
West Germany	Ireland			Sweden	Estonia		Turkey	Kosovo
Italy					Hungary			Montenegro
Luxembourg					Latvia			Serbia
Netherlands					Lithuania			Iceland
					Malta			
					Poland			
					Slovakia			
					Slovenia			

(d)
Comparisons between the population of the EU and other countries, 2008

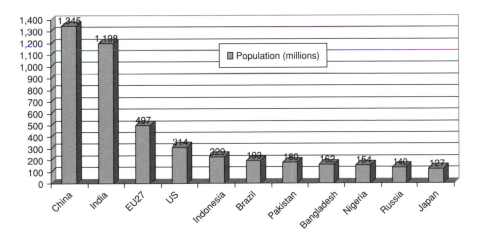

Source: World Population Prospects, The 2008 Revision, United Nations, 2009: http://www.un.org/esa/population/publications/wpp2008/wpp2008_highlights.pdf.

Document 36   COUNCIL VOTING AND EUROPEAN PARLIAMENT REPRESENTATION

The enlargement of the European Union prompted a reassessment of the weighting of votes in the Council and the distribution of seats in the European Parliament. Despite these adjustments, there is still a discrepancy in the distribution of Council votes and number of MEPs per member state.

Country	Population (millions)	Voting Weights		European Parliament Representation			
		Votes in the Council	Population per vote (millions) in the Council	5th term 1999–2004	6th term 2004–2009	7th term 2009–14	Population per MEP (millions)
Germany	82.4	29	2.84	99	99	99	0.83
France	64.057	29	2.2	87	78	72	0.88
Britain	60.776	29	2.09	87	78	72	0.84
Italy	58.147	29	2.0	87	78	72	0.80
Spain	40.448	27	1.49	64	54	50	0.80
Poland	38.518	27	1.42	0	54	50	0.77
Romania	22.276	14	1.59			33	0.67
Netherlands	16.570	13	1.27	31	27	25	0.66
Greece	10.706	12	0.89	25	24	22	0.48
Czech Republic	10.288	12	0.85	0	24	22	0.46
Belgium	10.392	12	0.86	25	24	22	0.47
Hungary	9.956	12	0.82	0	24	22	0.45
Portugal	10.642	12	0.88	25	24	22	0.48
Sweden	9.031	10	0.90	22	19	18	0.50
Austria	8.199	10	0.81	21	18	17	0.48
Bulgaria	7.322	10	0.73			17	0.43
Slovakia	5.477	7	0.78	0	14	13	0.42
Denmark	5.468	7	0.78	16	14	13	0.42
Finland	5.238	7	0.74	16	14	13	0.40
Ireland	4.109	7	0.58	15	13	12	0.34
Lithuania	3.575	7	0.51	0	13	12	0.29
Latvia	2.254	4	0.56	0	9	8	0.65
Slovenia	2.009	4	0.50	0	7	7	0.28
Estonia	1.315	4	0.32	0	6	6	0.21
Cyprus	0.788	4	0.19	0	6	6	0.13
Luxembourg	0.480	4	0.12	6	6	6	0.08
Malta	0.401	3	0.13	0	5	5	0.08
Totals	*497*	*345*		*626*	*732*	*736*	
	27 countries	27 countries	27 countries	15 countries	25 countries	27 countries	27 countries

Note: The population statistics for the member states has been rounded. As such, the total population column reflects the overall EU population and not just the sum of figures listed above.

VOTER TURNOUT IN EUROPEAN PARLIAMENT ELECTIONS

Document 37

This document chronicles the turnout in European Parliament elections since direct elections were first held in 1979. At the 2009 elections the average level of voting fell for the seventh time running.

State	1979	1981	1984	1987	1989	1994	1995	1996	1999	2004	2007	2009
Belgium	91.36		92.09		90.73	90.66			91.05	90.81		90.39
Denmark	47.82		52.38		46.17	52.92			50.46	47.89		59.54
Germany	65.73		56.76		62.28	60.02			45.19	43		43.3
Ireland	63.61		47.56		68.28	43.98			50.21	58.58		58.64
France	60.71		56.72		48.8	52.71			46.76	42.76		40.63
Italy	85.65		82.47		81.07	73.6			69.76	71.72		65.05
Luxembourg	88.91		88.79		87.39	88.55			87.27	91.35		90.75
Netherlands	58.12		50.88		47.48	36.69			30.02	39.26		36.75
UK	32.35		32.57		36.37	36.43			24.0	38.52		34.7
Greece		81.48	80.59		80.03	73.18			70.25	63.22		52.61
Spain				68.52	54.71	59.14			63.05	45.14		44.9
Portugal				72.42	51.1	35.54			39.93	38.6		36.78
Sweden							41.63		38.84	37.85		45.53
Austria								67.73	49.4	42.43		45.97
Finland								57.6	30.14	39.43		40.3
Czech Republic										28.3		28.2
Estonia										26.38		43.9
Cyprus										72.5		59.4
Lithuania										48.38		20.98
Latvia										41.34		53.7
Hungary										38.5		36.31
Malta										82.39		78.79
Poland										20.87		24.53
Slovenia										28.35		28.33
Slovakia										16.97		19.64
Bulgaria											29.22	38.99
Romania											29.47	47.67
EU total	61.99		58.98		58.41	56.67			49.51	45.47		43

Source: http://www.europarl.europa.eu/parliament/archive/elections2009/en/turnout_en.html.

Further Reading

Place of publication is London unless otherwise noted.

Websites

There are a huge number of websites devoted to the EU. The most useful is **Europa**, the official site of the EU: www.europa.eu.int (where a full list of member state governments can be found: www.europa.eu.int/abc/govern-ments/index_en.html). A helpful gateway to a great deal of information is **Intute**: www.intute.ac.uk/socialsciences/. Other relevant reference websites include the **BBC**: www.bbc.co.uk/ and the **Avalon Project**: www.avalon.law.yale.edu/default.asp at the Yale Law School, which provides a vast collection of twentieth-century documents in law, history and diplomacy.

Some of the most important organisations include the **United Nations**: www.un.org/, **North Atlantic Treaty Organisation**: www.nato.int, and **Organisation for Security and Cooperation in Europe**: www.osce.org/. A very useful source of information is the **European Union Institute for Security Studies**: www.iss-eu.org, which publishes the excellent Chaillot Papers. There are a number of organisations that are devoted to the study of the EU. These include the **University Association for Contemporary European Studies**: www.uaces.org/, the **European Community Studies Association**: www.ecsanet.org/, the **Centre for European Policy Studies**: www.ceps.be/index.php, the **Federal Trust**: www.fedtrust.co.uk, and the **Institute of European Affairs**: www/iiea.ie. Other research institutes include the **Royal Institute of International Affairs**: www.chathamhouse.org.uk/ and the **Royal United Services Institute**: www.rusi.org/. Research papers focusing on European integration can be accessed at **European Integration On-Line Papers**: www.eiop.or.at.

Key Texts

Most of the major publishing houses have series devoted to the EU and European affairs more generally. The best are the **New European Union Series** published by Oxford University Press and the **European Union Series** published by Palgrave. There are also a considerable number of academic journals that focus on European affairs; two of the best are the **Journal of Common Market Studies** and the **Journal of European Public Policy**. Two of the finest introductory texts are Alex Warleigh-Lack, **European Union: The Basics**, 2nd edition (Routledge, 2009) and Clive Archer, **The European Union** (Routledge, 2008). A very useful reference guide is Alasdair Blair, **Companion to the European Union** (Routledge, 2006). Comprehensive studies include Michelle Cini (ed.) **European Union Politics**, 2nd edition (Oxford: Oxford University Press, 2006), and Ian Bache and Stephen George, **Politics in the European Union**, 2nd edition (Oxford: Oxford University Press, 2006). Other classic studies include Desmond Dinan, **Ever Closer Union?**, 3rd edition (Basingstoke: Palgrave, 2005); John McCormick, **Understanding the European Union**, 4th edition (Basingstoke: Palgrave, 2008); and Neill Nugent, **The Government and Politics of the European Union**, 6th edition (Basingstoke: Palgrave, 2006). More advanced analysis can be found in Jeremy Richardson (ed.) **European Union: Power and Policy-Making**, 3rd edition (Routledge, 2006) and Helen Wallace, William Wallace and Mark Pollack (eds) **Policy-Making in the European Union**, 5th edition (Oxford: Oxford University Press, 2005).

History

For general historical overviews see John Pinder, **The Building of the European Union** (Oxford: Oxford University Press, 1998) and Derek Urwin, **The Community of Europe**, 2nd edition (Longman, 1995). Norman Davies, **Europe. A History** (Pimlico, 1997) is also worth a look. Desmond Dinan (ed.) **Origins and Evolution of the European Union** (Oxford: Oxford University Press, 2006) is a comprehensive collection of essays that chart the development of the EU. Andrew Moravcsik's **The Choice for Europe** (UCL Press, 1999) provides an excellent analysis of the evolution of the EU from the 1950s to the 1990s. One of the few accounts of US policy towards European integration is the excellent study by Geir Lundestad, **'Empire' by Integration** (Oxford: Oxford University Press, 1998). For an appreciation of the role played by the superpowers in the post-war reconstruction of Europe, see A.W. De Porte, **Europe Between the Superpowers**, 2nd edition (New Haven: Yale University Press, 1986).

For an analysis of the factors that were influential in promoting European unity in the post-war period, see Walter Lipgens, *A History of European Integration, Vol. 1, 1945–47* (Oxford: Clarendon Press, 1982); Alan Milward, *The Reconstruction of Western Europe 1945–51* (Methuen, 1984); and Ernst Haas, *The Uniting of Europe: Political, Social and Economic Forces, 1950–1957* (Stanford: Stanford University Press, 1968). Alan Milward's excellent *The European Rescue of the Nation State* sets the history of European integration within the system of European nation states after the Second World War. A personal account is provided in Dean Acheson, *Present at the Creation* (Hamish Hamilton, 1970); François Duchene, *Jean Monnet: The First Statesman of Interdependence* (New York: Norton and Company, 1994); Paul-Henri Spaak, *The Continuing Battle: Memoirs of a European 1936–1966* (Weidenfeld & Nicolson, 1971); Jean Monnet, *Memoirs* (Collins, 1978); and Robert Marjolin, *Memoirs 1911–1986* (Weidenfeld & Nicolson, 1989). Roy Jenkins recounts his experience in *European Diary 1977–1981* (Collins, 1989). The role played by many of the individuals in the construction of Europe is discussed in Martyn Bond, Julie Smith and William Wallace (eds) *Eminent Europeans* (Greycoat Press, 1996).

The 1980s were a turning point in the history of European integration with the resolution of the British budget problem and the signing of the Single European Act. One of the best studies of Britain's relations with the EU can be found in John W. Young, *Britain and European Unity, 1945–1999*, 2nd edition (Basingstoke: Macmillan, 2000). Jacques Delors Presidency of the European Commission from the mid-1980s has been viewed as a particularly dynamic period and a detailed analysis can be found in Charles Grant, *Delors: Inside the House That Jacques Built* (Nicholas Brealey, 1994) and Helen Drake, *Jacques Delors* (Routledge, 2000). On the internal market see Lord Cockfield, *The European Union: Creating the Single Market* (Chichester, 1994) and Paolo Cecchini, *The European Challenge, 1992: The Benefits of a Single Market* (Aldershot: Wildwood House, 1988).

For a review of the Cold War see John W. Young, *Cold War Europe 1945–89* (Edward Arnold, 1996) and John W. Young and John Kent, *International Relations since 1945: A Global History* (Oxford: Oxford University Press, 2004). An excellent account of the key issues in the post-Cold War period can be found in Robin Niblett and William Wallace (eds) *Rethinking European Order* (Basingstoke: Palgrave, 2001) and Ian Clark, *The Post-Cold War Order* (Oxford: Oxford University Press, 2001).

For a review of the Maastricht negotiations see Richard Corbett, *The Treaty of Maastricht* (Longman, 1993) and Finn Laursen and Sophie Vanhoonacker (eds) *The Intergovernmental Conference on Political Union* (Dordrecht: Martinus Nijhoff, 1992). The position of Britain is charted in Anthony Forster, *Britain and the Maastricht Negotiations* (Macmillan, 1999) and

Alasdair Blair, **Dealing with Europe** (Aldershot: Ashgate, 1999). A standard text on the intergovernmental pillars is Eileen Denza, **The Intergovernmental Pillars of the European Union** (Oxford: Oxford University Press, 2002).

On the Amsterdam Treaty see Nanette Neuwahl, Philip Lynch and Wyn Rees (eds) **Reforming the European Union** (Longman, 1999); Martin Westlake, **The European Union Beyond Amsterdam** (Routledge, 1998); Finn Laursen (ed.) **The Amsterdam Treaty: National Preference Formation, Interstate Bargaining and Outcome** (Odense: Odense University Press, 2002); and Jörg Monar and Wolfgang Wessels (eds) **The European Union after the Treaty of Amsterdam** (Continuum, 2001). On the Nice Treaty see Kim Feus (ed.) **The Treaty of Nice Explained** (Kogan Page/The Federal Trust, 2001) and David Galloway, **The Treaty of Nice and Beyond** (Sheffield: Sheffield Academic Press, 2001). To understand more about the Constitutional Treaty consult Clive Church and David Phinnemore, **Understanding the European Constitution: An Introduction to the EU Constitutional Treaty** (Routledge, 2005), and Finn Laursen (ed.) **The Rise and Fall of the EU's Constitutional Treaty** (Leiden: Martinus Nijhoff, 2008). An excellent account of IGC negotiations can be found in Derek Beach and Colette Mazzucelli (eds) **Leadership in the Big Bangs of European Integration** (Basingstoke: Palgrave, 2007).

Institutions

Some of the best books that are focused on the EU institutions include John Peterson and Michael Shackleton (eds) **The Institutions of the European Union**, 2nd edition (Oxford: Oxford University Press, 2006); and Simon Hix, **The Political System of the European Union**, 2nd edition (Basingstoke: Palgrave, 2005). An accessible introduction is Alex Warleigh (ed.) **Understanding European Union Institutions** (Routledge, 2002). The best introduction to the European Commission is to be found in Neill Nugent, **The European Commission** (Basingstoke: Palgrave, 2000). Other useful studies include David Spence and Geoffrey Edwards (eds) **The European Commission**, 3rd edition (John Harper, 2006) and Liesbet Hooghe, **The European Commission and the Integration of Europe** (Cambridge: Cambridge University Press, 2001). The increased powers that have been attributed to the European Parliament are covered in Francis Jacobs, Richard Corbett and Michael Shackleton, **The European Parliament**, 5th edition (John Harper, 2005); Amy Kreppel, **The European Parliament and Supranational Party System: A Study in Institutional Development** (Cambridge: Cambridge University Press, 2002); B. Rittberger, **Building Europe's Parliament: Democratic Representation Beyond the Nation State** (Oxford: Oxford

University Press, 2005); Roger Scully, *Becoming Europeans? Attitudes, Behaviour and Socialisation in the European Parliament* (Oxford: Oxford University Press, 2005); and Simon Hix and Roger Scully, *The European Parliament at Fifty: Special Issue of the Journal of Common Market Studies*, Vol. 41, No. 2, 2003. For a review of the Council of Ministers see Fiona Hayes-Renshaw and Helen Wallace, *The Council of Ministers*, 2nd edition (New York: St. Martin's Press, 2006); Martin Westlake and David Galloway, *The Council of the European Union*, 3rd edition (Cartermill, 2004); and John Peterson and Elizabeth Bomberg, *Decision-Making in the European Union* (Basingstoke: Macmillan, 1999). The best discussion of the European Court of Justice's role can be found in Anthony Arnull, *The European Union and its Court of Justice*, 2nd edition (Oxford: Oxford University Press, 2006). It is also worth consulting Karen Alter, *The European Court's Political Power* (Oxford: Oxford University Press, 2009); Renaud Dehousse, *The European Court of Justice* (Basingstoke: Palgrave, 1998); and L. Neville Brown and Tom Kennedy, *The Court of Justice of the European Communities*, 5th edition (Sweet and Maxwell, 2000). The complex legal system of the EU is examined by Josephine Shaw, *Law of the European Union*, 3rd edition (Basingstoke: Palgrave, 2000). Finally, the relationship between national courts and the Court of Justice is examined in Karen Alter, *Establishing the Supremacy of European Law* (Oxford: Oxford University Press, 2003).

Policies

On agricultural policy see Grace Skogstad and Amy Verdun (eds), *The Common Agricultural Policy* (Routledge, 2009). For environmental policy see John McCormick, *Environmental Policy in the European Union* (Basingstoke: Palgrave, 2001). The internal market is discussed in Kenneth Armstrong and Simon Bulmer, *The Governance of the Single European Market* (Manchester: Manchester University Press, 1998). For a review of social policy see Linda Hantrais, *Social Policy in the European Union*, 3rd edition (Palgrave, 2007). The politics surrounding the negotiation of monetary union in the Maastricht Treaty is tackled in Kenneth Dyson and Kevin Featherstone, *The Road to Maastricht* (Oxford: Oxford University Press, 1999). Good analysis of EMU can be found in Paul de Grauwe, *The Economics of Monetary Union*, 8th edition (Oxford: Oxford University Press, 2009).

Good overviews of EU foreign-policy capability can be found in Michael E, Smith, *Europe's Foreign and Security Policy: The Institutionalization of Cooperation* (Cambridge: Cambridge University Press, 2003); Hazel Smith,

European Union Foreign Policy: What It Is and What It Does (Pluto Press, 2002) and Brian White, **Understanding European Foreign Policy** (Basingstoke: Palgrave, 2001). The broader remit of the EU's external relations policy is discussed in John Vogler, Richard Whitman and Charlotte Bretherton, **The External Policies of the European Union** (Palgrave, 2010). The EU's relations with the Third World are covered in Martin Holland, **The European Union and the Third World** (Basingstoke: Palgrave, 2002). The impact of enlargement on the EU is examined in Helene Sjursen (ed.) **Questioning EU Enlargement: Europe in Search of Identity** (Routledge, 2006).

A cumulative effect of the growth in the number of EU policies is that they have significantly increased the impact that the EU has on world affairs. This is a topic that is examined in Christopher Hill and Michael Smith, **International Relations and the European Union** (Oxford: Oxford University Press, 2005), while it is also worth examining John McCormick, **The European Superpower** (Palgrave, 2007). On justice and home affairs, see Andrew Geddes, **Immigration and European Integration: Towards fortress Europe**, 2nd edition (Manchester: Manchester University Press, 2008). The erosion of the difference between domestic and European areas of policy has been analysed through the lens of Europeanisation and one of the most useful sources is Kevin Featherstone and Claudio Radaelli (eds), **The Politics of Europeanisation** (Oxford: Oxford University Press, 2003). Analysis of the British position is covered in Simon Bulmer and Martin Burch, **The Europeanisation of Whitehall** (Manchester: Manchester University Press, 2009). Some commentators also consider that there is insufficient democracy within the EU and for an understanding of this subject see Alex Warleigh, **Democracy in the European Union: Theory, Practice and Reform** (Sage, 2003) and Dimitris Chryssochoou, **Democracy in the European Union** (I.B. Taurus, 2000).

Theories

A good starting point is Ben Rosamond, **Theories of European Integration** (Macmillan, 2000). One of the most comprehensive accounts is Antje Wiener and Thomas Diez (eds) *European Integration Theory*, 2nd edition (Oxford: Oxford University Press, 2009). Federalist accounts can be found in Michael Burgess, **Federalism and the European Union** (Routledge, 2000). An introduction to intergovernmentalism can be found in Stanley Hoffman, **The European Sisyphus** (Oxford: Westview Press, 1995) and Andrew Moravcsik, **The Choice for Europe** (University College London Press, 1998). Constructivism offers a new approach to the study of European integration, of which the most useful text is Thomas Christiansen, Knud Erik Jorgensen and Antje Wiener (eds) *The Social Construction of Europe* (Sage, 2001). Simon Hix has argued that the EU is best understood from the angle of comparative politics in *The Political System of the European Union*, 2nd edition (Palgrave, 2005). A multi-level governance approach can be found in Ian Bache and Mathew Flinders (eds) *Multi-level Governance* (Oxford: Oxford University Press, 2005) and Liesbet Hooghe and Gary Marks, *Multi-level Governance and European Integration* (Boulder, CO: Rowman and Littlefield, 2001). Finally, for an institutionalist viewpoint, see Gerhard Schneider and Mark Aspinwall (eds), *The Rules of Integration* (Manchester: Manchester University Press, 2001).

Finally, if after having read any the books mentioned above you reach a conclusion that there is room for change in the EU then you should read the excellent account by Simon Hix, *What's Wrong with the European Union and How to Fix It* (Polity, 2008).

References

The place of publication is London unless otherwise noted.

Aldcroft, D.H. and Oliver, M.J. (1998) *Exchange Rate Regimes in the Twentieth Century*, Cheltenham: Edward Elgar.

Alter, K.J. (2001) *Establishing the Supremacy of European Law*, Oxford: Oxford University Press.

Alter, K.J. and Meunier-Aitsahalia, S. (1994) 'Judicial Politics in the European Community: European Integration and the Pathbreaking *Cassis de Dijon* Decision', *Comparative Political Studies*, Vol. 33, No. 4, pp. 316–46.

Archer, C. (1990) *Organizing Western Europe*, Edward Arnold.

Archer, C. (2000) *The European Union: Structure and Process*, 3rd edition, Continuum.

Armstrong, K. and Bulmer, S. (1998) *The Governance of the Single European Market*, Manchester: Manchester University Press.

Barker, E. (1971) *Britain in a Divided Europe*, Weidenfeld and Nicolson.

Blair, A. (1998a) 'UK Policy Coordination during the 1990–91 Intergovernmental Conference', *Diplomacy and Statecraft*, Vol. 9, No. 2, pp. 160–83.

Blair, A. (1998b) 'Swimming with the tide? Britain and the Maastricht Treaty negotiations on Common Foreign and Security Policy', *Contemporary British History*, Vol. 12, No. 4, pp. 87–102.

Blair, A. (1999) *Dealing with Europe: Britain and the Negotiation of the Maastricht Treaty*, Aldershot: Ashgate.

Blair, A. (2001) 'Permanent Representations to the European Union', *Diplomacy and Statecraft*, Vol. 12, No. 3, pp. 173–93.

Blair, A. (2002) *Saving the Pound? Britain's Road to Monetary Union*, Longman.

Blair, A. (2004) 'Diplomacy: The Impact of the EU on its Member States', in W. Carlsnaes, H. Sjursen and B. White (eds) *Contemporary European Foreign Policy*, Sage.

Blair, A. (2008) 'The United Kingdom and the Constitutional Treaty: Leading from Within', in F. Laursen (ed.) *The Rise and Fall of the EU's Constitutional Treaty*, Leiden: Martinus Nijhuff.

Blair, A. and Curtis, S. (2009) *International Politics: An Introductory Guide*, Edinburgh: Edinburgh University Press.

Börzel, T. and Risse, T. (2003) 'Conceptualizing the Domestic Impact of Europe', in Kevin Featherstone and Claudio M. Radaelli (eds) *The Politics of Europeanization*, Oxford: Oxford University Press, pp. 57–80.

Cameron, D. (1992) 'The 1992 Initiative: Causes and Consequences' in A.M. Sbragia (ed.) *Euro Euro-Politics: Institutions and Policymaking in the 'New' European Community*, Washington, DC: Brookings, pp. 23–74.

Cameron, F. (2004a) 'Widening and Deepening' in Fraser Cameron (ed.) *The Future of the Europe: Integration and Enlargement*, Routledge, pp. 1–17.

Cameron, F. (2004b) 'Europe's future' in Fraser Cameron (ed.) *The Future of the Europe: Integration and Enlargement*, Routledge, pp. 148–161.

Camps, M. (1964) *Britain and the European Community 1955–63*, Oxford University Press.

Cecchini, P., Catinat, M. and Jacquemin, A. (1988) *The European Challenge: 1992: The Benefits of a Single Market*, Aldershot: Wildwood House.

Clark, I. (2001) *The Post-Cold War Order*, Oxford: Oxford University Press.

Cockfield, Lord Arthur (1994) *The European Union: Creating the Single Market*, Wiley Chancery.

Cole, A. (2001) *Franco-German Relations*, Longman.

Corbett, R. (1994) 'Representing the People', in A. Duff, J. Pinder and R. Pryce (eds) *Maastricht and Beyond*, Routledge.

Cowles, M.G. (1995) 'Setting the Agenda for a New Europe: The European Round Table and EC 1992', *Journal of Common Market Studies*, Vol. 33, No. 4, pp. 501–26.

De Porte, A.W. (1986) *Europe between the Superpowers: The Enduring Balance*, New Haven: Yale University Press.

Dell, E. (1991) *A Hard Pounding: Politics and Economic Crisis 1974–76*, Oxford: Oxford University Press.

Denman, R. (1996) *Missed Chances: Britain and Europe in the Twentieth Century*, Cassell.

Diebold, W. (1959) *The Schuman Plan*, New York: Praeger.

Dinan, D. (2005) *Ever Closer Union? An Introduction to the European Community*, Palgrave, 3rd edition.

Duchêne, F. (1996) 'Jean Monnet – Pragmatic Visionary' in M. Bond, J. Smith and W. Wallace (eds) *Eminent Europeans*, The Greycoat Press, pp. 45–61.

Dunlop, J. (1993) *The Rise of Russia and the Fall of the Soviet Empire*, Princeton, NJ: Princeton University Press.

Dyson, K. and Featherstone, K. (1999) *The Road to Maastricht: Negotiating Economic and Monetary Union*, Oxford: Oxford University Press.

Forster, A. and Blair, A. (2002) *The Making of Britain's European Foreign Policy*, Longman.

Friis, L. (2003) 'EU Enlargement . . . And Then There were 28', in E. Bomberg and A. Stubb (eds) *The European Union: How Does it Work?*, Oxford: Oxford University Press, pp. 177–194.

Fukuyama, F. (1989) 'The end of history', *The National Interest*, Summer.

Fursdon, E. (1980) *The European Defence Community: A History*, St Martin.

Garthoff, R.L. (1994) *The Great Transition: American–Soviet Relations and the End of the Cold War*, Washington, DC: The Brookings Institution.

George, S. (1996) Politics and Policy in the European Community, 3rd edition, Oxford: Oxford University Press.

George, S. (1999) *An Awkward Partner: Britain in the European Community*, 3rd edition, Oxford: Oxford University Press.

Gillingham, J. (1991) *Coal, Steel and the Rebirth of Europe 1945–1955. The Germans and the French from the Ruhr Conflict to European Community*, Cambridge: Cambridge University Press.

Grant, W. (1997) *The Common Agricultural Policy*, Macmillan.

Haas, E.B. (1968) *The Uniting of Europe: Political, Social and Economic Forces 1950–57*, 2nd edition, Stevens.

Hallstein, W. (1962) *United Europe: Challenges and Opportunity*, Oxford University Press.

Hannay, D. (2000) (ed.) *Britain's Entry into the European Community. Report on the Negotiations of 1970–1972 by Sir Con O'Neill*, Frank Cass.

Harrison, R.J. (1974) *Europe in Question: Theories of Regional International Integration*, Allen and Unwin.

Heath, E. (1998) *The Course of My Life*, Hodder & Stoughton.

Henderson, N. (1994) *Mandarin: The Diaries of an Ambassador 1969–1982*, Weidenfeld & Nicolson.

Henig, S. (2002) *The Uniting of Europe*, 2nd edition, Routledge.

Hill, C. (1993) 'The Capability–Expectations Gap, or Conceptualizing Europe's International Role', *Journal of Common Market Studies*, Vol. 31, No. 3, pp. 305–28.

Hix, S. (1999) *The Political System of the European Union*, Palgrave.

Hix, S. (2008) *What's Wrong with the European Union and How to Fix It*, Polity.

Hoffmann, S. (1966) 'The Fate of the Nation State', *Daedalus*, Summer.

Huntingdon, S.P. (1993) 'The Clash of Civilizations', *Foreign Affairs*, Vol. 72, pp. 22–49.

Hyland, W.G. (1986) 'The Struggle for Europe: An American View' in Andrew J. Pierre (ed.) *Nuclear Weapons in Europe*, New York, NY: Council on Foreign Relations.

Jenkins, R. (1989) *European Diary, 1977–1981*, Collins.

Jenkins, R. (1991) *A Life at the Centre*, Macmillan.

Jordan, A. (2002) *The Europeanization of British Environmental Policy: A Departmental Perspective*, Palgrave.

Judge, D. and Earnshaw, D. (2003) *The European Parliament*, Palgrave.

Leonard, D. (1996) 'Britain's Indecision – from Macmillan to the Referendum', in M. Bond, J. Smith and William W. (eds) *Eminent Europeans*, The Greycoat Press, pp. 162–78.

Lindberg, L. and Scheingold, S. (1970) *Europe's Would-Be Polity*, Englewood Cliffs, NJ: Prentice Hall.

Lipgens, W.A. (1982) *History of European Integration, Vol. 1, 1945–47*, Oxford: Clarendon Press.

Lundestad, G. (1998) *'Empire' by Integration: the United States and European Integration, 1945–1997*, Oxford: Oxford University Press.

Lundgreen, A. (2006) 'The Case of Turkey: Are Some Candidates More "European" than others?', in H. Sjursen (ed.) *Questioning EU Enlargement: Europe in Search of Identity*, Routledge, pp. 121–41.

Macmillan, H. (1973) *At the End of the Day, 1961–63*, Macmillan.

Majone, G. (1996) *Regulating Europe*, Routledge.

Marjolin, R. (1989) *Architect of European Unity: Memoirs: 1911–1986*, London: Weidenfeld and Nicolson.

Marjolin, R. *et al.* (1975) *Report of the Study Group Economic Monetary Union 1980, 'Marjolin Report'*, Brussels: Commission of the European Communities.

May, A. (1999) *Britain and Europe since 1945*, Longman.

McCormick, J. (2008) *Understanding the European Union*, 4th edition, Palgrave.

Middlemas, K. (1995) *Orchestrating Europe: The Informal Politics of the European Union 1973–95*, Fontana.

Milward, A. (1984) *The Reconstruction of Western Europe 1945–1951*, Methuen & Co. Ltd.

Milward, A. (1992) *The European Rescue of the Nation State*, Routledge and Kegan & Paul.

Mitrany, D. (1946) *A Working Peace System*, Royal Institute of International Affairs.

Monnet, J. (1978) *Memoirs* (translated by R. Mayne), New York: Doubleday & Company.

Moravcsik, A. (1991) 'Negotiating the Single European Act', in R.O. Keohane and S. Hoffmann (ed.) *The New European Community: Decisionmaking and Institutional Change*, Boulder, CO, Westview Press.

Moravcsik, A. (1998) *The Choice for Europe: Social Purpose and State Power from Messina to Maastricht*, UCL Press.

Nugent, N. (2003) *The Government and Politics of the European Union*, 5th edition, Macmillan.

Nutting, A. (1961) *Europe Will Not Wait*, Hollis and Carter.

Padoa-Schioppa, T. (1987) *Efficiency, Stability and Equity: A Strategy for the Evolution of the Economic System of the EC*, Oxford: Oxford University Press.

Paterson, W.E. (1994) 'The Chancellor and Foreign Policy', in Stephen Padgett (ed.) *The Development of the German Chancellorship: Adenauer to Kohl*, Hurst and Company.

Pelkmans, J. and Winters, L.A., with Wallace, H. (1988) *Europe's Domestic Market*, Royal Institute of International Affairs.

Peterson, J. (1995) 'Decision-making in the European Union: Towards a Framework for Analysis', *Journal of European Public Policy*, Vol. 2, No. 1, pp. 46–65.

Peterson, J. and Sharp, M. (1998) *Technology Policy in the European Union*, Macmillan.

Pinder, J. (1998) *The Building of the European Union*, Oxford: Oxford University Press.

Pollack, M. (1997) 'The Commission as an Agent', in N. Nugent (ed.) *At the Heart of the Union: Studies of the European Commission*, Macmillan.

Prior, J. (1986) *A Balance of Power*, Hamish Hamilton.

Reynolds, D. (2000) *Britannia Overruled*, Longman.

Rosamond, B. (2000) *Theories of European Integration*, Macmillan.

Ross, G. (1995a) *Jacques Delors and European Integration*, Cambridge: Polity Press.

Ryan, D. (2003) *The United States and Europe in the Twentieth Century*, Longman.

Sandholtz, W. and Zysman, J. (1989) '1992: Recasting the European Bargain', *World Poliics*, Vol. 42, No. 1, pp. 95–128.

Schmidt, H. (1985) *A Grand Strategy for the West*, Henry L. Stimson Lectures, Yale, CT: Yale University Press.

Seldon, A. and Collings, D. (2000) *Britain Under Thatcher*, Longman.

Spaak, P.-H. (1971) *The Continuing Battle: Memoirs of a European 1936–1966*, Weidenfeld & Nicolson.

Stubb, A. (2002) *Negotiating Flexibility in the European Union: Amsterdam, Nice and Beyond*, Palgrave.

Thatcher, M. (1993) *The Downing Street Years*, HarperCollins.
Thody, P. (2000) *Europe since 1945*, Routledge.
Tranholm-Mikkelsen, J. (1991) 'Neofunctionalism: Obstinate or Obsolete? A Reappraisal in Light of the New Dynamism of the European Community', *Millennium*, Vol. 20, pp. 1–22.
Tugendhat, C. (1987) *Making Sense of Europe*, Harmondsworth: Penguin.

Urwin, D.W. (1995) *The Community of Europe: A History of European Integration since 1945*, 2nd edition, Longman.

Warner, G. (1984) 'The Labour Governments and the Unity of Western Europe, 1945–51', in R. Ovendale (ed.) *The Foreign Policy of the British Labour Governments 1945–51*, Leicester: Leicester University Press, pp. 61–82.
Weinberger, C. (1990) *Fighting for Peace*, Michael Joseph Ltd.
Weiner, A. and Neunreither, K. (2000) 'Introduction: Amsterdam and Beyond', in K. Neunreither and A. Weiner (ed.) *European Integration After Amsterdam*, Oxford: Oxford University Press, pp. 1–11.
White, B. (2001) *Understanding European Foreign Policy*, Palgrave.
Willis, F. (1968) *France, Germany and the New Europe 1945–1963*, Stanford: Stanford University Press.

Young, H. (1990) *One of Us*, Macmillan.
Young, J.W. (1991) *Cold War Europe 1945–1989: A Political History*, Edward Arnold.
Young, J.W. (2000) *Britain and European Unity 1945–1999*, 2nd edition, Macmillan.
Young, J.W. and Kent, J. (2004) *International Relations since 1945: A Global History*, Oxford: Oxford University Press.

Zurcher, A.J. (1958) *The Struggle to Unite Europe, 1940–58*, New York: New York University Press.

Index

SEMINAR STUDIES
IN HISTORY

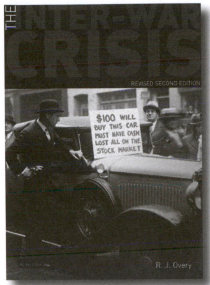

THE INTER-WAR CRISIS
REVISED SECOND EDITION

$100 WILL BUY THIS CAR MUST HAVE CASH LOST ALL ON THE STOCK MARKET

R. J. Overy

9781408223178

THE SECOND WORLD WAR IN EUROPE

9781405846998

THE SECOND WORLD WAR ON THE EASTERN FRONT

9781405840637

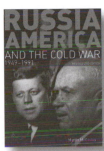

RUSSIA AMERICA AND THE COLD WAR 1949–1991

9781405874304

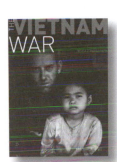

THE VIETNAM WAR

9781405874342

CAMPAIGN 1866–1928

9781408228234

THE ITALIAN RISORGIMENTO

9781408205167

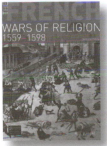

THE FRENCH WARS OF RELIGION 1559–1598

9781408228197

THE SCRAMBLE FOR AFRICA

M. E. Chamberlain

9781408220146

THE FRENCH REVOLUTION 1787–1804

9781408204382

THE ARAB-ISRAELI CONFLICT

Kirsten E. Schulze

9780582771895

ORIGINS OF THE COLD WAR 1941–1949

9781405874335

SEMINAR STUDIES
IN HISTORY